Brooks - Cork Library
Shelton State
Community College

P9-EMB-583

UNIVERSITY PRESS OF FLORIDA / STATE UNIVERSITY SYSTEM

Florida A&M University, Tallahassee
Florida Atlantic University, Boca Raton
Florida Gulf Coast University, Ft. Myers
Florida International University, Miami
Florida State University, Tallahassee
University of Central Florida, Orlando
University of Florida, Gainesville
University of North Florida, Jacksonville
University of South Florida, Tampa
University of West Florida, Pensacola

UNIVERSITY PRESS OF FLORIDA

Gainesville | Tallahassee | Tampa | Boca Raton | Pensacola | Orlando | Miami | Jacksonville | Ft. Myers

DISCARDED

COUNTING VOTES

Lessons from the 2000 Presidential Election in Florida

Brooks - Cork Library
Shelton State
Community College

Edited by Robert P. Watson

Copyright 2004 by Robert P. Watson
Printed in the United States of America on acid-free, recycled paper
All rights reserved

09 08 07 006 05 04   6 5 4 3 2 1

Library of Congress Cataloging-in-Publication Data
Counting votes : lessons from the 2000 presidential election in Florida /
edited by Robert P. Watson
p. cm.
Includes bibliographical references and index.
ISBN 0-8130-2714-4 (cloth : alk. paper)
1. Elections—United States. 2. Election law—United States.
3. Presidents—United States—election—2000.
I. Watson, Robert P., 1962–
JK1976.c645 2004
324.973—DC22   2004043737

The University Press of Florida is the scholarly publishing agency
for the State University System of Florida, comprising Florida A&M
University, Florida Atlantic University, Florida Gulf Coast University,
Florida International University, Florida State University, University
of Central Florida, University of Florida, University of North Florida,
University of South Florida, and University of West Florida.

University Press of Florida
15 Northwest 15th Street
Gainesville, FL 32611-2079
http://www.upf.com

Contents

Tables

Foreword

Let Every Voice Be Heard, Let Every Vote Be Counted

CAROLYN JEFFERSON-JENKINS, PAST PRESIDENT,
LEAGUE OF WOMEN VOTERS OF THE UNITED STATES

The presidential election of 2000 and its aftermath generated much conversation and consternation about the health of democracy in the United States. The question remains: What is the voter's role in this democratic process? Equally important questions are: How well are voters fulfilling their role? What impact does a low-quality system of election administration have on elections? What solutions to existing problems should be examined? The League of Women Voters has a voice in the conversation because of its reputation as a leading nonpartisan organization involved in civic and electoral issues, its eighty-four-year history of fostering effective citizen participation in elections, and its grassroots network representing every segment of society.

The role that voters play is critical to making democracy work. Thomas Jefferson believed that each generation must interpret and renew the relationship with its government for itself. Each generation must make its own commitment to protect that relationship, which is at the heart of a free democratic system. Jefferson also believed that it is citizens who ultimately determine the success of representative government. Citizens in a democracy can do this by holding their government accountable, taking part in the political debates that affect their lives, engaging in the decision-making process of government, working for change they believe in, and exercising their First Amendment rights to speak out and to participate in public life. These are some of the obligations citizens have in our political system. Over time, and especially today, new information technologies have significantly transformed the possibilities, and practice, of democracy. First television and now the Internet have made possible electronic town hall meetings and interactive teleconferencing, replacing the traditional town meeting and the type of campaigning and civil discourse that was prevalent during the early days of the republic.

The compact between the government and citizens is a sacred trust. Unless we make the system set up by the Constitution and the Bill of Rights work, our democratic foundation will lose its potency. When the founders created the federalist system with separation of powers and checks and balances, democracy was practiced very differently than today. Women couldn't vote, African Americans couldn't vote, people without property couldn't vote. One need only read history to hear the extraordinary excuses advanced to block efforts to give women the basic right to vote: Women, according to antisuffragists, would increase the "irresponsible vote," since they always choose the best-looking candidate. Voting, the critics contended, would take women away from their duties as wives and mothers.

The expression of the citizen's will is the basis of democracy. Democracy provides citizens with an opportunity to influence how their government will serve them. But democracy also imposes obligations on citizens to participate in the political process. Americans are both frustrated with and downright angry about the state of the current political system. They do not believe that they are living in a democracy now. They don't believe that "we the people" actually rule. What is more, people do not believe this system is able to solve the pressing problems they face. In moving from yesterday's Industrial Age democracy to today's Information Age democracy, both direct and mediated democracy can and should be enhanced. Voters' frustration with the political system continues to grow, as does animosity toward the media. But the anger doesn't stop there. The public also has become more polarized on issues of social policy and cultural change. And after the 2000 election, people wonder whether or not their votes really count.

Is There Hope amid the Anger?

Assuming that citizens do still believe in the system, the League of Women Voters commissioned a survey in 1996 to uncover the mood of the nation. The league found that electoral turnout reflects more clearly the character of our culture than the character of our politics. A key finding of the league's survey was that the alienation and cynicism many observers blame for recent declines in electoral participation in the United States are not deciding factors in nonvoting. Rather, among the major factors that distinguish voters from nonvoters are that nonvoters are less likely to grasp the impact of elections on issues that matter to them; nonvoters are more likely to believe they lack information on which to base their voting decisions; nonvoters are more likely to perceive the voting process as difficult and cumbersome; and nonvoters are less likely to be contacted by organizations encouraging them to vote.

Another of the survey's key findings is that voters and nonvoters have nearly identical levels of mistrust in government, with both groups expressing profound cynicism and political alienation. Taken together, these findings imply that, while political alienation and cynicism are widespread among the population, alienation cannot be considered a factor in nonvoting.

The league's survey tested several hypotheses to explain why so many Americans don't vote. One of the explanations appears to be that voters and nonvoters differ in their perceptions of the importance of elections. Specifically, voters were more likely than nonvoters to recognize the impact of various elections on issues of direct and personal concern. There is a clear message here that people aren't getting the information they need so they can understand the consequences of elections in their lives.

According to the league, these findings support a second hypothesis tested in the survey: that people are more likely to vote if they believe they have accurate information about the election. There is a clear connection between voting and people's belief that they have good, unbiased information on which to base their decisions. The survey also suggested that people are more likely to vote if they feel encouraged to do so by friends and family.

As a follow-up to the 1996 survey, in 1999 the league conducted another study and found an American populace that is involved in and attached to its communities. Contrary to conventional wisdom, a significant share of Americans would like to become more involved in their communities, including a sizable pool of people who are not currently involved. We identified barriers to community involvement, among them the perception that getting involved requires a high level of information and a significant, inflexible time commitment. People also fear that their work will not have an impact.

The league suggested strategies to overcome barriers to community involvement, such as creating opportunities for volunteer work that people can fit into their schedules at their convenience or complete from their own homes. Activities that people can do with their children and families also are likely to be met with enthusiasm. Organizations seeking to mobilize volunteers should be certain to provide concrete details about the beneficial impact of the efforts as well as information about the organization itself.

A majority of people feel they can make a difference in solving community problems. Americans have more confidence that groups of people can have an impact in solving community problems than in influencing politicians. Americans may be "bowling alone," but they are joining with others to work on community activities and issues. In their hectic lives, people do not want community involvement to be another rigid commitment to juggle.

In sum, Americans are connected to their communities. Contrary to conventional wisdom, many people are interested in becoming more involved. However, in an era when people are faced with time constraints and competing priorities, groups and organizations that want to mobilize volunteers need to offer flexibility, information, and a compelling reason to get involved. Most of all, people need to feel that their efforts will make a difference.

The Unfinished Business of Democracy

American democracy, indeed democracy worldwide, is at a critical juncture. American citizens feel angry and shut out of the democratic process. The key to renewing democracy lies in empowering citizens to shape better communities worldwide. They shape those communities by letting their voices be heard. They do this by voting.

Democracy is founded on the belief in the common good. As more people opt out of the process and some people are denied access, the concept of the common good is eroded rather quickly. In a participatory democracy, citizens must have access to information and access to the process. Citizen participation is the thread that holds together our political system's ability to serve the common good. It is also a thread that is currently very frayed and in danger of breaking.

Meaningful election administration reform is not just about politicians and money. It is about a more representative decision-making process. The league of Women Voters has renewed its appeal for meaningful election administration reform, in the wake of the voting irregularities in Florida during the 2000 presidential election. In testimony before the U.S. Senate and the U.S. House of

Representatives, I had the opportunity to emphasize the importance not just of promoting voting, as the mechanism to increase citizen participation, but of having every vote that is cast counted accurately.

What happened in Florida confirms what the league has known for years— that many components of our election systems are dysfunctional and in need of significant action from federal as well as state and local governments. We need to ensure that basic voter protections, like the Voting Rights Act of 1965 and the National Voter Registration Act of 1993, are fully enforced. We need to develop new protections to ensure that people with disabilities have access and that discriminatory purges are stopped.

The right to vote and have one's vote counted is one of our democracy's most fundamental principles. Congress and the president must act together to provide the funding that is needed to make election reform a reality at every polling place in the nation. Effective reform legislation should balance the need to fix the ills of our electoral system with the preservation and protection of voting rights. Years of indifference and inadequate funds have left our election administration systems vulnerable and placed the right of American citizens to vote, and to have their votes effectively counted on an equal basis, at risk.

Many of the problems in election administration are problems of implementation rather than of public policy. Implementation issues have effects on real people and voters. All too often, these implementation issues have a disproportionate impact on the participation of voters from racial and ethnic minorities. To alleviate these problems, we need effective reform to reinforce compliance with our nation's most basic voter protection laws, affording states and localities the resources to enforce these laws fully and completely.

Bipartisan support is crucial to achieve significant funding and continuing prioritization of three concerns essential to passage of effective election reform: (1) Voting system standards must ensure that voters can verify and correct their ballots, as well as be notified of overvotes. These standards also protect against high voting machine error rates and enhance access for people with disabilities. (2) A national standard must ensure that voters can receive provisional ballots. This fail-safe system means that if a voter's name is not found on the registration list at the polls, or if other problems occur, the voter can still cast a ballot that will be counted if the voter's eligibility is confirmed. (3) Statewide computerized voter registration lists must be required. This facilitates removal of duplicate registrations across jurisdictions, provides greater assurance that names will be on the rolls, and streamlines administration while combating fraud.

In 2001 the league conducted a survey of our fifty state leagues. The problems most often reported were that many motor-voter applicants were not listed at the polling place, that polling places were too crowded and lines too long, and that voters were not given written notice of their polling place location. A major problem appears to be the increasing shortage of poll workers, coupled with insufficient poll worker training. This is a serious problem in many jurisdictions. Poll workers tend to be retired people. Poll worker recruitment programs should offer seven- or eight-hour shifts, particularly for older volunteers, rather than the fourteen-hour days that are common today. Congress should consider tax incentives for retirees to participate. Recruiting of high school seniors and college students should be encouraged, perhaps by offering academic credit. All poll workers should be paid at least minimum wage and be given the training that this important job requires. We must look for ways to recognize and reward the civic contribution of these unheralded workers.

Opinion polls also show that most Americans believe that our government is run for the benefit of special interests rather than for the good of all people. Our political system is based on the consent of the governed, but the campaign finance system is undermining public confidence and increasing cynicism. We need campaign finance reform so that citizens can regain their rightful place at the center of our political system.

What has brought it all together is the overarching goal of restoring the health of American democracy. It is time to respond to the needs of the public. The 2000 presidential election called the nation's attention to the urgent need for improvements in the methods, practices, and technology through which our elections are administered, and such challenges as election reform, campaign finance reform, and the direct election of the president. We are tackling these challenges at all levels because we firmly believe that *representative* government is the foundation of our democratic process, and the unfinished business of the nation. Democracy is not static. It is ever changing and continues to evolve even in the world's oldest democracies.

Creating a Democracy Where Citizens Come First

The suffragists' campaign to win ratification of the Nineteenth Amendment offers a guidebook on how to make the system work for citizens. Self-government is hard work. The league of Women Voters has long supported the right of every citizen to vote. Implicit in that statement is the right to have one's vote properly counted. Election 2000 focused the public's attention on the fact that our election systems do no always operate effectively or efficiently, but *they should* and *they can* and *they must.*

At the federal level, the league is lobbying for legislation (1) to create a substantial multiyear grants program to upgrade election systems including, but not limited to, voting technology, voter education, and poll worker training; (2) to identify and provide funding for the jurisdictions with the most significant problems; (3) to establish "best practices" to ensure accessibility, convenience, accuracy, and nondiscrimination, including provisional ballot opportunities and protections against arbitrary purges; (4) to protect and ensure compliance with the Voting Rights Act, the National Voter Registration Act, the Americans with Disabilities Act, and other voter protection laws; and (5) to mandate that state and local jurisdictions receiving grants ensure that disabled voters can vote privately and independently.

Most citizens show little interest in the process, not because they dismiss its importance, but simply because they do not recognize the extent to which the current election system impairs the right of all Americans to engage in self-government. The public generally believed that the system worked well in the past and they used to trust it to work well in the future. Regrettably, the present election system has not worked well. It still bears the mark of forces that originally appeared at the turn of the last century—fear of the then widespread corruption and fraud at the polls, and a desire to control the voting participation of millions of European immigrants who threatened the political status quo. Although these particular forces have largely ceased to exist, the system remains saddled with many unnecessarily restrictive laws and exclusionary procedures. It has become an administrative maze in which many of the abuses it was designed to prevent can, in fact, be more easily hidden and through which the average citizen must painstakingly grope in order to exercise his or her fundamental right to the franchise.

Fear of fraud is often advanced in opposition to proposed reform of the present election system. It could be argued, however, that such abuses are a function of community mores and will exist in some communities no matter what election procedures are established. More noteworthy, it would seem, is the fraud perpetrated on the American people by a system that excludes millions of eligible voters from the electoral process in the name of preventing a few who dishonestly cast votes.

One of the many articles printed in the months following Election 2000 accurately stated: "Our national civics lesson is over." But what, if anything, have we learned from the closest presidential election in more than a century? We have learned a lot. Whether we now do something about it is the more important question. From the beginning, the right to vote has been a source of constant debate. Benjamin Franklin said in *Wit and Sentiment:* "Today a man owns a jackass worth fifty dollars and he is entitled to vote; but before the next election the jackass dies. The man in the mean time has become more experienced, his knowledge of the principles of government, and his acquaintance with mankind, are more extensive, and he is therefore better qualified to make a proper selection of rulers—but the jackass is dead and the man cannot vote. Now gentlemen, pray inform me, in whom is the right of suffrage? In the man or in the jackass?"

Election 2000 has lifted the veil on the many problems that face the U.S. election system, from election administration issues, such as counting mechanisms and ballot design, to constitutional issues such as the Electoral College. These issues fall into two basic categories: those where the problems and solutions are clear, so that we can move forward quickly and effectively, and those where there is no agreement on either the scope and nature of the problems or on their solution. Among the problems are these: Fear of fraud is often cited to keep certain people away from the polls. The poor, the elderly, the uneducated, and racial and ethnic minorities are particularly burdened. Registration lists are often incomplete, and registration procedures are too complex. So are the procedures for absentee voting, as well as the procedures for actually casting a ballot. Staff at the polling places are poorly trained. Bilingual staff aren't available when needed. Officials too often act as if voting were a privilege, rather than a right.

New Challenges Bring New Solutions

The League of Women Voters believes in representative government and in individual liberties established in the Constitution of the United States. We believe that democratic government depends upon the informed and active participation of its citizens and requires that governmental bodies protect the citizen's right to know by giving adequate notice of proposed actions, holding meetings, and making public records accessible. Further, we believe that every citizen should be protected in the exercise of these rights. Fundamental to this participation is the citizen's right to vote. In order to increase participation, the league believes that election officials have a responsibility to encourage the exercise of the vote, promote citizen confidence in and understanding of the electoral process, and provide equal access to the ballot.

The league believes that voters have the ability to make reasonable judgments if they have the proper tools. Politicians believe negative campaigning works, even though the efficacy of questionable campaigns is unproven. Voters need to change the environment so that it is in the interest of political parties and candidates to conduct more positive campaigns. Improving election systems is a difficult and complex endeavor. Activities work best at state and local levels. And let us not forget the citizens of the District of Columbia, who still do not have full congressional voting rights. Our election administration systems are in dire need of repair and adequate funding.

The goal of election reform must be to make the vote of every American citizen count. This is the criterion by which every federal election reform proposal must be judged. Election 2000 made it clear that we need effective standards to fully protect voters' rights. At the dawn of the twenty-first century, in the most vibrant democracy in history, we must address the persistent lack of attention and lack of resources that conspire to bar people—all people—from equal protection in the electoral process.

Public office is a public trust. Candidates must meet their obligations to the voters. I ask that every citizen play his or her part in promoting election reforms. To do this, we all must arm ourselves with knowledge. I applaud you for reading this book and encourage you to take the lessons shared in these pages to heart. A book such as this plays a role not only in furthering our national civic education in elections but in fostering a public dialogue on the need for election reform, something to which the League of Women Voters dedicates itself and something that is absolutely essential if we are to truly reform the system.

Preface

It was truly an election like no other. The United States had never elected a president the way it did in 2000. Following the election on November 7, 2000, a thirty-six-day drama ensued, complete with intrigue, suspense, and scandal. It is doubtful Hollywood writers could have written a more intriguing, suspense-filled script than that produced by the elections officials, voters, and candidates in Florida. It featured ugly allegations of racism that harkened back to the pre–civil rights days of the Deep South, heretofore unknown election workers—some honest and well-intentioned, others colorful and scandalous—thrust suddenly into the spotlight, and a plot thick with spoiled ballots, faulty voting machinery, and miscast votes.

What started off as a ho-hum campaign between two uninspiring presidential candidates turned into an election day where *each vote* literally did matter. Although the lawyers and courts took control of the election, the process bogged down in a legal terra incognita. The experts seemed befuddled and unable either to predict or to explain the outcome. The media got it wrong, twice—calling Florida first for Gore and then for Bush—and later rescinded both reports. And the public was treated to a national civics lesson about the Electoral College and the Constitution. Perhaps befitting the unprecedented events surrounding the contested result, Election 2000 ended with yet another controversy.

Several worthy books have been produced telling the story of the 2000 election. But they tell only part of the story. The voices of many of those involved in the election have not been heard, and the events of the 2000 election are still unfolding. Election 2000 has become both the focal point and the impetus for an array of interesting and important electoral reforms. Indeed, in the wake of the 2000 election, a host of reforms have been proposed—and a few instituted—that could fundamentally change the way public officials are elected. Moreover, we have yet to fully assess the significance of the 2000 election; its meaning will continue to be debated and its effect felt in future reforms and elections. What did we learn from 2000? Are elections conducted in a fair and accurate manner? What of the integrity of the ballots, voting technology, and officials that make up our electoral system? What reforms are needed? These are the questions that truly define the legacy of Election 2000, and they are but a few of the questions this book addresses.

With an eye to future elections and mindful of lessons learned, this book examines the state of elections in the wake of Election 2000. It offers readers a behind-the-scenes look at the controversial election in Florida in the words of those intimately involved in it. The book presents a nuts-and-bolts account of how the 2000 election was run and how elections in general are administered. Finally, it examines the reform movement Election 2000 helped usher in.

Although noted authors wrote books about the 2000 election, political pundits debated it in the media, and workers discussed it around office water coolers throughout the world, what has been largely absent from the dialogue on the election is the voices of those who ran it—those who designed the ballots, ran the voting machines, administered the election, brought the lawsuits, and served on the canvassing boards that counted the votes. One of the goals of this book is to provide the words of those involved in the election in Florida, unfiltered through reporters or commentators. Another is to offer a mix of scholarly essays and commentary written by a wide array of individuals with expertise and experience in elections. These include well-respected scholars who study the presidency, the Electoral College, voting behavior, and elections; attorneys involved in the lawsuits that defined the 2000 presidential election; activists with nonprofit organizations leading the reform movement; and local political party and elections officials from Florida who were in the trenches in 2000.

A third goal of the book is to offer readers a fair and balanced account of the 2000 election, and of the state of elections and electoral reforms. A final objective has been to produce a study of elections suitable for a wide audience, including professors and college students, local and state elections officials, and, most important, concerned citizens and voters in Florida and elsewhere. The contributors worked hard to produce highly readable and timely essays in both of the essay formats in the book: first-person insights of the 2000 election and the experiences of those involved in running elections, and scholarly analyses of the state of elections and election reforms.

A number of local election and political party officials in Florida contributed to this book, and many graciously allowed me to interview them. Thank you to Mitch Ceasar, Cathy Dubin, Jess Gittelson, Mark Hoch, David Leahy, Gisela Salas, and Thomas Spencer, and many others who will be unnamed. Thank you for sharing your story. Thank you also to Blair Bobier for compiling a list of important reports that have been produced about the 2000 election controversy and post-2000 election reforms (parts of this list appear in appendix D), and for his work to improve the functioning of this democracy. I wish also to acknowledge Joan Karp, head of the South Palm Beach County League of Women Voters, for providing information on the league's efforts both locally and nationally to improve the integrity of elections. A special thank you to Carolyn Jefferson-Jenkins, past president of the League of Women Voters of the United States and one of the country's leading voices on election reforms, for taking the time out of her demanding schedule to contribute a foreword to this project.

An impressive group of scholars contributed to this book and they have my sincere appreciation for writing such readable and informative essays.

As always, I wish to acknowledge Claudia, Alessandro, and Isabella for their patience and support.

Most important, this book was written to empower voters. Two things we all share—readers and contributors—is our status as participants and stakeholders in the electoral process. All reforms start with thoughts, words, and proposals. May the contents of this book be beneficial in that regard, for perhaps no other political issue is as vital to the proper functioning of the American democratic "experiment" as fair, open, and reliable elections.

INTRODUCTION

The State of Elections: People, Politics, and Problems

ROBERT P. WATSON, FLORIDA ATLANTIC UNIVERSITY

> The world would come to know us as the baffling center of a baffling state, helplessly unprepared to overcome the dual limitations of our old technology and casual citizenship, which was expressed in tens of thousands of indecipherable votes.
>
> —*Palm Beach Post,* December 14, 2000

Dateline: Florida, November 7, 2000

Three things became clear to the nation on the morning after the November 7 election: (1) the election was still undecided; (2) the media and political commentators did not know what was going to happen; and (3) the outcome of Florida's contested election would determine the next president. After the initial vote was counted in Florida, Republican George W. Bush led Democrat Al Gore by 1,784 votes, an uncomfortable and intriguingly thin margin given the nearly six million votes cast in the Sunshine State. The concept of a recount entered the public consciousness when it was announced that Florida law required an automatic recount in the event an election was as close as this one, unless the loser of the initial count declined his or her right to a recount.[1] Al Gore did not, so the recount proceeded.

Widespread reports of voting fraud, mistaken votes, and voting machine error began to surface, raising questions about the legitimacy of the entire state's election. Three counties in particular—Broward, Miami-Dade, and Palm Beach, which happened to be three of the state's largest, all located along southeast Florida's "Gold Coast"—were at the center of the storm. African Americans came forward with accusations that they had been turned away from voting in Broward County and elsewhere around the state. Voters attempting to cast a vote for Gore in Palm Beach County feared they had mistakenly voted for Reform Party candidate Pat Buchanan because of a confusing ballot design, the famous "butterfly ballot," which placed Gore's name second on the left-hand page of the ballot but the punch-hole for Buchanan second overall on the ballot.[2] Many voters, the elderly in particular, reported being confused by the ballot design, and Democrats expressed concern because of the importance of the vote in Palm Beach County to a Gore victory. Palm Beach County is home to a large Jewish population prone to voting Democratic, and if this important Democratic base inadvertently cast votes for Pat Buchanan—a right-wing candidate who even publicly acknowledged his surprise at the large number of votes he received in Palm Beach County—it could prove fatal to a Democratic victory. High levels of unrecorded votes and spoiled ballots were registered in all three southeast Florida counties and around the state. In a high-stakes game of he-said-she-said, Democrats accused Republicans of tampering with absentee ballots in some of Florida's northern counties, while Republicans accused Democrats of trying to change the outcome of the state's vote. Democrats accused Republicans of purging Democratic voters from the state voter registration rolls, while Republicans accused Democrats of helping unregistered citizens to vote.

The presidential election in Florida remained inconclusive and contested. The state's twenty-five electoral votes were enough to guarantee the election to whichever candidate could claim victory in the disputed state.[3] Following the election, an historic and unprecedented thirty-six-day controversy ensued (see chronology in appendix A).

The Thirty-six Days

And the Winner Is . . .

Campaign pollsters and political commentators had predicted Florida would have both a close election and a key role in determining the winner of the presidential race. Early exit polls and returns seemed to point to Gore winning the state. Indeed, the national media announced late on Election Day that Gore had won the state. With returns still coming in and errors emerging in some of the early data, their pronouncement proved premature. They would later call Bush the winner, then be forced for a second time in the same night to retract their report. The media were not alone in their undue haste, as candidate Al

Gore called his opponent after the second media report to concede defeat, only to see Bush's lead in the state become negligible and marred by discrepancies. Gore called Bush back and retracted his earlier concession in a famously terse and tense phone call that mirrored the feelings of many and perfectly reflected the mood in Florida.[4]

As mandated by Florida law, a recount was taking place. Soon, however, the extent of the discrepancies, the closeness of the race, and allegations of machine error that might or might not be corrected in the automatic recount (along with lobbying by Democrats hoping to elicit a different result) produced a hand recount. Bush filed suit to prevent and then stop any recount from occurring. While unsuccessful initially in blocking the hand recount, the Republican strategy of delaying any response by the counties or state to the unresolved outcome would ultimately prove to be one of the deciding factors in Election 2000.

Al Gore called for a hand recount in four counties—Broward, Miami-Dade, Palm Beach, and Volusia. Bush claimed the move was partisan and biased, as Gore had won these four counties comfortably. Gore claimed that the counties had a high incidence of undervotes and allegations of voting irregularities, and old voting technology had been used. As the hand recount progressed, Bush's lead shrank to a mere 327 votes. Yet Bush benefited from the overseas vote, encompassing many military personnel serving abroad who vote Republican. This vote, which was still being counted after the polls closed on Election Day, extended Bush's 327-vote lead to 930. The Bush campaign team saw this as a sign their candidate had won, and renewed efforts to certify their man as the winner. The Democrats pressed on with their claims that the undervotes, overvotes, and spoiled ballots needed to be recounted by hand. All the while, even the experts and the county canvassing boards that were ultimately charged with conducting the hand recounts were uncertain as to just how a hand recount should be conducted, from a legal, logistical, and "chad" perspective. And by state law the votes were to be submitted by November 14, one week after Election Day.

The only county to complete the initial hand recount in time was Volusia County, and the state's top elections officer, Secretary of State Katherine Harris, did not permit the other counties extra time to complete their recount. The canvassing boards of the three large, and now pivotal, counties in southeast Florida—Broward, Miami-Dade, and Palm Beach—sued Harris for adequate time to complete their recounts. The request was denied, and Harris declared her intention to certify George W. Bush the victor. However, the Florida Supreme Court intervened and, on November 21, overturned Harris's refusal to extend the recount. Florida's high court gave the counties until November 26 to complete their recounts. The plot thickened as it was revealed that Harris, even though she was the state's director of elections, had simultaneously been serving as cochair of George W. Bush's Florida campaign. Democrats alleged a conflict of interest and saw partisan motives in the secretary of state's seemingly pro-Bush decisions during the postelection ordeal. The fact that candidate George W. Bush's younger brother Jeb Bush was governor of Florida only added to the tangled plot and the concerns of Democrats.

Even though the deadline for completing the recount had been extended, the Bush campaign team's strategy of delaying action, filing suits, and flying in top Republican politicians to oversee the process seemed to be working. Miami-Dade County failed to complete its recount even by the extended deadline, and Palm Beach County submitted its numbers a few hours after the deadline. Only the Broward County Canvassing Board completed a recount in the time allotted. For reasons that remain uncertain, Miami-Dade's canvassing board had decided not to attempt to complete their recount by November 26. Gore ultimately picked up roughly four hundred votes from the recount in Broward County and at least two hundred in Palm Beach County, but the secretary of state refused to accept partial recounts or Palm Beach County's late numbers. The race was again a dead heat.

The next day, November 26, Secretary of State Katherine Harris certified George W. Bush the winner in Florida. On November 27, Al Gore filed suit to challenge the certification. On December 4, the presiding judge ruled against Gore's request, upholding Harris's certification. But on appeal the Florida Supreme Court overturned the ruling and agreed to Gore's request to halt the certification of a winner until a viable hand recount was completed. The court also ordered that, in view of possible problems with the unrecorded votes, the 60,000–plus undervotes registered in the state be hand counted. By this time, the partial hand recount had reduced Bush's lead to just 154 votes.

Whether by design or by mistake, Florida's Supreme Court specified neither how to conduct the recount nor what constituted a vote. The counties, with only vague legal guidelines to assist them, had varying standards for what constituted a vote and how to proceed with their task. George W. Bush asked the U.S. Supreme Court to review the Florida Supreme Court's actions in allowing the hand recount and in denying his certification by the secretary of state. The U.S. Supreme Court considered the issue but delayed ruling. On December 4 the nation's high court declined to make a decision, sending the case back to the

Florida with a request that the state court review its earlier decision and clarify its ruling to extend the deadline for the hand recount. Many of those eagerly watching the unfolding events were initially uncertain whether the actions of the U.S. Supreme Court favored Bush or Gore. But the delays of the recount process and delays by the U.S. Supreme Court would, because of the limited time remaining, ultimately prove to be Gore's undoing.

Election Controversies

Either way, for many the recount did not dispel the controversies surrounding the administration of the election; nor did the subsequent decision by the U.S. Supreme Court that gave Bush the victory. The press was reporting that Florida counties were experiencing high numbers of unrecorded votes, including both undervotes—ballots with no vote in one or more races—and overvotes, with votes for more than one candidate in a race. The presence of unrecorded votes is a common occurrence in elections and is usually not a problem. Unrecorded votes had never been a possible factor in the outcome of a presidential election, but in the case of Florida, the number of unrecorded votes was unusually high and exceeded the margin by which Bush had purportedly won the state. Moreover, while one might expect voters to abstain in some races on the "bottom" of the ticket—such as municipal races—eyebrows were raised when exceptionally high numbers of voters did not record a vote for the race on the "top" of the ticket—the presidential contest. This and related problems led commentators and scholars to ask whether the phenomenon was a result of machine error, a flawed ballot, or fraud. As we see in this book, studies have shown that certain types of older voting technologies are prone to producing higher rates of unrecorded votes or spoiled ballots.[5] For instance, punch-card voting machines tend to be less accurate than electronic or touch-screen systems, and many of the contested counties in Florida were using antiquated voting technologies. Moreover, certain communities—poorer, African American precincts—have traditionally experienced higher than average rates of the same problems. Additional questions about violation of equal protection clauses arose with allegations that African American voters in the 2000 election were turned away from the polls and had been purged from registered voter rolls, often by unjustified application of already draconian laws precluding felons from voting.[6]

The American public was also treated to the jargon of elections when a controversy erupted over "chads." The chad problem became a central issue in the thirty-six-day controversy following the election. In the counties using punch-card voting machines, voters were required to insert their ballot into the machine and then, using a small, pencil-like stylus, make perforations in the boxes appearing next to their preferred candidates' names. Sounds easy enough. But complaints surfaced that the ballots did not align well in the machines, making it difficult to "punch" through the appropriate mark. Ideally, the hole would be punched clean through the ballot and the tiny piece of paper—the "chad"—would fall into a tray under the ballot. Such punch-card systems record votes by scanning the ballot and reading the holes left by the detached chads. Yet if a chad remains attached, the light sensor can fail to read the vote— which appears to have been a problem with some of the undervoted ballots in Florida, especially for the presidential race. During the hand recount, the issue emerged of how officials might use a partially detached or punched chad as an indication of the intent of the voter, and thus whether or not to count certain types of chads as votes. (See appendix B for the types of chads.)

Decided by the Court

On December 9, 2000, the U.S. Supreme Court supported George W. Bush's suit by a narrow 5-4 vote and once again held up the recount until a thorough review could be completed. Because of the limited time remaining, this spelled another setback for the Gore team. Finally, only three days later on December 12, the high court by another 5-4 vote ruled in favor of Bush and stopped the recount on grounds that insufficient time remained and the recount and actions of the Florida court were unconstitutional. Five justices supported Bush—Chief Justice William Rehnquist, Sandra Day O'Connor, Antonin Scalia, Anthony Kennedy, and Clarence Thomas. The four dissenting were John Paul Stevens, David Souter, Ruth Bader Ginsberg, and Stephen Breyer. Justices Souter and Breyer had agreed that the Florida Supreme Court's decision was lacking adequate clarification and justification, but they felt the proper course of action was to send the case back to the state for a decision.

What had started out as a political battle had, after the election, quickly become centered on the accuracy of voting systems. The effort to address the election controversy was, however, usurped by lawyers who split hairs over election law and definitions of chads.

Election 2000 became a legal battle. For instance, the Democrats filed motions to disqualify thousands of votes in Seminole and Martin Counties on grounds that the elections offices permitted members of the Bush campaign and local Republicans to correct mistakes on ballots cast by Republicans and to fill in mandatory voter information on absentee ballots on behalf of the voters. But the courts ruled against Gore and allowed those ballots to be counted for Bush. During the fight over the recount, Gore both won and lost various motions to provide a hand recount, while Bush both won and lost various motions to stop the recount.

Although numerous scholars and media commentators—joined by Democrats—alleged that the Supreme Court had acted in a partisan manner, on questionable constitutional footing, and in direct contradiction to their previous position of favoring the principle of federalism by not overturning or interfering with state matters, it was already over.[7] The high court questioned the rationale used by the Florida court in extending the recount deadline and pointed to Article II of the Constitution granting state legislatures the power to determine how the state's presidential electors would be chosen. In the end, Gore ran out of time, legal options, and supporters on the Supreme Court. Arguably the most intriguing election in modern history had been decided, for better or for worse, by the highest legal authority.

Bush v. Gore, the court case, had been decided, and thus Bush versus Gore, the campaign, had been decided. Even though Al Gore had won the popular vote by more than 500,000 votes, George W. Bush had won the Electoral College 271-266, passing the constitutionally mandated majority mark by one vote. On January 6, 2001, as required by the Constitution, the electoral votes were counted before a joint session of Congress, bringing the dispute to closure. In one final plot in the Election 2000 saga, a group of African American members of the House of Representatives attempted to formally object to Florida's electoral votes being cast for Bush on grounds that many allegations had been brought by African Americans claiming to have been denied their right to vote. However, in order for such an objection to move forward, it needs bicameral support.[8] Because no member of the U.S. Senate would join the representatives in the protest, the votes were counted and Congress certified George W. Bush as president.

The Meaning of Elections

The Importance of Democratic Participation

Elections assume many different forms, but for an election system to be viable it must provide opportunities for citizen participation and opposition to the ruling regime. Democratic electoral systems permit both opposition and widespread if not universal citizen participation. Though these were previously restricted largely to the United States, Canada, and Western Europe, progress has been made throughout the world in recent decades in making elections truly democratic. Still, however, some authoritarian electoral systems do not permit opposition—or allow for only token opposition—and provide no means to assure openness and accountability through an independent body or one free from influence or control by the authoritarian regime. The prevalence of such nondemocratic electoral systems might come as a surprise to some Americans, who long ago grew accustomed to presumably fair, accurate, and democratic elections at home. An occasional headline about a "rigged" election in a less developed nation or efforts by the United States to monitor suspect elections abroad reminded Americans that such problems with elections still existed. Yet after the 2000 election in Florida the reality of inaccurate and questionable elections was brought to the forefront, and much more attention is now paid to how elections are run.

Elections provide citizens with a means of participation. Elections also provide an important reminder of accountability: the government must be responsive to the citizenry or face the threat of defeat in the next election. Because citizens in a democratic election have some degree of influence on who governs, elections also confer a degree of legitimacy on the ruling or winning regime, which provides an important counterbalance to any legal or constitutional forms of authority.

Voting is a fundamental component of a healthy democracy and is generally seen as a virtue and a civic duty. The very process of voting may help to promote a civic culture in society, and the outcome of a vote determines the parameters for what is generally considered acceptable behavior in political life—the candidates, programs, and policies "chosen" by the electorate. A healthy election presents candidates and political parties offering voters different positions on important issues—that is, offering choices. Thus this opportunity for expression—whether of support or of disagreement—affords voters a peaceful means of registering any social or political discontent.

Universal Suffrage and Enfranchisement

Even in the most democratic electoral systems, the government or ruling regime plays a role in regulating the processes that comprise the election. Such concerns as voter registration requirements, composition of the electorate, development of a ballot, date established for the election, means of casting a vote, and even the counting and verification of the vote are typically the responsibility of government. Historically, a number of approaches have been employed by governments and rulers to influence the outcome of elections. One of the main ways to do this is to manipulate the composition of the electorate. Requirements and barriers in the form of property requirements, for instance, have been used to deny certain citizens and groups the right to participate. This occurred in the United States, where property, sex, and race were employed to construct the electorate. Even after women and African Americans gained the right to vote, mechanisms such as the "white primaries" were used in the South until the civil rights movement manipulated the electorate.

Another perhaps less transparent means of influencing the outcome of elections is the manipulation of electoral districts. Because political bodies such as state legislatures are responsible for determining the character and composition of electoral districts, a temptation exists to reorganize—or, technically, "reapportion"—the districts to advantage a certain political interest or group. This is known as gerrymandering. Districts have been redesigned to contain many liberal voters so as to create a safe district or seat for a Democrat. In the South, districts were often drawn to resemble a wagon wheel, with the center of the wheel located in a large community of African American voters. This had the effect of dividing the community (through the spokes of the wheel, which were the borders of other districts) into several different districts, rather than allowing the group in question a district of its own. In theory, and usually in practice, this dilutes the power of the group of voters in question—African Americans in this example. If the community were organized as a district, the result would likely be the election of an African American. The gerrymandering, however, would likely result in the election of Caucasians in the district in question and neighboring districts (the ones between the spokes of the wheel). Because the number of electoral districts is often fixed, yet the population expands and migrates, districts are typically reapportioned every ten years using population data from the decennial census. This occurs in the two-year election cycle following the census and has been used by both major political parties to serve their own interest. When the Democrats control state legislatures, the apportionment process generally favors Democrats, and the opposite occurs when Republicans are in power.

The United States has overcome a history of efforts to disenfranchise certain citizens, notably slaves and women. Advancing the concept of "universal suffrage" by the Framers of the Constitution was momentous, even if it took a long time and great struggle to achieve in practice. At the time of the founding, essentially only white males owning land could vote or run for office. After the Civil War, the Fifteenth Amendment in 1870 extended the right to vote to black males. Yet after Reconstruction ended in 1877, southern states denied the basic rights of voting and citizenship through a variety of mechanisms including poll taxes, grandfather clauses, literacy tests, and outright terror and intimidation. Indeed, it was not until the 1960s, with the passage in 1964 of the Twenty-second Amendment, which outlawed poll taxes, and the 1965 Voting Rights Act, which provided a means for assuring open and inclusive elections, that many of these undemocratic practices were eliminated. And women did not gain the legal right to vote until 1920, with the passage of the Nineteenth Amendment.

Voting and Election Systems

Voting is a political activity that tends to have the impact of democratizing citizen participation or even constituting democracy, without which only a few privileged individuals or groups would have access to political power and participation. The process of casting a vote is simple, and is designed to accomplish the aforementioned goal of democracy. The time and energy required to cast a vote is minimal, less than that needed to write a letter to a candidate or organize a political debate or rally. Dates are established for elections, although they may vary from county to county, state to state. Voter and election education programs are also available, designed to further clarify the process and encourage participation by informed voters. Generally, electoral systems require a prospective voter to register, which is usually without cost and can be done in a simple and timely manner. The 1993 National Voter Registration Act signed by President Bill Clinton, for example, provides citizens with the convenience of mailing registration forms or registering through a number of government offices that provide social services as well as through state driver's license offices—thus the nickname "motor voter."

Even though voting is a fundamental right and the struggle required to attain this right was long and marked by great sacrifice, tens of millions of citizens in the United States fail to participate in the electoral process. Turnout in presidential elections hovers around 50 percent, while nonpresidential elections such as congressional races usually draw perhaps a third of eligible voters. Local elections around the nation suffer even lower voting rates. Turnout varies considerably around the world, and a number of nations surpass the U.S. turnout of roughly 50 percent in national elections. For instance, other mature "western" democracies such as Australia, Britain, Denmark, Israel, Germany, and South Africa typically enjoy voting rates in the 70–90 percent range, while U.S. neighbors Canada and Mexico also experience turnouts in the sixties and seventies.[9] Voting turnout in the United States also varies considerably with income, education, race, and even region, with many ethnic minorities and groups lower on the socioeconomic ladder generally recording lower rates of participation. While there are a number of reasons for this, it undeniably influences electoral outcomes and the distribution of political power. Relatedly, issues such as the disenfranchisement of former felons and the reliability and integrity of elections—as seen in the 2000 controversy in Florida—pose threats to the notion of universal suffrage and the viability of open, fair, and democratic elections in the United States.

Many voters simply cast a vote on Election Day without thinking about the complex system of running an election and the people involved in administering it. In the United States, elections are largely the responsibility of the states, and a role exists for local government. The principle of federalism is quite apparent in elections, where the lack of a uniform election system confuses many voters. This constitutional design explains the existence of a seemingly endless variety of voting machines, ballot designs, and dates for elections. Even up until the 1970s, prospective voters moving from one state to another were likely to find different residency and registration requirements. Officials and, in some cases, election boards at the state level are charged with administering elections and working with local elections supervisors, some of whom are elected and partisan, some of whom are not. Voters are assigned to a particular precinct, a geographic region where the voter lives, designed expressly for the purpose of voting. State and local elections officials are charged with registering voters, maintaining accurate rolls of registered voters, setting up the precincts, designing the ballot, selecting a voting system or machine, recruiting and training volunteer poll workers, and actually conducting and then counting the vote.

There are a variety of electoral systems, each with its own potential advantages and disadvantages. The United States tends to rely on a "plurality system," although no standard, universal system exists. In a plurality system, the candidate winning the most votes wins the election, whether or not those votes constitute a *majority* of the votes cast. For instance, if four viable candidates run in an election, the vote may be split 40-30-20-10. The winner, with 40 percent of the votes cast, did not achieve a majority. This candidate did, however, receive the *most* votes, and in a plurality system is thus elected. In order to win election in a "majority system," a threshold of "50 percent plus one" is required. Because of the higher standard for victory, a runoff election between the top two candidates is required if no single candidate meets the "50 percent plus one" requirement. Both systems make it difficult for a minor-party or third-party candidate to win. The most common electoral system in Europe is "proportional representation." In such a system, various parties are awarded seats proportional to the percentage of the popular vote they win. Thus, the party of the fourth candidate in the aforementioned scenario would receive 10 percent of the seats in the election. In some states in the United States, candidates in the presidential primary are awarded delegates based on the proportion of votes they receive in that election.

Reform and the Fallout from Florida 2000

The Florida Effect

Florida is what political scientists and campaign consultants call a swing state. In addition to being the fourth most populous state in the country, Florida is one of those states that is truly competitive. Unlike Hawaii, which is a strongly Democratic state, or Wyoming, which is a strongly Republican state, Florida is generally considered to be "up for grabs." The state elects both Democrats and Republicans in local and state races and has split its vote in recent presidential contests. So scholars and public opinion polls were predicting a close contest in the Sunshine State. Accordingly, both George W. Bush and Al Gore made it a priority for their campaigns.

Neither presidential candidate seemed to generate much enthusiasm in the electorate, and the same can be said for many candidates competing at the local and state levels in the 2000 elections. Barely 51 percent of the voters bothered to vote in 2000, making the turnout rather average for recent elections. Although it was an important election, the public was largely uninspired, even bored with the entire process.[10] Perhaps the lack of enthusiasm was in part due to the candidates. This would be the "best-case" scenario one could hope for. On the other hand, it is possible the public did not understand the intricacies of the Electoral College. This suggests a "worst-case" scenario, wherein the public's apathy was the result of feeling that they are not a part of the process or outcome, that their vote does not matter. Eventually, such a concern may have appeared to have been justified. After all, it appeared that the electors, lawyers, and courts were making the decisions. Scholars have generally agreed that the judiciary played too much of a role in the 2000 election, more than is proper, and perhaps so much so that it impacted the public's confidence in the system, after the fact; relatedly, it is generally agreed that what happened in Florida was important and the 2000 election was a turning point in U.S. politics.[11]

The Florida controversy overshadowed the thousands of other races held throughout the country in 2000. But the controversy in Florida also brought to the public's attention the implications of having inadequate and outdated election and voting systems. Election 2000 produced many close elections, divided government at the national level, and no clear majority or minority party. It was contested by uninspiring, centrist candidates and determined by an uninspired, centrist electorate. Perhaps the most ironic outcome of the election—or perhaps the most reassuring, depending upon one's perspective—was that, in the months before the tragic terrorist attacks on the United States of September 11, 2001, the nation seemed to be running much as it had. George W. Bush did not experience the problems of legitimacy that many scholars and commentators had predicted as a result of a controversial election, partisan bickering defined a divided Congress, and the public remained apathetic. On the tail of the election controversy the economy faltered after years of unprecedented growth. However, the by-product of Election 2000 seemed to be business as usual, which might be the result of the election being decided by the lawyers and courts.

It appears that no crime was committed, with the possible exception of incidents of voters being turned away from the polls, which remain under investigation. It appears that there was no overriding conscious attempt to manipulate the system, with the possible exception of a few isolated cases. So, why was election 2000 a watershed in U.S. politics? Why the controversy?

With hindsight, it appears that the real culprits were simple human mistakes and misunderstanding, along with a poorly designed and poorly administered election system. As a result, there were a number of casualties in the wake of the election. For many involved—courts and individual judges, the two parties' attorneys, journalists covering the election, scholars and commentators thought to be experts on elections—the controversy was a lose-lose situation. Neither Bush nor Gore displayed or admitted to any other desire than thinly veiled attempts to direct the legal fight in his own interest, and the same can be said about the political parties.[12] The courts showed they were not above partisan politics; journalists acted too quickly in calling the election while whipping events into a sensationalistic frenzy; scholars and commentators demonstrated their lack of understanding of the U.S. electoral system; and the nation's system of elections showed itself to be inadequate and antiquated.[13] The whole process and all involved were tarnished.

There are some long-term consequences of the historic election, and simmering beneath the surface are unresolved concerns. Many scholars and commentators have pointed out the divisions among the public, and damage to our faith in elections and other institutions of government such as the courts, in the wake of Election 2000. In particular, the U.S. Supreme Court's actions have been attacked as "unmistakenly partisan" and "incomprehensible."[14] Supreme Court Justice John Paul Stevens admitted his disappointment with the Court's decision, suggesting the real losers in 2000 were the Supreme Court and "the nation's confidence in the judge as an impartial guardian of the rule of law."[15] Reports have noted the public's eroding faith in everything from the media's objectivity and quality of reporting to the reliability of polls to voting systems and elections officials.[16]

The Palm Beach County elections supervisor Theresa LePore was vilified for designing the grossly flawed butterfly ballot that may have given Bush the election, and the Palm Beach County Canvassing Board bore the brunt of Democrats' rage and late-night comedians' jokes for its inability to conduct a timely recount. However, in yet another irony, it would appear that this canvassing board was one of the few actors involved in the infamous election to have conducted itself above self-interest. Although this Democratic-leaning board conducted a recount in a Democratic stronghold that might have turned the election to Gore's advantage, the board diligently developed strict criteria for counting the votes and awarded to Gore an amazingly low 8 percent of questionable ballots, both of which actions worked against the Democrats.[17]

The Electoral College under Fire

It had been more than a century (1888) since the Electoral College failed to give the election to the winner of the popular vote, and although another such outcome loomed in the shadows, the country had grown complacent. The United States had not experienced a deadlocked election and major Electoral College controversy since the 1876 race between Rutherford B. Hayes and Samuel J. Tilden.

Few citizens understand the mechanics of the Electoral College, yet opinion polls have consistently shown that a majority of citizens want to replace it with direct popular election.[18] Indeed, more constitutional amendments have been proposed dealing with the Electoral College than with any other issue. The topic was debated hotly by the Framers, and it has continually captured the attention of reformers.[19] Yet it would seem that the nation needs a "misfired" election or crisis before reform enjoys widespread or serious support.

Whether the events of Election 2000 will result in Electoral College reforms remains to be seen. A practical answer would be that, regardless of how rational and attractive such reforms might be, it is doubtful real reform will result. Changing the Electoral College requires an amendment to the Constitution, and the current system benefits not only the two major political parties (by making it hard for a third-party candidate to win) but also the largest states (to which candidates devote more attention) and the smallest (which are assured at least three electoral votes).

The Electoral College was born of conflict and compromise as the Framers, wrestling with the question of how to pick a president, debated and rejected many proposals. Its genesis was also less than noble, as it favored the interests of slaveholding states. Only white males owning property could vote at the time, and because most slaveholding states were smaller in white population than their northern counterparts such as Massachusetts, New York, and Pennsylvania, the direct popular election of the president would have placed the slave states at a disadvantage. In the Electoral College, however, each state's electoral votes are proportional to its congressional delegation. And the size of that delegation, except for a fixed contingent of two senators, reflects the state's total population. Since each slave was counted—albeit as three-fifths of a person—the southern states with large slave populations enjoyed greatly increased clout.

The Electoral College was also a compromise between large and small states. Rather than being based on a grand design or political philosophy, it reveals a practical compromise that balanced such interests as those of large and small states as well as those leery of a popular election and those desirous of the states having a major role. It was the view of the Framers that such a mechanism would place the right person in the office.

As the system allocates electors to each state on the basis of its congressional presence, Florida with its twenty-three representatives and two senators in 2000 had twenty-five electoral votes. In general, the candidate who gets the largest popular vote in a state receives all of that state's electoral votes in a winner-take-all system. The exceptions are Maine and Nebraska, where the winner in each congressional district receives that district's vote and the overall winner receives the two "Senate" votes. Some states "pledge" their electoral votes so that the winner of the popular election in the state must receive the support of the electors. Other states are unpledged, meaning that, theoretically, the electors could ignore the popular vote when casting their votes.[20]

A candidate need only carry a plurality of the state's popular vote to win all the state's electors. So whether a candidate wins the state by a handful of votes or a landslide, by a plurality or a majority, he or she receives all of the state's electoral votes. A candidate needs a majority—at least 270—to win the presidency. If no candidate receives a majority in the Electoral College, the House of Representatives picks the winner, with each state's delegation getting one vote to cast. This happened in 1800 and 1824. Because of the design of the Electoral College—requiring only a popular plurality to receive all of a state's votes—the winning candidate might lose the popular vote nationally, as happened in 1876, 1888, and 2000.

Technically, the voting on Election Day does not determine the presidency. Rather, it elects a slate of electors who meet in each state capitol on the Monday after the second Wednesday in December and cast ballots. These ballots are then read in early January in a joint session of Congress where the winner is announced.

Reform

Much attention has been devoted in recent years to the need for campaign reform, most notably in the area of campaign financing. The seemingly countless financial scandals and abuses of "soft money" donations and so-called issue advocacy ads highlighted a concern among the public that many facets of campaigns and elections were in need of reform. Systematic campaign reforms did not occur until the early 1970s, with the creation of the Federal Elections Commission to oversee campaign practices and with the establishment of limitations on individual and PAC (political action committee) contributions to candidates and the political parties.

But little has been done to improve how elections are run. The Florida controversy in 2000 kick-started the reform process, as a number of state and local initiatives both in Florida and around the nation have been introduced and some passed since 2000. Indeed, the election amounted to a national civics lesson and a cruel exercise in how *not* to run an election. It cast doubt on the accuracy, fairness, and overall viability of elections. Problems with undervotes and overvotes were discovered to be quite normal, despite the fact that they could alter the outcome of elections. It was also discovered that outdated voting systems, prone to error, were still being used throughout the nation, and so were flawed ballot designs that research has shown produce spoiled ballots. For instance, the butterfly ballot used in Palm Beach County was a two-sided ballot, a type known to produce unrecorded votes and undervotes. The same can be said of punch-card and lever voting machines, yet they are still used.

Even though it was public knowledge that Florida's elections supervisors were elected officials and partisan, and even though most elections officials in Florida and nationwide are honest professionals, alarms were sounded at the possible conflict of interest raised by this occurrence. To be sure, controversy swirled over the actions of Katherine Harris, Florida's secretary of state. The fact that she served both as head elections official for the state and as the Bush campaign's cochair in the state gave, at the least, the appearance of impropriety, which in turn cast doubt upon the integrity of the election. That she saw no reason to excuse herself from one of her jobs, that her official decisions during the controversy uniformly favored Bush, that she made a lot of money on a book after the election, and that she chose to run for the U.S. House of Representatives as a Republican after the election (she was elected), did little to help the matter.

Widespread allegations of fraud in the 2000 race remain unresolved. These include: bribes to get the homeless and college students to vote for a particular party; voters voting in more than one precinct; Florida's zealous effort to purge felons from voter rolls, resulting in the purge of nonfelons too; poll workers in Florida and elsewhere tampering with ballots and casting votes where citizens left ballots empty (undervoted).[21]

Not surprisingly, the call for reform has been sounded. A host of scholarly conferences have been convened and books published on the topic. Organizations from the League of Women Voters to the National Association of Secretaries of State have issued reports outlining an ambitious agenda of reforms. Voters, think tanks, and commentators have advocated reform. A high-profile National Commission on Federal Election Reform cochaired by former presidents Jimmy Carter and Gerald Ford issued a scathing report advocating a number of reform measures.[22] But reform is a complex matter, and there exists the need to think through the reform measures, conduct further research on election practices and systems, and promote a national dialogue on the issues.[23]

Any election reforms will need to be in line with the decentralized nature of elections in the United States. The Constitution grants states the right to play a lead role in their elections, and even presidential elections are not run by the federal government. Instead they are a collage of local and state contests that often vary considerably in their functioning and format. Even within a state, a range of voting equipment and technologies is encountered, from lever machines to punch-card systems to optical scanners. Does this mean the federal government can do nothing? While it cannot mandate uniformity of voting systems or a national ballot design or other reform measures, it can, for example, offer funding for states and localities to procure new voting technology. Relatedly, the precedent the U.S. Supreme Court used for overruling a state in an election matter might leave room for more federal oversight in elections.

Numerous reform measures have been proposed by scholars, electoral reform committees, and nonprofit advocates of election reform. Perhaps foremost among the reform recommendations is a systematic, aggressive, and uniform evaluation of election systems. The goal of making voting as simple, appealing, inclusive, and democratic as possible must be prioritized in our efforts to research and evaluate elections. Here are some of the proposed initiatives:

- Standardize statewide voter registration systems
- Institute same-day registration and voting
- Automate registration systems
- Extend voting hours
- Make Election Day a holiday
- Improve poll workers' training
- Improve poll workers' pay
- Improve poll workers' working conditions
- Shorten poll workers' work shifts
- Use college students and government personnel to staff polls
- Restore voting rights to disenfranchised former felons
- Encourage absentee voting
- Encourage early voting
- Permit unrestricted absentee voting without requiring reason
- Institute Internet voting
- Permit "provisional voting" on Election Day by any voter claiming to be eligible
- Mail ballots to voters' homes
- Improve and augment voter information and education
- Simplify the voting process
- Simplify the ballot design

- Use newer, more accurate voting systems and technologies
- Set uniform benchmarks for assessing elections and voting system performance
- Standardize election laws, processes, and forms
- Set federal standards for voting equipment
- Increase federal money for elections administration
- Increase state assistance to poor counties for elections administration
- Prevent news media from reporting early returns and exit polls until polling places close
- Install nonpartisan elections officials or require them to run as "nonpartisan" candidates
- Establish a new federal elections administration commission
- Rethink the Electoral College

Such a measure as the National Voter Registration Act of 1993, or "motor-voter bill," seems to be a step in the right direction inasmuch as it has removed obstacles to voting and encouraged registration. In Florida, for example, one million new voters were registered in 1995–96.[24] Even though the Republican Party opposed the measure and then-president George Bush vetoed a similar bill in 1992 (Republican opponents claimed the new system would be ripe for fraud and abuse; also, it would help register likely Democrats), the measure did pass and is a recent example of a major election reform.

Many of the reforms can be done simply and at low cost. Others will cost money, which will continue to be a major roadblock in a tight economy. An example of simple reforms at work is the nonprofit, nonpartisan Project Vote Smart, which collects information on thousands of candidates around the country and provides a free voter education and information service to the public. Thanks to grant funding, it is able to offer a toll-free hotline and an informative Web site. Another example is the publication and distribution of voting guides by nonprofit agencies, universities, and elections offices.[25] Nationwide, programs such as Kids Voting USA are promoting voter participation and a civic ethos by allowing K–12 students to participate in mock elections and learn about voting and elections in the classroom.

The 2000 election changed history. Indeed, the United States has never chosen a president quite the way it did in 2000. Contemplating the long-term significance of Election 2000, the *Chronicle of Higher Education* asked a group of well-regarded scholars to predict how the election will be viewed in a half century. Reflective of the mood and opinions of the nation, the scholars responded with a number of interpretations of the event, some from perspectives supportive of Bush and some of Gore, and most of them critical of the courts and the electoral system. However, the commentary echoed a note of optimism that the election controversy may have helped to "reinvigorate America's interest in democracy."[26] Certainly many of the issues and controversies from the 2000 election in Florida go to the very heart of the country's democratic experiment and raise fundamental questions about fairness and equality. These questions must be answered and legitimacy and confidence in elections must be restored for democracy to function. The effect of the 2000 controversy was to create a "Florida movement," which is helping to raise consciousness about the need for reform.[27]

Notes

1. Florida Statute 102.141(4) requires an automatic recount if the margin in an election is less than 0.5 percent of the total votes cast.

2. Critics had a field day with the flawed butterfly ballot. When this author handed sample ballots to some of his college students and asked them to vote, a few intending to vote for Gore unintentionally voted for Buchanan.

3. Florida had twenty-five electoral votes in 2000, but after reapportionment in 2002 the state has twenty-seven electoral votes.

4. The famous Gore-Bush exchange is discussed in the *New York Times*. See "Contesting the Vote," December 6, 2000, A27.

BUSH: Let me make sure I understand, you are calling to retract your concession.
GORE: You don't have to get snippy about this. Let me explain something, your younger brother is not the ultimate authority on this.

5. There are numerous studies of voting machines and technologies that raise concerns about accuracy. See, for instance, the Report of the National Commission on Federal Election Reform, 2002. The subject is also discussed in this book in chapters 9–11.

6. Since African American males suffer disproportionately high rates of incarceration, laws precluding felons from voting result in higher percentages of African American males being disenfranchised, in Florida and elsewhere. And Florida happens to be one of the toughest states in the nation in stripping former felons of the right to vote—along with the ability to run for public office and even to be licensed by the state as required by certain occupations, all of which has a detrimental impact on this segment of Florida's population. The rigorous purging of Florida's rolls, it was claimed after Election 2000, eliminated not only felons but many qualified black voters.

For detailed discussion of the many allegations of possible racism and equal protection violations that were raised, see the list of election reform sources in appendix D, most notably the report of the U.S. Commission on Civil Rights at www.usccr.gov/. See reports "Has Election Reform Gone Far Enough" at www.usccr.gov/press/archives/2002/061302.htm, "U.S. Commission on Civil Rights Continues Review of Florida Election Reform" at www.usccr.gov/press/archives/2002/052302.htm, or "U.S. Commission on Civil Rights Concludes that 'No Count' is Real Issue in Florida Votes" at www.usccr.gov/press/archives/2001/030901.htm

7. For a good discussion of this issue, see Ceaser and Busch, *The Perfect Tie*, and Dionne and Kristol, *Bush v. Gore.*

8. See U.S. Code, Section 15, Title III.

9. Lowi and Ginsberg, *American Government,* 431.

10. See Ceaser and Busch, *The Perfect Tie,* prologue.

11. Dionne and Kristol, *Bush v. Gore,* 1–2.

12. McWilliams, "Meaning of the Election."

13. For a fuller discussion, see Posner, *Breaking the Deadlock.*

14. Greenhouse, "Collision with Politics."

15. This appears in Judge Stevens's dissent in the *Bush v. Gore* court case and can also be read in the *New York Times,* December 13, 2000, A1.

16. See Ceaser and Busch, *The Perfect Tie*; Dionne and Kristol, *Bush v. Gore.*

17. The author bases his opinion on numerous interviews with individuals and officials involved in the 2000 election in South Florida counties. The Palm Beach County Canvassing Board—like the county's electorate—is Democratic in its political leanings. The canvassing board was composed of the county's elections supervisor, Theresa LePore, Judge Charles Burton, and County Commissioner Carol Roberts.

18. Cronin, Foreword, viii.

19. Best, *Choice of the People,* 1.

20. The notion of unfaithful electors has not been a problem in the modern era. In fact, since 1948 fewer than ten electors have voted in ways not dictated by their state's popular vote. In 1988 an elector from West Virginia cast a vote in reverse order of the Democratic ticket, electing to vote for Lloyd Bentsen and Michael Dukakis rather than Dukakis and Bentsen. One elector in the 2000 race did not vote as pledged in an apparent protest of the election.

21. For an excellent discussion on these allegations of fraud, see Ceaser and Busch, *The Perfect Tie,* 245–47.

22. The National Commission on Federal Election Reform was cochaired by Jimmy Carter, Gerald Ford, Lloyd N. Cutler, and Robert H. Michel. See their *To Assure Pride.*

23. Ceaser and Busch, *The Perfect Tie,* 241.

24. From the news briefing by former Senate majority leader Tom Daschle held through the U.S. Senate Democratic Policy Committee on May 20, 1996.

25. The League of Women Voters' report (that is presented in the Appendix) found that, "Voting guides serve a very useful purpose, providing moderately conscientious voters with a great deal of relevant information in a very convenient form." See Bartels and Vavreck, *Campaign Reform,* 37–39.

26. The comments were made by Professor Cass Sunstein, a legal scholar with the University of Chicago. See "What We'll Remember in 2050."

27. Dionne and Kristol, *Bush v. Gore,* 3.

THE FLORIDA ELECTION CONTROVERSY

2 ☐

☐

☐

The Election, Miami, and the Recount

THOMAS R. SPENCER, COUNSEL, REPUBLICAN PARTY
OF MIAMI-DADE COUNTY

A political campaign has basically two main components: financial[1] and political. Both are administered by experienced, capable professionals with expertise in these areas. I participated in both components of George W. Bush's campaign. My first function in late 1999 was not only to donate substantial funds to the Bush Exploratory Committee but to raise substantial funds as well. Since contributions to the presidential committee are limited and must be personal contributions, a wide-ranging effort has to be undertaken to raise sufficient funds for the campaign. These personal contributors are known as "hard" dollars. They are called hard because they are *hard* to raise!

For individuals such as myself working to raise money, it is necessary to request funds from every friend, family member, and business associate you know. The finance committee keeps precise records of how successful one is, and sets contribution "levels" or goals. It should be noted that almost $100,000,000 in hard contributions must be raised in a presidential election cycle. Most of this money is spent on media campaigns. Thus the leaders of finance committees must necessarily be very aggressive in "encouraging" committee members to raise hard contributions. Those who raise the most money inevitably receive the most preferential invitations to events and access to the candidate at finance committee events, which is a nice incentive to meet the fund-raising goals, but not necessarily the reason most of us become involved in such difficult work.

The finance committee activities for the Bush campaign in Florida consisted of hundreds of fund-raising events to raise the necessary hard-dollar campaign contributions. At the same time, political activities began in late 1999 and were coordinated and run simultaneously with finance activities.

"Political" activities are designed to raise the awareness, name recognition, and issue identification of the candidate among the public and potential voters and inspire a "grassroots" base support and excitement. This is done through media campaigns, direct mail, phone banks, and door-to-door solicitation. Also, constituent groups are formed, such as Veterans for Bush, to assist in this matter.

The Florida Campaign

One of my first political activities pertaining directly to George W. Bush's presidential campaign in Florida was to accompany Florida governor Jeb Bush to New Hampshire to stump for his brother in the New Hampshire primary. The finance committee chartered a plane, filled it with supporters and campaign volunteers from Florida, loaded it with oranges and strawberries grown in the Sunshine State, and landed in New Hampshire one cold morning in February of 2000. We went from house to house, soliciting votes and dropping off oranges and strawberries to anyone who would open the door. This accomplished two important things: First, we raised the awareness of voters that Floridians were behind George W. Bush. Second, it reinforced our gratitude for living in warm, sunny Florida!

Our committee continued both finance activities and political activities through the spring and summer of 2000, culminating in the Republican National Convention in August 2000. There the Florida state delegates met to plan a strategy for the final stretch of activities leading up to Election Day. Moreover, our state Republican finance committee began the aggressive solicitation of "soft" campaign dollars to support our state Republican Victory Committee.

Soft campaign dollars are those raised from businesses and very wealthy individuals. They are generally substantial in number and directed to activities that support the campaign indirectly. They are very important contributions that usually come late in the campaign, after the hard dollars are raised.

As soon as the Republican Convention was over in August 2000 with vice presidential candidate Dick Cheney selected, we began to carefully plan out the final Florida campaign activities. The Florida Republican Party has a well-run team that is supported by county Republican committees from around the state. Each county has elected district representatives who represent and organize each neighborhood.

While the professional campaign teams put together the television and radio commercials, our party began to plan our grassroots campaign strategies. These included:

- Appointing precinct captains to monitor the actual vote
- Organizing phone banks to make sure that our voters went to the polls
- Establishing transportation committees around the state to get voters to the polls on Election Day
- Having absentee voter teams available to make sure absentee voters completed the proper applications and submitted their ballots
- Preparing legal teams to monitor possible cases of vote fraud and any other legal problems that they might encounter on Election Day as they worked in precincts around the state
- Creating general teams charged with making sure campaign workers were properly trained

Prior to Election Day a legal team was appointed to be on duty throughout the day to ensure that campaign precinct workers had someone to talk to. Generally, attorneys supportive of the Republican Party are used for this task. If a problem arose, campaign workers could call a legal team member and have that lawyer record a complaint with the elections office. Administering an election is a complicated task governed by a detailed system of laws and rules. Many voters do not understand all the intricacies of how elections work or even the full extent of their rights as voters. Also, it is necessary to have such legal teams available because official poll workers are not trained in the full range of election laws and procedures. Many poll workers are simply civic-minded citizens doing their part to make the election work, but they only work sporadically as elections are held.

For example, during the 2000 election some voters were turned away at the polls for lack of sufficient identification. Apparently some poll workers insisted that prospective voters have two forms of identification containing photographs in order to vote, even though the law required only one such identification! The function of the legal team was to instantly work out this and other problems with the Department of Elections, with the goal of correcting the problems so that voters could cast their ballots.

Election Day

Election Day in 2000 was, like all elections, defined by pandemonium. From the moment the polls opened at 7 a.m. on November 7 until they closed at 7 p.m., the political party workers toiled feverishly to turn out the vote. Assuring that the party's faithful members get out to vote on Election Day is an important duty of the political party officers.

Since I was serving as the Miami-Dade chairman for the U.S. Senate campaign of U.S. Representative Bill McCollum as well as an officer in the Republican Party and a member of the Bush presidential campaign in Florida, I had triple duty on Election Day. After the polls closed that evening, I flew to Orlando to "celebrate" victory. Unfortunately for the Republican Party, at around 9 p.m. Bill McCollum conceded defeat in his Senate bid, and we commiserated together until 11 p.m., watching the final results of the Bush-Gore race unfold with great theater and suspense. To our great dismay, at one point during the evening it appeared that the race in Florida was lost. The numbers being called by the media were painful.

I went to sleep at 12:30 a.m. after a long, hard day of work, dejected at the prospect of losing the presidential election.

The Recount Controversy

At 1:30 a.m. November 8, my cell phone rang and on the other end was the legal team coordinator for the Bush-Cheney campaign. She requested that I fly back to Miami and be at the Department of Elections at eight. When I arrived at the Department of Elections that morning, I encountered nothing short of a media frenzy. A machine recount was in progress, which I was requested to monitor. The election remained in dispute and appeared to be too close to call. The recount took all day. It produced results virtually identical to the initial count. However, the Democratic Party demanded that the Miami-Dade County Canvassing Board order a manual recount of three heavily Democratic precincts that had been selected by the Democratic Party.

Florida election law requires a canvassing board to review the election results and adjudicate (subject to appeal) vote tabulation and absentee ballot issues. The Miami-Dade Canvassing Board consisted of two county court judges and the supervisor of elections for the county. After the three aforementioned precincts were manually counted, a change of only six votes (out of five thousand) was shown. This net change was in Gore's favor.

By a 2–1 vote, the canvassing board declined to manually recount the six-hundred-odd precincts that existed in Miami-Dade. This was because Florida law did not require a manual recount unless the machine count for the entire county was materially defective. The canvassing board reasoned that the Republican Hispanic precincts would more than even out the Democratic precinct changes. However, three days later on November 17, after a Democratic Party motion for rehearing, the canvassing board reversed itself and decided to manually recount the entire county, including the 10,700 "undervotes" registered by the machines. The reason for deciding to recount the whole county was that the vote difference between Gore and Bush, in the three South Florida counties the Gore campaign had decided to contest through recounts, had grown very small.

I was designated by the Bush-Cheney campaign team to monitor the computer sorting of the 10,700 "undervotes" and to challenge the canvassing board's handling of the undervotes. An undervote is a ballot on which a voter votes in some or most of the races but, for some reason, does not register a vote in one or more of the races on the ballot. The Democratic Party wanted to find out why some voters did not vote for any presidential candidate, and was concerned that some of these voters might have intended to vote for Gore but their votes were not counted. The Republican Party filed a lawsuit to stop the recount on grounds related to the discretion of the canvassing board, since we did not believe there was any legal standard to judge alleged undervotes, but the suit was dismissed by the Miami-Dade Circuit Court.

The Miami-Dade manual recount dragged on for many days. After only 15 percent of the votes had been counted, the Miami-Dade County Canvassing Board decided that it could not properly finish the recount by the deadline of November 26 that had been established by the Supreme Court of Florida. The recount was stopped. Because many of us in the Republican Party believed the recount was being conducted without legal standards or agreed-upon standards of what constituted a vote or undervote, we were delighted to learn that the recount was ended. The Democrats filed a lawsuit to overturn the canvassing board's decision and restart the recount. However, like the earlier lawsuit by the Republican Party, it was dismissed. The circuit court held that the canvassing board had legal discretion to start or stop a recount under the circumstances.

In the meantime, another issue occupied the attention of the Republican Party. We challenged the decisions of the canvassing board pertaining to military absentee ballots. Military personnel voting by absentee ballot tended to favor the Republican Party. But some critics alleged that irregularities surrounded some of these ballots, and that others had arrived too late to be counted. We did not believe there was a problem. Yet some of the absentee ballots from military voters were thrown out by the canvassing board on a motion filed by the Democratic Party.

Lawsuits and Court Action

By November 26, 2000, Secretary of State Katherine Harris, the head of Florida's elections office, had certified the Miami-Dade County vote. But the work of local political party officers was not yet over. I flew to Washington, D.C., on November 30 to present a speech on the court proceedings of the recount to a group of European statesman. The issue of recounts in Palm Beach, Broward, and Miami-Dade counties was at this time before Tallahassee's circuit court judge Sanders Sauls, being attacked on various grounds by the Democratic Party.

The U.S. Supreme Court was at the same time in session concerning the first appeal by Al Gore over the controversies in Florida. The U.S. Supreme Court ended up reversing the Supreme Court of Florida, allowing the election results in Florida to stand. A total of thirty-five lawsuits were then before various courts in Florida over the election.

On December 1, 2000, the Bush-Cheney legal team called me to Tallahassee to testify before Judge Sanders Sauls on the matter of the Miami-Dade County recount. As it turned out, I was the only lawyer who had participated in every aspect of the recount in Miami-Dade. The judge seemed particularly interested in my observation of the standards used by the canvassing board with respect to undervoted ballots. I explained to Judge Sauls that there were no standards used, in my observation. The issue of objective standards was very important because Palm Beach, Broward, and Dade counties approached the analysis of undervotes in three entirely different ways. Florida law did not provide a standard for assessing undervotes. Judge Sauls ruled against Al Gore, who wanted the recount to proceed and wanted further consideration of undervotes, but Sauls was then reversed by the Supreme Court of Florida. The legal escapade ended when the U.S. Supreme Court finally reversed the Florida Supreme Court.

My testimony was utilized as the basis for the Bush-Cheney campaign's arguments in the Supreme Court of Florida and in the Supreme Court of the United States. The majority decision in the second and final U.S. Supreme Court decision rendered December 12, 2000, referred to my testimony as a factual basis for its decision finding the "standardless recount" unconstitutional.

Al Gore conceded the election that evening. I was finally able to celebrate George W. Bush's victory in Florida, which amounted to his election as president.

Concluding Thoughts

It is my firm belief that Florida was unfairly criticized during and after the election for issues that were overstated by critics. Countrywide, there were more than two million undervotes. This is a large number. Moreover, there are always numerous problems in voting and in the use of voting machines in every election. What happened in Miami-Dade County, or in Florida, was not unusual for elections in the county or state—or, for that matter, in most any county or state. On average, in the United States, over 3 percent of the vote ends up being discarded for various reasons. Florida is neither better nor worse than the rest of the country.

The problem in this particular election in Florida, however, was that 2000 ended up being an incredibly close election. Our system for conducting elections and counting votes does not do well in elections where the vote difference is less than 1 percent. Machine ballots are not made to be manually recounted.

As we have seen, there are often no standards, laws, or systems in place to deal adequately with such concerns in very close elections. There are opportunities for outright fraud. The United States as a whole has not properly addressed the limitations of voting technology and devised techniques to make voting more accessible, more convenient, and easier. We have the technical ability to solve these problems. And, as a result of the media focus on this election, things are improving. Improved voting technologies and procedures are finally happening. Most importantly, voters now recognize the danger in not voting.

Notes

1. This article was written before the substantial changes in the federal election law commonly referred to as the McCain-Feingold Act.

3 ☐

☐

☐

Some Things Are Not Meant to Be

The Florida Controversy and Vote Recount

MITCHELL CEASAR, CHAIR,
DEMOCRATIC PARTY OF BROWARD COUNTY

Broward County is the strongest Democratic county in Florida. Proportionately, it is one of the strongest Democratic counties in the United States, clearly one of the strongest in the South. It is a relatively large and populated county. If you were to go to King's County, New York, which is Brooklyn, the county organization would produce more votes in the aggregate for the Democratic Party. However, the margin of victory for Democrats over Republicans in Broward County, compared to other counties around the country, makes us significant. For instance, if you look at the margin of victory enjoyed by President Bill Clinton in his reelection in 1996—a relatively comfortable and easy reelection for an incumbent—Clinton succeeded by a margin of 177,000 votes in Broward. In the 2000 race, which was much more competitive, Al Gore won the county by a margin of 210,000 votes. That is, the county bested the Clinton margin of victory by almost 20 percent, a significant number. Vice President Gore and our local party won in Broward County not only by appealing to our Democratic base but by reaching out to independents as well.

Let me be very honest. If the 2000 election in Broward County and voting procedures had been handled more honorably, Al Gore would have been elected president of the United States in 2000. The Democratic Party approached the election as it always had: multiple campaign headquarters throughout the county were established, party operatives were trained and prepped for the election, and we expected a strong victory. It is incredible to think that Gore should have been president of the United States and that a single state, Florida, would have been responsible for his election. More interestingly, Broward County, as a single county, would have been responsible for electing Gore due to the gigantic 210,000-vote margin of victory he enjoyed locally. Gore received approximately 68 percent of the vote, far higher than the registration numbers for the party in the county. From a historical perspective, it is hard to pinpoint another county that might have swung a presidential election. A possible example was the 1960 race between John F. Kennedy and Richard M. Nixon, where it was alleged that voting irregularities in Cook County provided Kennedy with victory in Illinois, and the presidency. I do not know of another case in our political history where a single county elected a president.

My view is that Broward County elected Al Gore. It took a Supreme Court action to nullify victory and change the will of millions.

Election Day 2000

Much work goes into preparing for an election. The political parties are preoccupied with get-out-the-vote drives, polling, position development, and message delivery coordinating efforts with local candidates and the Gore campaign team in Florida. Party officials such as myself spend the entire day of the election "driving around," ensuring that these tasks are being completed and dealing with last-minute problems. Broward is a large, densely populated county. I began to see irregularities very early in the day. I was also notified of problems with the "butterfly ballot" in neighboring Palm Beach County, but we had many problems of our own to address.

In twenty-six years of political activity, I had never seen irregularities of the magnitude and extent that I saw in Broward County that day. It was so bad that in the late morning I received a phone call from the *Miami Herald* about the widespread reports of voting difficulties. They inquired if I had come across such problems. I told them I had, and provided numerous examples. Being an attorney, I was sure to give my account with both evidence and specifics. Because it was still early in Election Day, most reporters and most members of the public—except for those voting in certain Florida counties—did not know what was occurring.

The *Herald* had no motive other than a good story—while uncovering the truth, of course—so they were going to break the story of confusion and irregularities. The *Herald* notified me that after checking the contentions I had alleged and interviewing people experiencing problems, they had concluded that it was all true. Everything. The story ran the day after the election.

By the afternoon of Election Day I had seen enough glaring problems to know a crisis was at hand. For example, I went to a predominantly African American precinct in Lauderhill in response to an array of complaints. I saw people being turned away because their names did not appear on the voting rolls furnished by the supervisor of elections. Many people were complaining. The system I observed, set up by the Republican supervisor of elections, was outrageously inadequate, which led me to believe that she was either totally unprepared for the election or perhaps there were darker motives. I still do not know the answer. I have never seen an election where so many facets of administering an election were so poorly done. One of the measures undertaken by Jane Carroll, the elections supervisor, was setting up cell phones at different precincts. If a problem arose, precinct workers could contact the supervisor's office. But the problems were so numerous that precinct workers and frustrated would-be voters could not get through. The elections office had only thirty to thirty-five phone lines for a county of 1.5 million people. Calls simply went unanswered. After an hour or so of calling by countless precinct workers, the cell phones went dead. No one was furnished with rechargers, so the elections office employees in the field were not able to notify the office of complaints or obtain answers to the pressing problems. The day ended, and many people had still not been able to vote.

I traveled from precinct to precinct documenting the problems and trying to find solutions. Wherever I went, I found many items unaddressed, frustrated citizens and poll workers, and dead cell phones. In fact, after visiting approximately one dozen precincts, I did not find a single precinct where the cell phones were still working and poll workers were able to get through to the elections office. Most of the complaints were from staff, frustrated that they could not verify if people were registered to vote. Most wanted to encourage the citizens to vote, but could not reach the elections office for instructions because of the inadequate number of phone lines and the dead phones. This also raises the issue that those in charge of the precincts were inadequately trained in dealing with such an emergency.

Several poll workers at different precincts asked me if they could borrow change so they could use a nearby pay phone and contact the supervisor of elections. So I went to the nearest convenience store to obtain several dollars worth of coinage. In the end, the majority of these individuals never would be able to get through to the elections office. Sadly, we later learned that the county emergency center, which was centrally located, could have been used to provide hundreds of phone lines free of charge. The supervisor of elections did not utilize that service. As a result, the "phone problem" caused many prospective voters to be denied their right to vote.

So extensive were the problems with the voting lists, and so disproportionate were the problems of "unregistered" Democrats and African Americans, that attention must be turned to the person and office responsible for producing the voting lists: the secretary of state for Florida, Katherine Harris, and the Division of Elections. Incidentally, Ms. Harris was a Republican cochairing George W. Bush's Florida campaign while serving as the "impartial" supervisor of elections for the state. The lists had been prepared under contract by a consultant and were incorrect, inconsistent, and grossly inadequate, missing many eligible voters.

I still remember a particularly glaring example. At one of the precincts I visited, I encountered a woman complaining to poll workers about being turned away. She told us that she entered the precinct with her son, who was eighteen. He was on the list. He voted. She was not on the list. The woman informed the poll workers that she had voted at the very same precinct only two months before in September's primary election. This was later confirmed by the clerk. The woman tried to make her case by showing that both she and her son had all the proper identification. They lived at the same address and had driver's licenses and valid voter registration cards showing their address in that precinct and the precinct number. Everything appeared to be in order, but for some reason her name, like so many others, had been omitted from the voting lists and she was not permitted to vote. The poll workers were unable to contact the elections office for instructions and did not know how to handle such problems.

The Recount

I cannot help but question the work of the Broward County elections supervisor. Ms. Carroll had been the supervisor for twenty-eight years prior to the 2000 election. Frankly, she had been a very partisan Republican, although she tried to portray herself as neutral and apolitical. To me, her partisanship was proven when the recount arose. By this time the eyes of the United States, if not the world, were on a handful of Florida counties, and specifically on Broward County. How did the elections supervisor respond? She decided to go out of town for days, claiming she had a vacation planned and had already bought the tickets. Her behavior at such a critical time, with so much at stake, was utterly incredible. Whatever legacy she may have established during her career from previous elections was washed away in the sea of indifference and possible incompetence.

Coincidentally, the supervisor of elections was retiring shortly after the November election. But she had not yet relinquished her position. Her position included showing up and attempting to resolve the crisis. I am reminded of the comedian who said that half of life is showing up. Well, this did not happen in Broward County.

As I mentioned earlier, I first learned of the voting irregularities early in the morning of Election Day as reports flooded into my office, and I later saw them firsthand. My concerns were shared by others, becoming the subject of local and national media reports.

Many of us involved in the election were up all night following the returns. It was certainly a political roller coaster of emotions. We had been consistently told by party officials and pollsters that if Broward County produced 200,000 Democratic votes, Al Gore would win Florida—which still technically may be true. Political analysts and commentators had also said that if the Democrats could win Michigan, Pennsylvania, and Florida, the presidential election was certainly over. Gore would win.

While we watched the networks' coverage during the evening, it was reported that Gore had won Michigan and Pennsylvania. Certainly, I thought when the networks gave Florida to Gore, the election was over. I left about two-thirty in the morning with my son and went home. It had been a long, exhausting day and I went to sleep.

Throughout the night, the reports apparently contradicted one another. When I awoke around 7:30 a.m. after a few hours of sleep, I turned on the *Today Show,* as I do every morning, and heard that Gore was down by roughly 1,700 votes in Florida. I found this unbelievable. Gore had won, then had lost, and now it was a virtual tie. It was such a small amount of votes, given the one hundred million votes cast nationally. Anything could happen at this point. News programs claimed it was the closest election since 1960, but it was the closest election in history. It was clear that there was no precedent for what was about to transpire.

I began talking to my then fifteen-year-old son, David, about what would and could happen. He has always been interested in politics, surrounded by campaigns and elections. We realized that, given all the irregularities I had witnessed, there was the possibility that some votes had not been counted. I was thinking in a vacuum. I had not spoken to the Gore staff or other party leaders, except in passing. At the time our priority had been to document the irregularities from a legal perspective. We had not been thinking from a political perspective. My son, who is very computer literate, unlike his father, suggested that we go on the Internet and start looking for information on the votes. So he punched up the Supervisor of Elections Web site. David (my son) assisted me in obtaining a printout of the votes received by Gore, Bush, Buchanan, and other candidates in Broward County. In the official numbers provided, we found a discrepancy in the vote totals in excess of 14,000 plus change. It had to be a mistake. Such a number would certainly be significant, given the virtual tie between Bush and Gore. But David double-checked and recounted. Sure enough, there was a discrepancy. My son scribbled the number on a 3" x 4" piece of scratch paper on his desk.

Armed with this scratch paper and some new knowledge, I contacted a supervisor of elections from another county. We started to brainstorm and discuss the possibility of undervotes and overvotes. At that point I called Mitchell Berger, a Democrat from Broward County who served on the National Finance Committee of the Gore campaign. I met with Berger and a handful of Gore campaign aides, discussing the discrepancy in numbers.

I announced my theory about the overvotes, undervotes, and the need for a recount, while inviting their feedback. Many more votes had been recorded for other races on the ballot than for the presidential race. This just did not make sense. Why would a voter go to the trouble of casting votes for all the races on a ballot, with the exception of the premier race? All studies on voting indicate that citizens are much more likely to vote in presidential races than in other races. Votes were incorrectly counted. We spent almost an hour discussing different scenarios, realizing there was something to the theory. We discovered that a recount was an option, but it must be requested through the chair of the party in the particular county in question. I made the formal request.

The Gore folks took our message and proposal up the channels of the national campaign hierarchy. We discussed overvotes and undervotes and the discrepancy in totals. They agreed that it did not make sense that people coming to vote would skip the first race on the ballot. I believed that, given the fact that Broward County is solidly Gore country—Gore carried the county with roughly 68 percent—it would make sense that the majority of the 14,000-plus missing votes would have been cast for Gore. The number of votes Gore would pick up in the event of a valid recount would more than make up the margin, and that would be "the ball game."

With the Gore advisers, we checked the language of the statutes and made the formal request for a recount. I signed the first document and hand-delivered it to the office of the judge who was the chair of the canvassing board.

Obviously, the statute providing for the recount is applicable statewide. When other counties discovered what was occurring in Broward County, they obtained my documents and used a version of my petition in their respective counties. Now we were involved in a recount, stemming from my son's ideas on the computer, conjuring up numbers. In fact, when I appeared at the first hearing, I had in my hand the little scrap of paper bearing my son's handwriting and numbers—numbers that should have determined who the president of the United States would be.

The response by the press to the idea of a recount and missing votes was, obviously, a journalistic feeding frenzy. They found it exciting, as did I, never before having had media dealings of this magnitude. The recount went through many processes. First, the canvassing committee contacted Jane Carroll, the supervisor of elections, who was in North Carolina. She informed them that she would not return to Florida. Meanwhile attorneys were pleading, "You can't stay there. We'll get you on a plane. We'll get you on a train." Her response was basically, "Well, no, I'm here on vacation." It was the most arrogant display of indifference I have ever seen by an elected official.

It was surprising that the press did not make more of this issue. At first the idea of a recount was opposed by the canvassing board. They finally agreed to a limited recount, but only in a few, selected precincts. Most of this was based on an opinion from Katherine Harris, the Republican secretary of state charged with overseeing elections. So even though there were enough votes in question to decide the outcome of the presidential election, they were only reluctantly willing to make the decision based on a sampling. The Democrats fought the secretary of state's opinion, which cited no case law or credible standard. It was purely a political instrument. Another differing opinion was drafted through the attorney general's office countering the secretary of state's opinion, basing its view on case law and sound statutory positions.

Eventually the recount began, and we endured weeks of chaos. The Republicans pursued a strategy of flying in powerful Republican governors and members of Congress from other states to intimidate local officials and stall the process. There was not a day during this recount when I did not view a prominent Republican politician from *outside* Florida. The Democrats brought in a few officials. I had my son with me so he could witness history. Moreover, the idea of a recount had started with him. My son enjoyed meeting prominent politicians such as Senator Barbara Mikulski of Maryland, who enjoyed speaking with him about the recount and how it originated.

During a recount, the parties are allowed observers to monitor the process. Such Republican heavyweights as Mark Racicot of Montana, who would later become chair of the Republican National Committee, and George Pataki, Republican governor of New York, loomed over the process. I do not believe, however, that this effort to intimidate the canvassing board, local officials, or the Democratic Party succeeded. Most individuals involved in the recount worked hard with little regard to the figures present. This effort to intimidate and delay the process is what I personally found most despicable about the recount. I referred to these teams of lawyers and politicians from outside of the state, sent to disrupt the process, as the "brie brigade." Sporting double-breasted suit jackets, the high-priced attorneys and politicians were flown in by the Republican National Committee specifically for the purpose of creating confusion and intimidation. The same strategy occurred in other counties, such as Miami-Dade County. Indeed, there was even the threat of a riot in Miami when people were whipped into a frenzy by the brie brigade there. After moving in one direction, the Dade County Canvassing Board suddenly canceled all work and called off the recount. I recall seeing a van parked nearby and operatives handing out cell phones to disrupt the process. T-shirts with pro-Bush slogans and preprinted signs were also distributed. It was well orchestrated, well funded, and played well to the cameras covering the events.

Intimidation and delay. It would later become obvious that the Republican goal was to delay the process sufficiently to derail it. A conscious decision was made by Al Gore not to match these tactics. I believe this was to Gore's credit, although it may have cost him the election. Time passed, until the U.S. Supreme Court took jurisdiction, overruling the Florida Supreme Court and disallowing a recount to proceed. As soon as the highest court weighed in, I knew it was over, before the arguments began. Even though conservatives on the high court and conservative scholars talked about states' rights as their call to arms, they contradicted themselves and imposed a pro-Bush ruling on the state. Courts that are usually governed by precedent ignored prior rulings. The actions surrounding the 2000 election ignored history, the cornerstone of our judicial system.

Consequences of 2000

Perhaps what is most frustrating are the scars left on our political system and the future consequences of this event. Potentially, several things could happen, based on Election 2000. It might encourage people to vote, so that each vote "really counts." Or it might discourage people from voting. Polls and studies have shown that when greater numbers vote, Democrats are benefited. It is hard to stem the constant decline in voter participation when the public believes that institutions of government are not people-oriented. Faith in our government will suffer. The Supreme Court will also suffer some image decline. Our perception of these institutions will continue to erode, and confidence and voter participation will suffer. As a result, we get the elected officials we do not necessarily want, but deserve.

Another lesson learned is that voters need training on how voting machines operate. The party could play a role in this. We never really focused on educating people on the mechanics of voting, but now with the new technology, the party will need to do so. In the past, the party focused its attention on getting out the vote. The elections office has offered training to voters, but it was never a priority with the previous supervisor of elections. Broward County has a new supervisor of elections, and her office is in all communities educating voters.

To assure a good turnout on Election Day, the party must be active in the county many months prior to the election. We conduct training for party volunteers, work to get out the vote, and prepare party representatives to serve as poll monitors. In the past, we have offered training sessions for party volunteers and precinct workers once or twice a year, and we stage seminars for candidates on how to run for office.

I remain totally frustrated because I am convinced that the recount effort, whether it was conducted in select counties or the entire state, would have given Gore the victory. In Lake County, which is very conservative and voted overwhelmingly for Bush, the recount allowed Gore to pick up roughly a hundred votes. Upon hearing this, I thought, "I hope we recount all the counties." Obviously it was not my call, but I believe it would have been fairest to recount as many votes as possible, given the problems and consequences of the voting, not only in large Democratic counties such as Broward and Palm Beach but statewide.

Election 2000 proved that certain groups, particularly minorities, were and still are disenfranchised in one way or another. Many votes cast by African Americans that should have been recounted were excluded. It was claimed that those disqualified had voted twice. On examination, however, it became clear these were people who voted twice for Gore on the same ballot. There were hundreds of instances where a voter had checked off or punched "Gore" (depending on how the particular county recorded votes), but then, perhaps because of ambiguous instructions on the ballot, had also written Gore's name in the "write-in" space on the ballot. That is not voting twice. Elections officials are supposed to determine the intent of the voter in such instances, something that was quite clear. So if a canvassing board were to look at these ballots, what decision would they or should they have made? If Gore could pick up a hundred votes from small, Republican counties, what would have happened if the votes of roughly 26,000 disenfranchised voters in Duval County, mostly African Americans, had been counted?

There were many other improper actions and activities surrounding the election. For instance, in two Florida counties Republicans were permitted access to ballot-related materials prior to the vote. Specifically, in Seminole County the supervisor of elections allowed Republicans access to materials weeks prior to the election in order to correct absentee ballot lists. This was outrageous. In another county, Republican party officials were permitted to take the requests out of the office and return them in a modified form later. These appear to be illegal acts, but there was no penalty.

Looking to the Future

The next presidential election will undoubtedly attract significant media focus on Florida. The counties such as Broward that experienced problems will receive ample coverage. Florida will also continue to receive added attention from the press and both parties because it is "the" key state. Of the four biggest states—California, New York, Texas, and Florida—Florida is the only swing megastate. Recent presidential elections in Florida have been very close and competitive. The state continues to grow, so its importance will only increase. Florida and Broward County continue to be where the political action is.

Many party leaders, including myself, offered suggestions on reforming the process and preventing another debacle like 2000. The Republican-controlled legislature made a few reforms, but they were largely a Band-Aid approach, because real reform would not work in the Republicans' interest. Some of the needed reforms would empower and increase turnout for minority voters, which not only would be the right thing to do but would benefit Democrats.

One reform was allotting money for new voting technology, but it was a fraction of what was needed. And while the voting technology was in many cases antiquated, the technology was not the only problem in 2000. Many of the reforms advocated by independent groups such as the League of Women Voters have never been addressed by the Republican legislature or the Republican governor. The legislature acted very quickly, but for purposes of public consumption and appearances only. The tide of election reform seems to have ebbed in Florida. Meaningful reforms were never accomplished.

The lesson is that you cannot take the politics out of voting. In Florida, the secretary of state, the supervisors of elections, and some others involved in administering elections are themselves elected, making these fundamentally partisan political offices. At the least, the secretary of state should not be permitted to serve simultaneously as a campaign officer for one of the major party candidates in an election.

The elections officials do not have a great deal of power—when elections are done correctly. There is, however, power in the office when elections are run incorrectly. This is what occurred in Broward County. The failure to act by one person—Broward's supervisor of elections—changed the outcome of a presidential election.

4

Public Information

Dealing with the Media in an Election Crisis

GISELA SALAS, ASSISTANT SUPERVISOR OF ELECTIONS,
MIAMI-DADE COUNTY

When Election Day concluded in 2000, those of us with the elections office in Miami-Dade County were satisfied that we had had a successful election. Throughout the day, things seemed to be going well. It was actually a very smooth election, very normal. Or, perhaps not normal because we really did not have the usual problems during the day. I arrived home near four o'clock in the morning, and was trying to wind down for a brief nap before going back to work the following morning. This is the busiest time of the year for the elections office, and the day after the election can be hectic for those of us charged with public relations. At home I turned on the television briefly. That was the point when I first heard the word *recount*. The nation's attention seemed focused on Florida, and once I heard that, I knew Dade County would have a major role. According to the news, Florida would be the deciding factor.

Once I heard about the recount, I knew that whether or not an actual recount was taken, the elections office would have a lot to do. Most of us go into an election working long hours, and now we suspected that it would be some time before we could get caught up on our sleep. I basically had an hour and a half of sleep on election night, dressed, and went back to work.

I was prepared to work with the media and expected a little media presence. But nothing could have prepared me for what I encountered as I arrived at the elections office in downtown Miami. When I drove past our building to get into the parking lot, the entire west side of the building and parking lot was filled with media vans, trucks, and their satellites. Never in my wildest dreams would I have expected this. CNN. ABC. Local media. International media. Everyone was here, already waiting, first thing in the morning. It seemed like something out of a movie and, even as I was pulling into the parking area, I still wondered what was going on. This was the greeting that the Miami-Dade County elections office had the day after Election 2000.

As the public information officer for the elections office, I already had a good rapport with the media. Many knew me personally. This helped. I did not receive any phone calls immediately upon coming into the office. I did not have the chance. Basically, as I walked into the building, the media were waiting in person. "Here is the lady we're waiting for!" Then the questions started: "Okay, what's going on? How are you going to handle this?"

My first thought upon hearing these questions was: I have to find out what is going on. I must admit that I really had no clue as to exactly what was happening. We had run the election the way we were supposed to do it. By the book. So I went immediately to see the supervisor of elections, David Leahy, when I arrived at the office. He stated that we were going to have some work to do! It seemed that we were required to do a recount before we had a chance to assess the situation. Nonetheless, at that point, it still seemed it would be a routine recount, except that this one would decide who would be the president of the United States. This was something we had never done before. Still, it seemed the best approach would be to treat it as a routine recount. The Miami-Dade elections office had been through many recounts in our history. It is not uncommon. And that was good news.

What was not routine and what became unique about this recount was the extent of the media coverage. Strikingly, as one considered the whole state of Florida, which is the fourth largest state in the nation, the number of votes we were talking about that would decide the outcome of a presidential election was incredibly small. I wondered what kind of impact Miami-Dade County was going to have on the election. At the time, we did not know that we were one of the counties that they were focusing on, one of the counties that might decide the election. But we knew this race was really going to be close.

Miami-Dade's Response

The obvious priority was finding out first of all what was going on. We needed information so that we could accurately inform the rest of the elections office, the public, and the media. The way to approach this was in line with what the elections office has always done, which is to have control over who addresses the media. This prevents conflicting messages. In this case, the supervisor of elections, David Leahy, and I, as the assistant supervisor of elections and public information officer, would be the spokespersons for the department. Fortunately, David had a lot of experience as supervisor and we worked well together. The arrangement the department tended to use was that I would work with the Spanish-speaking media and David with the English-speaking media. However, because David was also on the canvassing board charged with the recount, to prevent a conflict of interest it was decided that essentially I would assume most of the media work.

My goal was to become thoroughly informed. Clear, accurate communication was essential. There was no precedent for what we were facing, so basically we went play-by-play. The fact that we had never handled this type of situation before made it even more important that our information be accurate. I worked closely with the supervisor and followed closely the work of the canvassing board. I kept the media informed as soon as information was available, so that in many circumstances they knew what was going to happen rather than having to wait for developments. At this point, I not only wanted to do the right thing but I wanted our department to look good in the eyes of the nation and the world, so I kept the lines of communication with the media as open as possible.

Given the number of media outlets wanting information and updates every minute of the day, I found myself understaffed. When the media did not get what they wanted as soon as they wanted it, they would get frustrated. Sometimes information could not be provided because the recount was in a holding pattern. And the only thing worse than a frustrated journalist is many frustrated journalists. The supervisor assigned another staff member in the department to assist me with appointments, requests, and my schedule, which had fast become overwhelming. With the volume of requests we had, it was a challenge simply to keep tabs on who needed what and who wanted an interview and when. To deal with this, we tried to give relative priority to each of the requests and to approach the situation as if it were any old election. In this respect, my office is accustomed to providing information after an election, making copies of votes and precinct results available to the public, the media, and the parties. To stay ahead of certain types of requests, we adopted the practice of making many extra copies of everything we did, on the assumption that, for every request, someone else would soon make a similar request. The bottom line for us was always to be consistent and to provide as accurate information as possible and in the fairest manner. All this helped somewhat, but at times the sheer avalanche of requests was unbelievable and we fell behind.

The elections office needed to inform not only the press corps but the public and politicians as well. Both campaigns wanted information and, in addition to the contested presidential election, there were the many local and state elections on our ballot. We could not forget about them. They too had a right to information and ballot results. The Democratic and Republican Parties sent officials to the county to monitor the process. There was so much at stake. These officials were present throughout the process and made many requests. The office was careful to provide information in a nonpartisan manner. Of course, we would not give something to the Republican Party without giving it to the Democratic Party. A way to assure that this happened was to provide information to everyone involved on a first-come-first-serve basis.

The physical setup of the elections office is such that the offices are open and fairly accessible. The tabulation room where votes are counted on election evening has television monitors, so all work can easily be observed, and contains a wall of glass windows where most of the people from the political parties and media as well as the candidates are invited to stand. The process is completely open. Police officers are posted in the building to keep people away from workers' desks and restricted materials. The elections office also contains a large lobby area where all concerned parties are invited to congregate, and there is a media room on a nearby floor of the building. The office provides phones, computers, and other helpful items. Information is distributed to everyone in this room and the main lobby.

At 7 p.m. we start preparing for the results process. Our public phone lines shift from a voter-question-and-assistance operation to a reporting-of-results operation. Once again the office focuses on informing the candidates and the public of the results as they begin to come in from the precincts. The candidates, their campaign managers, and the parties use this information to make projections about total votes and whether they have won. The elections office provides them with information at the precinct level until total votes are counted, and our staff assists them in understanding the results. The journalists are provided with phone lines and a computer so they can file their reports. In short, we provide many services to many constituents.

I believe we acted with no favoritism and worked hard to assure fairness in the way we interacted with both parties. We were evenhanded throughout the process.

The Job of Public Information Officer

The job of assistant supervisor of elections and public information officer in Miami-Dade County is an appointed position, and the appointment is made by the supervisor of elections. It is not a fixed appointment for a certain number of years, nor is it an elected position for a certain term in office. I basically serve at the pleasure of the supervisor and remain until the supervisor leaves office or no longer needs my services. I have been employed by the county for twenty-five years and, in this current job, I am considered a county employee.

A public information officer in an elections office, besides working with the public and the media, has a number of other duties. But first and foremost the officer is charged with providing information on elections. This requires many skills, patience being one of the most indispensable. It is important to look at things from the point of view of how you would like to be treated if you came through this door and you were running for office or if you were just looking for information. The elections office serves public officials, students, the general public, and so on, and its services range from answering inquiries about how to vote to furnishing previous election data.

One of the main aspects of the job is working with the media. I have found it helpful to try to be proactive rather than reactive whenever an election cycle is coming up or any special event. The press appreciates this and it makes my job both easier and more effective. It is important to keep the media informed. This is generally how the public and voters acquire their information. I provide routine press releases on a variety of matters from recruiting prospective poll workers to reminding voters to update their registration information. The elections office does regular public service announcements using radio, newspaper, and television. This requires us to "solicit" the media for this service and determine what types of announcements to run and how often. In Miami-Dade County, we work especially closely with the newspapers and have developed a good rapport with our local newspapers. For instance, rather than purchase an ad or run a public service announcement, at times we try to get the newspaper to cover the election issue as a story.

Finally, my position requires me to work closely with the political parties and politicians. The elections office provides many services to candidates for public office. We provide information on how to file to run for office, previous voting results, and technical information on election laws and voting systems. My office keeps candidates abreast of what we do and of changes in voting procedures. Our "qualifying package" basically outlines everything one needs to know to become a candidate for a particular office. In the package, we actually break down and tailor the information to the office and include an A-Z type of approach to what is needed for each public office, from election laws to how to file for candidacy.

There are many state laws and local ordinances pertaining to voting, and these are prone to change. It is a complicated process. The Miami-Dade County Commission has been aggressive in passing ordinances that deal with campaign finance. So just in that one area there are a number of ordinances that affect our local candidates, and it is very important that these candidates know what is going on and what the law says they can and cannot do even before they consider running for office. Information of this sort is a free service the elections office provides to anyone requesting it. This is public information. The Internet has been a great tool in informing the public. The elections office has a helpful Internet site that is frequently updated, and we continue to make improvements to it as we go along. One current project is to make all the candidate packages available online, along with all the forms needed to file as a candidate.

Even a "normal" election day is a long and tiresome day for those people working in elections. Elections administrators have many responsibilities beyond counting votes after the polls close, and public information officers do much more than just deal with the media or the public after an election. Planning an election takes months, and the work of an elections office is year-round, contrary to what some individuals might think. An elections office has sections with designated areas of responsibility, but there are many tasks involved in all areas and much overlapping of the work done. For instance, I am in charge of what are known as the public phones, a phone bank for people who call into the elections office on Election Day with any number of problems or questions that they might have regarding the election. This requires that my staff and I be prepared to answer a wide range of questions and know the election inside and out. The elections office makes that number available to the public prior to

Election Day and undertakes a campaign to get the number out to as much of the population as possible. We receive hundreds or even thousands of calls on Election Day.

There are approximately thirty workers assigned to that particular area of the election. Aside from that, I am also responsible for the poll workers. The Miami-Dade elections office has more than six thousand poll workers. In addition to their working the polls on Election Day, these workers must be recruited, trained, placed, and monitored. I am responsible for that as well. Clearly, the work of administering an election starts months before the actual day of the election. The elections office has roughly one dozen people assigned to the area of poll workers. Of course, what happens on the morning of the election is that a lot of people do not show up to work at the polls. This means we have to find replacements and will have to do some rearranging and juggling of precincts and workers. The office tries to allow for this beforehand and tries to limit such no-shows through our recruitment and training process. But it is a typical Election Day when poll workers do not show up.

For the elections staff, Election Day begins at 6 a.m., with the polls opening at around seven. The poll workers must be at the site by six, however. This means that many of us who work the elections are up well before then. We have staff at each polling place to make sure the site is open, clean, and ready and the workers are showing up on time. Phones are available at each site so that the staff can contact the main elections office with this information and any problems that might arise.

The elections office will also start getting calls from the press at an early hour. Prior to and during the day of the election, we offer a variety of services from voter education to public information on the candidates and items on the ballot to previous election results. One thing we do on Election Day is provide a series of projections on voter turnout. This is done by the Systems Division within the elections office, but ordinarily I would be the one who handles the task of distributing the information and turnout forecasts to the press, parties, and politicians. That is a time-consuming task throughout the day. Everybody involved in an election wants to know what is going on, whether there are any problems or anything unusual, and what the early projections suggest. The turnout forecasts start at 11 a.m. and are then announced at 1 and 3 p.m. After the last afternoon (3 p.m.) forecast is distributed, there is typically a slowdown in the office for a little while. The elections office will provide information for the media for the five or six o'clock news. After this point, the main focus is preparing to receive the ballots in the evening. The polling sites close at 7 p.m.

Just prior to 7 p.m. when the polls close, the public phones really start ringing with questions and requests. Typically, voters will call in with complaints of being told that they cannot cast their ballots because they are in the wrong precinct, because they just found out the polls closed or they needed their identification, or that they are not a registered voter. There are a wide range of complaints and questions that come in. So as a supervisor in charge of that section, I am busy handling the voter complaints and trying to make decisions. This is difficult. Do we let this person vote? Is there anything we can do for this person? Can we verify the allegation? Of course, if there is anything we can do for voters within reason, we will go ahead and take care of them. We try to be accommodating but fair within the parameters of election law.

The number of calls varies, but each call is usually very time-consuming. The office tries to give everyone as much time as possible and our undivided attention. In some instances, a voter will need to get to another polling site before it closes, and we will verify that the person is registered to vote, identify the polling site, and provide directions to it. This presents a difficult situation. Will the person have enough time to get to the correct precinct? Do we allow them to vote if they do not?

Election Day ends once the ballots are all tabulated and once all the final results are in. At that point I am basically free to go home. However, usually we have to do what is called a "logic and accuracy" test to end the evening. We like to confirm that everything went as planned before calling it an election and a night. After the final tabulation is finished, the Systems Division—our computer people—stay in the office along with David Leahy, the supervisor of elections, to run a final check. An accuracy test is done both before and after the vote as a way of testing the system. Once the supervisor is satisfied with the process and the accuracy test, the results are accepted. For a presidential election, it is not unusual to remain in the office until 5 a.m. It is a long day.

I am not sure that things have calmed down yet from the 2000 election. It was very hectic for several months afterward. Nor am I sure the office has returned to "normal" even after more than two years. By the time some sense of normalcy emerged, it was time to begin preparing for the 2002 election and the series of elections we run throughout the year for municipalities. Elections are an ongoing process. People tend to think of elections as occurring in four-year cycles, with elections offices doing nothing in between: elections officials earn great paychecks and take good, long vacations during nonelection years. This is especially not the case in Miami-Dade County, where we have more than thirty municipalities and they all run elections on various schedules. Special elections are also held from time to time. So, in effect, there is an ongoing cycle of preparation and then election every few months.

Lessons from 2000

One of the lessons from the 2000 election is that reform is needed. Some reforms have already been put in place. One problem with the 2000 election was that we did not have "provisional ballots." We now have these, which will allow such voters to vote and us to verify the legitimacy of the vote later. I believe this will be a positive change. I think that, if nothing else, when voters ended up trying to vote in the wrong precinct, elections officials will know that they tried to vote and, if there is not sufficient time for them to get to the correct precinct, they can use the provisional ballot and possibly be given credit for voting. A lot of times people end up in the wrong place and it becomes a last-minute decision. These new ballots might help. This is an example of election problems that could be avoided. This is a goal of the elections office, and much can be done through voter education and having helpful, trained precinct workers. Reforms can start with those problems that can more easily be avoided.

It seems that the lessons from Election 2000 are still being learned. At the same time, there are some good things to come out of this historic election. One of the good things is that people are now looking at elections as an important part of government and democracy. The elections office has received additional funding that allows us to expand our efforts to educate voters and keep the public informed. Part of these funds will be used to produce educational brochures and increase our presence in the community through community-based events and programs. Another portion of the money will allow us to hire needed staff that we did not have before. The main priority after the 2000 election has been voter education. So far, I believe we are reaching a wide section of the community and have had a tremendous impact in informing citizens of the importance of voting, how to vote, and the services we provide.

In the wake of the 2000 election, there has been a real public outcry for education on voting and elections. As a result of that, we now have the ability to do what we wish we could have done all along. In the past, the elections office had its hands tied in terms of providing the types of educational programs we wanted to provide because the budget was so limited. We literally did not have the money for new programs. We were scraping to complete existing projects. For example, all the public information literature and "brochures" I provided in the past were photocopies. Now the office is finally able to produce documents that look official and credible and we can print materials in the quality and quantity we need. Having a larger budget has helped, but it is still a limited budget and there is a lot to do. The office must still work within its means.

The elections office has historically gone to schools, unions, libraries, and a host of other locations in the community to make presentations and distribute literature. Getting the public interested in these events or the elections office was not always easy. However, because of the 2000 election, we are finding that everyone is now interested in voting and elections. The new voting technology we procured after the 2000 election has generated a lot of publicity. Everyone wants to see it and practice on it. The system has been working well so far, and the reception by the public has been strong. The elections office has been taking the new voting machines around the county. We also have one set up in our lobby for people to see and use, as well as in all the municipal city halls. We are hoping the new technology will have a positive impact on future elections. At times we have had daily events and demonstrations of voting equipment. More people phone our office, come to our office, access our Web site, and want our literature than ever before. To assist the public, we publicize in advance all our appearances and events. The schedule is also available on the department's Web site.

Additionally, the elections office has established outreach sites around the county to further our presence in the community and provide easy access to election information for the public. These sites include a lot of places where people would ordinarily go to receive other services. While at these locations they will see and can try out the new voting machines. We set up a booth at the county fair, so thousands of people were reached by such a nontraditional undertaking. The next step we hope to take is to set up machines and events at shopping malls. The outreach effort is extensive. Generally, the reaction by the public has been positive, and most people find the new technology very easy to use. So the good news is that the controversy of 2000 should help us better educate voters for future elections.

Another area that has been problematic is volunteers. Not enough people have volunteered their time. People are working longer and harder, and it is difficult to ask someone to give up an entire workday to volunteer. Poll workers make roughly $84 for working on Election Day. But while the money might seem to be an enticement to work, it is a long day, lasting from roughly 6 a.m. to 8 p.m. The work also requires a training program, so the rate basically works out to almost minimum wage. I am hoping that more people will volunteer with the elections office as a result of 2000 and this is something we are working on.

The public perception of how elections are run is important. If people do not have confidence in the system or office, they might not vote. The 2000 election obviously did not help our image or that of fair elections. It left a bad taste in many people's mouths, and I am not sure the public has a good perception of the whole process even after our post–2000 efforts. Generally, people distrust government, so an event like Election 2000 simply fed off that perception and made matters worse. I wish it were different. The elections office needs to consider the type of image we convey to the media and the public. That is why we are working so hard to improve the image and instill confidence in the public. It is not necessarily bad to be under public scrutiny or to have the public suspicious of the actions of government. But such views need to be moderated and healthy. We really hope people will turn out at the polls in future elections and the public outcry will be channeled into voting and other positive democratic actions.

Unfortunately, even in presidential elections, half the voters stay away from the polls on Election Day. I hope that will change. It is possible that many people who never voted might feel compelled to vote, if for no other reason than simple curiosity. So my sense is that Election 2000 will produce an increase in voter turnout, although I doubt it will be a dramatic increase to, say, 90 percent. The surge of patriotism and sense of civic duty arising after the tragedy of 9/11 might also help improve turnout. My personal goal is that a majority of voters participate in all elections, but I do not know if this goal will ever be reached in the United States.

The impact of the 2000 election was felt personally by all those involved. I learned lessons from the election. I always had a good rapport with the press and felt that I was effective in my efforts before 2000, but there was nothing like the media onslaught during Election 2000. Though I learned a lot, I did not walk away from that experience with a bad feeling toward the press. I understand their need to get the story and why they approached it as they did, although it was challenging for us to convey the message we wanted to convey to them. At times journalists seem not to want to listen to you. For instance, one thing I kept reiterating time and time again was that the situation with undervotes and overvotes was not an unusual one. This happens all the time. To help make my point, I actually cited for the press other elections where we had a greater number of undervotes or overvotes than in 2000. However, this information received no coverage whatsoever and was lost in the bigger picture. Unfortunately, had the public received such information, it might have helped them to better understand the election and put it into context. So, that experience was a little aggravating for me, considering how much I emphasized that point to the media.

Another lesson I learned was that the press and public needed to be educated on the fundamentals of voting and election terminology. Often people do not know as much about elections as they should. So throughout the coverage of the 2000 election I attempted to include in my briefings and interactions with the press and public an education on the basics of elections and exactly what was happening step by step. This helped them to understand that certain aspects of what was occurring were expected, while other aspects of the election were unusual.

In working with the press, one finds oneself misquoted and stories inaccurately reported. I was misquoted. An example that ended up causing anxiety among some people in the community was that ballot boxes had been left throughout Miami-Dade County. What happened was that the elections office has boxes that are labeled "ballot box" and, yes, they are left throughout the county. That is regular procedure, but ballots are actually removed from those cases and placed in other small metal cases called "transfer cases." Those are the ones that are used to transport the ballots to the collection centers. Well, misinformation made the headlines. It was reported that ballot boxes were left around the county, making people think that we literally left ballots unaccounted for and uncounted. The story came off as if ballots had been strewn throughout the county. Once the first media outlet reports such information, it creates a domino effect.

I walked away from the election tired and somewhat more recognizable than before the election. People recognized me from my interviews and press briefings and would come up to me at places like supermarkets and ask about the election. I remember ordering a ready-made Thanksgiving dinner because we were not sure if we would be working in the office during Thanksgiving or if we were going to be home. While I was standing in line at the supermarket to order, the manager recognized me and asked me about the election. Such experiences were odd for someone not used to having fifteen minutes of fame.

In the end, most elections officials did their jobs, responded to the challenge with integrity, and remained committed to their work even after the 2000 election. I found that people assumed, because I worked in an elections office, that I wanted to talk about politics and politics was my passion. Others assumed we were excessively political. The truth is that most of us do not spend our time talking about politics and most of us are rather apolitical. We actively try to remain neutral, as we are not paid for our opinions. We are motivated to serve the community and the electoral process.

RUNNING AN ELECTION

5 ☐

      ☐

      ☐

Running an Election and the Work
of the Elections Office

DAVID LEAHY, FORMER SUPERVISOR OF ELECTIONS,
CONSULTANT TO MIAMI-DADE COUNTY ELECTIONS DEPARTMENT

The Miami-Dade County Elections Department has a total of sixty-nine employees. The department is organized around five basic functional areas known as divisions, each headed by an assistant supervisor of elections.

The first area is Voter Registration, which is rather self-explanatory. The assistant supervisor in charge of registration also oversees voter demonstration and voter education.

The second area is Public Services. This division is required to wear many hats. It works with the candidates for office, taking requests from them for election results and producing lists of candidates running for office. The Public Services Division is also responsible for campaign finance and financial disclosure requirements. And it maintains the elections office Web site and disseminates information to the public.

A third division is Systems, which is responsible for the tabulation of votes, disseminating election results, and all of the computer programs and equipment throughout the elections office.

The fourth division is Election Support. This is another large umbrella operation, responsible for numerous services. It performs all the administrative functions for the office—purchasing, personnel, bill paying, and other tasks. The Election Support Division also takes care of our fleet of motor vehicles, identifies and secures the use of polling places, prepares the polling sites for the election by installing phone lines and other preparation, and makes sure each polling site is ready and running on Election Day. This division delivers voting machines and ballots to the precincts and then picks them up at the end of the election.

The fifth and final section is the Absentee Ballots and Voter Fraud Division. This division handles ballot requests and issues new ballots. It also manages the petition process, verifying any petition for municipal or county candidates, as well as constitutional petitions. This is a large undertaking. The department might do 500,000 signatures this year, and for constitutional amendments in the county they are verified one by one. The division also has a small unit that looks for voter fraud. To prevent and clean up fraud in elections, the staff examines registration records, absentee ballots, petitions, and other records, looking for irregularities. They also anticipate and correct problems that might arise, so that we do not have to read about it in the newspapers. A goal of mine is to be a little more proactive in addressing election fraud.

Among the many services it provides, the elections office is continually involved in public outreach, training, voter education, and an array of other elections projects. For example, we host training programs for voters and candidates and sponsor an in-house training program for employees. We recruit poll workers, voters, and possible polling sites. The office runs voter registration drives, absentee ballot programs, petition programs, and other initiatives. And we are updating, maintaining, and providing education about voting machines and technology and vote tabulation equipment. It is our office that physically tabulates the votes after an election and records the results, which are also filed in our office and made available to the public. To fulfill all these responsibilities, the elections office has a warehouse where we store everything—all our supplies that go out on Election Day, all our voting equipment, and numerous other items. This warehouse is maintained by the Election Support Division.

Supervising an elections office is like running a big company. We have a large number of employees and two facilities within the agency. We also organize hundreds of precincts at election time. One thing I am quite proud of is the integrity of the department and our employees. To me, that is the most important characteristic of an elections office and my goal as supervisor. I take this work very seriously and so do my employees. I am registered nonpartisan. I do not have to be—it is not required by law or by my contact—but I am because it sends a message and I like to have the ability to work with all political parties on equal footing. I work hard to get along professionally with leaders of the parties. I attend events for the Democratic Party and I attend events for the Republican Party in a nonpartisan capacity. The office offers voter education programs and demonstrations of voting equipment to all parties and the whole county without preference. This office needs to be viewed as totally nonpartisan, apolitical, and possessing great integrity. This is the most important facet of the elections office and it is my goal. Without such, I could not do my job effectively.

Running an Election

Of course, the main responsibility of the elections office is to administer elections. A lot of work goes into this, and we sometimes run several elections a year for a variety of public offices around the county. To do this, the elections office used 617 precincts, but because the county is growing we now are working with 754 precincts. Every ten years a census is taken, and the results influence the political jurisdictions represented by elected officials. The process of redistricting occurs every ten years, two years after the census is taken, giving everyone enough time to assess the census data. Not only does the elections office help with the redistricting process, but the process of reapportioning political districts requires us to change ballots, precincts, and elections. So the perception that we run one election every two or four years is far from true. The elections office stays busy throughout the year either preparing for or running elections. After the 2000 election we also procured a new voting system. Educating voters about this new system and making the internal adjustments to it have required a considerable amount of time and energy.

The process of planning for an election takes months. For instance, we must secure polling sites throughout the county. Every precinct has a voting site, which could be a library, school, park facility, or fire station. As a county agency, we use a lot of county government facilities, schools, and churches, but we also use apartment complexes and other convenient buildings. There are two main problems we face in identifying, securing, and preparing polling places. The first is making sure they can physically accommodate our needs. All facilities must be accessible to the disabled and must be available from six o'clock in the morning until eight at night. And even among the limited sites that are accessible to the disabled and can be used solely for the election all day long, not all have the space needed to accommodate voting machines and well over a thousand people coming to vote, not to mention adequate parking.

The other big problem in this area is finding people to work the election. We need a large enough number to staff hundreds of polling places, and these individuals must be capable of doing the assigned work. The county pays only $82.40, and the election workers put in a very long and demanding fourteen-hour day. Plus, they must attend two or three hours of training. This basically works out to minimum wage. Most of our poll workers are senior citizens. A lot more senior citizens would like to serve as poll workers but are unable to work the full fourteen-hour day. We also need poll workers who speak other languages.

Some of these workers volunteer their services and approach us, but our main approach to staffing the election is to recruit and do so aggressively. It is very difficult to find enough capable people, even though we are located in an area with a large senior citizen population. In working-class neighborhoods it is especially hard to find enough poll workers. In fact, our recruiting starts many months prior to the election. To recruit workers, we go to the chambers of commerce and an assortment of civic and community groups and ask them to encourage their members and staff to work the election. The elections office also places advertisements in the newspapers. We also try to get a diverse group of workers to reflect our population and recruit workers geographically from communities around the entire county. All told, for the general election we will need at least seven thousand poll workers. Regardless of our best efforts to recruit the right type of people, some will not show up for the training program, a vitally important part of preparing citizens to run a complex election. Others will come down with an illness or simply not show up on Election Day. So, our work does not end once we identify seven thousand prospective workers.

It is not important for voters or persons working the election to know all the different elements that go into running an election. However, they should be familiar with how to vote, the candidates and issues on the ballot, and the basic services and work of the elections office. The elections office exists to make sure an election is run properly.

It often seems to be a classic case of the squeaky wheel getting the grease. When the elections office does a good job, it is scarcely noticed by the public or media. Previous elections received a fraction of the media coverage that the November 2000 election received. Of course, the fact that a presidential race was being decided by a small number of votes rather justifies the coverage, but when problems are perceived to have occurred, the press will report them. When there are none, however, the press does not report on the success of the election. This phenomenon is true in other areas. For instance, let us say that everything goes well in an election during a given year. At the end of that year when the elections office shows up at the county budget hearing, the commissioners will take the fact that everything is running well as a sign that we do not need additional funding. Our budget might even be cut. If the election experiences some challenges but we manage to survive it, then there is a better chance of getting more funding. This happened in the wake of the 2000 election when the elections office received additional funding from the county as well as funds from the state of Florida, something that never happened before. In fact, we continue to receive funds and might get more from sources we never received public money from before. Historically, the United States government has done a great job ensuring that funds were provided to other countries so that they might improve their registration and voting systems and therefore hold fair and accurate elections. The federal government, however, has never provided a cent to our office, although they have passed many bills requiring us to do certain things, and the county taxpayers end up funding the initiatives.

One of the biggest challenges I faced as the supervisor of elections was dealing with such limited resources. Miami-Dade County ensures that the supervisor has enough money to do what he or she is mandated to do, but the county is not a rich county. It does not have the resources to provide extra money to try new initiatives or use the latest technology or increase our voter education and get-out-the-vote programs. Every year the county commission deals with a huge list of unmet needs and simply does not have the money to fund them all. So a challenge of my job in running elections is to make sure that I get done what is legally required of us and then do a little more, such as getting more people to register to vote, educating voters, and so on, with whatever funds I can secure. Ironically, because of what happened in 2000, the elections office is getting more money to improve the voting process and do these extra things.

Election Day

Election Day is a very long day at the elections office. I typically wake up at 4 a.m. and try to be in my office by five-thirty. My employees are supposed to be in the office around six. I like to be here at least thirty minutes before them to think things over and check the network, phone lines, and so on. On the morning of elections, there are two main concerns that command our attention. The first one is to make sure that all our polling places open up on time. Somebody is at the facility opening it up for the poll workers. We must coordinate beforehand all the details—who opens the facility, the time, making sure they have the key. In a few instances the poll workers have a key to the facility. It is always a worry to depend on somebody who normally does not work with us and we do not know well to be at the polling place on election morning. The elections office plans this well in advance and sends reminder letters, but there will always be some who do not show up on the morning of the election. So this is one of the first potential problems I concentrate on that morning.

Another major concern is making sure the polling places have the right ballots. In major countywide elections, there are often different types of ballots at different precincts. One commission seat will feature certain candidates and another commission seat will feature other candidates. In the September 2000 primaries, there were 523 different types of ballots in Miami-Dade County. So I must make sure that every precinct has the right ballot, and this causes a lot of worrying and requires a lot of planning. The elections office institutes controls to make sure that everyone has the right ballot, but I end up sitting in my office on the morning of the election just hoping that we did not make a mistake. It helps that we have been through so many elections and have perfected the system. It also helps that I have a very good staff and the Miami-Dade elections office has not had many of those types of mistakes occur over the years. But I still sit in my office on election morning and worry.

By 8 a.m. I will know that all the polling places are open. Our office is in touch with everyone by phone. By this time my staff assigned to the ballots will have informed me whether all the ballots are in all the right places or whether we have a problem. If all goes well—and it usually does—I can relax a little bit and prepare then to handle the problems that will pop up throughout the day. Most of the problems that I have to deal with during Election Day are not problems in the polling place with voters, but rather problems outside the polling place with campaigns. The campaigns complain, make allegations, and worry about whether the other campaign is violating some rule. I also deal with reporters all day long. Much of my day is thus spent answering questions and putting out fires. The job involves a lot of troubleshooting.

In order to address so many potential problems, I do not assign myself a specific job on Election Day. This frees me up to respond to an array of issues once we ensure that the polling places have opened on time and the ballots are where they are supposed to be. The elections supervisor needs to be free to address pressing problems—whatever comes up. Some previous elections have been nice and quiet and I was able to stay in my office and actually get work done. But other elections have been spent running from one fire to the next and answering questions all day long. Each election is different in this respect. During the major countywide elections, I rarely am able to sit at my desk.

In a way, the elections supervisor spends the election monitoring all the different networks we have running. An administrator from the office is assigned to each of these many networks. For example, one of the networks in my office—the administrative network—is set up to handle the solicitation problems, work with candidates, and answer questions from the news media. Another one is devoted to absentee ballots. Another is established solely to deal with unforeseen problems. We have forty troubleshooters spread out countywide on Election Day prepared to go to polling places that have problems. A phone network is in place to take the last-minute calls from the public asking where they go to vote, whether they are registered to vote, and other questions. The elections office maintains a huge phone and computer bank on the eighteenth floor of the office building that includes up to a hundred phones and twenty-five computers and is designed to take care of an assortment of voter questions and problems. Still another network is set up at the voting equipment warehouse to take care of any problems with voting machines and equipment. In short, the election process is meticulously planned and networks are in place to handle all problems. We also ensure that each network has the knowledge, staff, and resources to get the job done. In general, I try to have all facets of the election planned and scheduled at least 120 days prior to Election Day.

The polls close at 7 p.m., and at this time the elections office really starts day two of the election. The focus of our work shifts to getting the results. This involves bringing all the ballots in, counting the votes, and making sure the vote is tabulated correctly. From there the elections office again shifts gears to reporting the vote. We need to inform the candidates, press, and public of the results. The same worry I experience when the polls are opening appears again when the polls close. Did all the precincts close at the correct time and according to procedure? Are the ballots being turned in according to schedule? Are we missing any? Have we accounted for all the ballots and equipment or did any of the poll workers forget to bring something back to the office? The poll workers are good citizens who put in a long, hard day. But most are just average citizens doing their civic duty, and it is possible that some mistakes will be made. We are all tired by this time.

Poll workers and ballots are coming from all over the county at hundreds of different sites. The process of simply getting all the ballots from so many sites and according to procedure is a challenge. This is why Election Day is often a full twenty-four-hour day for many of us involved in running an election.

Lessons from the 2000 Election

There were many lessons learned from the 2000 election. This is true not only for those of us working in the elections office in Miami-Dade County but for the entire nation. We all realized that it is a challenge to run an election where every aspect works according to plan. The lesson is that one cannot cut corners, cannot underfund, cannot afford to plan elections poorly. Miami-Dade County used to have in our precincts poll workers whose sole job it was to show voters how to vote. This was because there are always new voters who have concerns and need assistance, new voters from other countries, and so on. Unfortunately, that service was cut a few years before the 2000 election because of budget cuts. Again, it is difficult to run an election according to the highest standards if the budget for doing so is cut back by 5 percent every year. I think we in Miami-Dade County learned that we cannot skimp on the funding of elections.

There are many aspects of an election that cannot be cut because they are mandated by law, but many of the other services I believe are essential to the health of an election are not funded. For example, the law might say that elections offices are required to offer voting demonstrations, but it does not say how much emphasis should be placed on them or that the precinct is required to have a separate person assigned to the task. These extra measures were cut from the budget, and we had to move the voting demonstration over to the check-in table where voters are signing in. The poll workers at the check-in table had to try and do both tasks. When a line is forming to vote, there might not be enough staff or time to devote to voting demonstrations for every voter needing them. Also, the check-in table is not the best site in which to conduct such assistance. In effect, little occurred in the way of offering voting demonstrations.

Because of the problems with the 2000 election and thanks to the extra funding it generated, the elections office is now able to again provide a poll worker whose job is specifically to provide voting demonstrations. This is good news because the person charged with this has the time to ask voters if they have questions or would like to see how to use the voting system. Also, because of the 2000 election, we now have new voting machines and a new voting system. Voters in the next elections will certainly have questions about these. My sense is that, at least for a few years, the elections office will be properly funded. This will enable us to offer the full range of services and expand existing services such as voter education programs.

However, this is not to say that everything is perfect after the experience of

2000. For instance, the elections office received a nice-sized grant from the state so that each county could conduct voter education programs in 2002. The elections supervisors from Florida's counties together asked the state legislature for grant money for 2003 so that the voter education programs might continue. We received nothing from the legislature. There was nothing in any of the bills in the 2002 legislative session to provide elections offices with funds to conduct voter education in subsequent years. Yet every county has elections coming up. These elections in 2003 might not be major, countywide elections, but there are numerous municipal elections slated. If the commitment to funding elections was already dwindling by 2002, those lessons from 2000 were not learned. Some memories are too short, and the lessons from 2000 were acted on only in the short term.

Another lesson from the 2000 election was that it helps to have the latest technology and best equipment for voting. This lesson was learned. Some of the voting technology being used was badly outdated. Many elections offices were conducting elections with voting technology and equipment that was thirty years old. The new technology is designed to prevent common voting errors. All elections offices need to obtain that equipment and technology and continually update the voting systems used.

There were not as many impressive advances in voting technology as one might expect, given the technological breakthroughs in other industries. Part of this was because of the market. Most elections offices were not funded to acquire expensive new technology, and county, state, and federal governments did not prioritize it. Miami-Dade County was still using the old punch-card system we had used back in the 1970s. There were few advances to replace it in the 1980s except for the optical scan systems. In the 1990s touch-screen systems were invented. Basically three new voting technologies were introduced in thirty-plus years. That is not a lot. Consider the technological advances since 1970 in other areas, and elections technology comes up short. It is my hope that new systems are invented that continue to improve the voting process and that a commitment to inventing, funding, and using these new technologies continues.

Herein lies one of the major lessons from the 2000 election: Elections need to be adequately funded.

6

A Look at Voting Machines and Voting Systems

JESS GITTELSON, DIRECTOR, VOTING EQUIPMENT CENTER
OF BROWARD COUNTY

The main job of the Voting Equipment Center supervisor is to maintain the warehouse. In general, I am part of a team that is responsible for making sure that all elections in the county run smoothly. The supervisor's position requires me to be well rounded and to troubleshoot in the event of any problems. The Voting Equipment Center has a staff of five part-time workers, one full-time assistant, and a secretary.

A person in my job does not need a certain specific educational background or skills. For instance, the job does not require a bachelor's degree from college. Rather, employees of the Voting Equipment Center need to have a general background and must be flexible, willing to do a variety of tasks. It helps to like what you are doing, which I do. The position in which I started, that of a warehouse worker, likewise did not have a specific set of qualifications. From doing maintenance and about every job in the department, I learned enough about the position that, as people retired, I was able to move up the ladder and become the supervisor.

In addition to troubleshooting any problems that might occur during an election—and the array of potential problems is limitless—the staff of the Voting Equipment Center must interact with the public. We field a lot of questions before and after elections, especially after the 2000 election. We also give tours of the operation, meet with community groups, and visit sites around the county to inform the public about elections. For instance, throughout the year we met with the public and took the voting machines to public places to test them and to allow people to practice voting. The machines performed well initially, but experienced a few kinks later. We continue to attempt to address all potential problems.

Voting

Broward County is a large county, both geographically and in terms of population. So I run a large warehouse with hundreds of voting machines and all the additional supplies and materials to support and service the voting process. The cost of the new iVotronics voting system was estimated at around $17.5 million. We procured some 5,300 voting machines at an item cost of approximately $3,400. This is a lot of money compared with the old Votomatic punch-card machines. So the change to a new technology was both a dramatic and an expensive change for the elections office.

The process of voting is very simple, and that is part of the job of the elections office. We need to make the process as accessible as possible for every voter. From what I have seen so far, the new technology accomplishes this. It is much easier for voters to use the new machines. When voters pick up their ballot, they simply insert it into the machine. Directions appear on the screen and are self-explanatory. The voter needs only to touch the screen with a finger in order to vote. There is always the possibility that some individuals—perhaps senior citizens—who are intimidated by computers might have a concern about the technology. However, these voters always have the option of getting help from a voter assistance official working at the precinct or of voting at home by absentee ballot. Also, in tests so far conducted on a number of people around the county, the feedback has been positive, including the feedback from older voters.

Broward County provided funds for replacing the voting system. Part of the funding came through an "outreach" program aimed at working with the His/panic and African American communities in the county. Historically, there have been problems associated with guaranteeing the right to vote of Hispanics and African Americans, and voter turnout has been low in these communities. Broward County has large Hispanic and African American populations, and we have been mandated to reach out to these communities to introduce them to the new technology. This is part of the work of the Voting Equipment Center. We physically take the machines around the county to participate in voter education programs and voting displays at churches and special events. It takes time—and it took us time—to learn new voting systems, but we began community outreach and educational programs immediately after the 2000 election and again after adopting the new voting technology. The elections office takes the machines out to the public almost on a daily basis in preparation for the next election.

One of the most challenging aspects of an election in a county the size of Broward is the sheer number of the voters and precincts. The county recently expanded from 600 precincts to probably 800 precincts. The simple logistics of setting up voting machines that work in hundreds of precincts around a geographically large county, and then staffing each precinct, is a huge undertaking. A science. My department must then be prepared on Election Day to service or replace malfunctioning machines at any one of these locations.

The old punch-card voting system on the Votomatic machines, which was used for many years, required about six weeks to prepare for a presidential election like the one in the year 2000. The Voting Equipment Center tested and serviced nearly 6,500 machines and then had them placed at precincts around the county. The ballots and frames for the machines had to be matched. In other words, each precinct might have a slightly different ballot, depending on who was running in that jurisdiction. And the ballot and frames on the machines had to match for every precinct. The old process was handled manually. The new touch-screen system requires that the PED—the ballot that goes into the machine and causes the candidates' names to appear on the screen—be programmed to match the ballot with the corresponding precinct in every machine. It involves technology but is easier to do.

The process of physically moving all the machines to hundreds of precincts around the county is a large logistical undertaking. This must be coordinated so that the right machines and ballots are taken to the right precinct. There are a number of little details. We must make sure we have the proper keys to access each building, the buildings must be clean and set up beforehand, the machines and ballots must be secure throughout the process, the precincts must open on time, the machines must work correctly—and then we must do the whole process in reverse while collecting the machines and ballots after the election. The Voting Equipment Center works with other departments in the elections office to coordinate this process, and we contract out with a company that actually delivers the machines to the precincts. We have used a company called AAA Gold Coast that bids for the contract. Some counties do this service themselves.

For example, I believe Miami-Dade County does this itself. Either way, a lot of coordination and planning is involved.

Election Day

Election Day is a very long day for the Voting Equipment Center and all involved in the election and comes after a very busy and demanding time. Most of us are tired going into the election. A typical day for me is to be in the office by 5:30 a.m. in order to start work at six. During the 2000 election, the phones started ringing at 6:00 a.m. and did not stop for one full hour. As soon as I hung up, the phone was ringing again. This went on for much of the day thereafter. A range of problems can typically occur at this point in the process. Often ballots would get stuck in the machines and we would have to instruct the precinct workers on how to correct the problem. Or, if it could not easily be remedied, we would dispatch a worker to the site to fix the machine. If the problem continued, we would have to replace the machine. Sometimes it is the fault of the machine. Sometimes voters insert the ballot incorrectly. Many voters are first-time voters, after all. Another problem is making sure each precinct has enough blank ballots. If not, we need to furnish them with a sufficient number of ballots. We try to work this out before the election, of course, by looking at the size of the precinct and previous voting trends.

The office stays busy for the entire day. At 7:00 p.m. the polls close, but our day is only half over. There are several prearranged drop points throughout the county, and ballots and machines are taken there after the election. We need to make sure the process is done in a secure, timely, and legal manner. From there, we check to make sure the ballots are where they are supposed to be, and the sheriff's office brings the ballots to the Voting Equipment Center in cases. Numerous observers are present to monitor our work to make sure everything is done fair and equitably. The League of Women Voters joins us in the warehouse to oversee the process. The ballots are checked and then counted in our computer room. In 2000, we had 617 precincts to count. The counting takes some time, and we make sure it is accurate. After the 2000 election, I arrived back home around 4:30 a.m. the day after the election. It is a long day. I always contemplate simply sleeping in the warehouse!

The 2000 election ended unlike any other election. It was not over the day after Election Day. A new dimension to the job was working with the press corps from around the world. Every television station from CNN to the local news had cameras and reporters at the Voting Equipment Center. Broward County, after all, was one of the counties where the outcome of the presidential election would be decided. Normally, we could clean out the boxes containing ballots and clean the voting machines. But after November 2000 we could not touch the ballots for legal reasons.

There were problems that occurred on Election Day in 2000. It is inevitable that some problems will occur in a county the size of Broward and when humans are involved. The responsibility of the Voting Equipment Center is to try and minimize problems associated with the machines. This includes malfunctions, having the right machines in the right locations, and other concerns. Ballots will get stuck in the machines, whether by fault of the voter or from machine error, ballots will be torn off while still in the machine, the lights on the machine will stop working, a stylus breaks, and other problems will occur no matter how much we test them and service them. When we sent out over 6,400 voting machines, we tried to keep the malfunction rate at zero, but realistically a 6-percent failure rate was not uncommon.

In anticipation of such problems, we station troubleshooters throughout the county typically at six central, convenient locations. The precincts and troubleshooters call me and I coordinate the service response. It is my responsibility to determine the nature of the problem from the poll workers at the precinct, contact the troubleshooter nearest to the problem, inform him (or her) of what the problem is, tell him how to repair it, and send him to the precinct in question. All machines are tested prior to the election, and we test them for all these possible problems. With the Votomatics we would put the ballots in the machines, check the lights, test the stylus, and so on, making sure there were no problems with the machine. Once they had been approved, they were loaded on pallets and readied for the precincts. Of course, with the new voting machines we might not have the same type of problems, but we will approach the testing and preparation in the same way. We are all hopeful that the voting-machine-related problems will be minimized with the new touch-screen iVotronics.

Lessons Learned from the 2000 Election

I have seen a lot of elections in more than fifteen years with the Voting Equipment Center. In a way, the 2000 election was unique. Its implication for the outcome of the presidential race and the overwhelming coverage by the national media were unlike anything I had experienced. However, we have had contested elections before, close elections before, lawsuits, and coverage by journalists in the past. So in some ways the election was not completely without precedent, but simply an amplified version of some previous elections.

While the 2000 election was perhaps the most interesting for me, I recall a previous election where a candidate lost by about five votes. The election was contested, and we were required to recount each ballot by hand. We even had to look at the holes—"chads" as the world learned in 2000—to make sure there were no concerns about them. The candidate who had won the election still ended up winning after we recounted the votes. The losing candidate's campaign felt that the machinery we were using was not counting the votes correctly. As it turned out, the machines did a good job. There were other memorable elections. A few years ago there was another election decided by roughly eighty votes. For this one we also had to hand count the votes and, fortunately, we again came up with a similar outcome.

Many states and counties have laws mandating a recount in the event an election is decided by a certain small percentage. We have such a requirement in Broward County and have ended up doing numerous recounts. There have been instances where we have had to recall the staff, fire up the machines, and count all the ballots a second time. So, one lesson to be learned from the 2000 election is that it was not completely unique. Some of the "problems" that happened in 2000 had happened before, and some had happened many times before.

All of us who work in elections accept such challenges. There have been times when the challenges were equivalent to those during the 2000 election and recount. For instance, we have had elections in three consecutive months—September, October, and November—with the third of the three being the large general election. That was stressful and difficult because we did not have the prep time leading up to each election to prepare only for that particular election. Less than a month is a short amount of time in which to prepare for another election. This was one of the biggest challenges in my career. Another was four years prior to that when we had a primary for only a handful of candidates for a handful of elected officials. Nevertheless, we had to go through the whole election—countywide, machines, precincts, and ballots—for just a small number of candidates. However, the law has since changed and such primaries are no longer held.

I would say the most rewarding aspect of my job is the day or the week following an election. To know that the job that we have done on the election was successful, with no mistakes and no problems, is rewarding. For me, the time before and during the election is stressful because I am continually checking and double-checking to make sure I sent all the machines to the right locations. If a mistake was made, not only would it have an impact on the election, but the press would be there to report on it. This is especially true in the wake of the 2000 election. Any mistake made from now on, no matter how small or insignificant, or whether it was our fault, will be reported. That part of the election will dominate the election coverage rather than all that was done right. The allegations whenever something goes wrong that it was done on purpose or that the election was unfair has been and will certainly continue to be a stressful part of the job. When we do things well, no one notices because the election runs as expected. There are few congratulations passed along. I always tell my staff that when we do the best job possible, no one will know. But, that one time when you do something wrong . . . it is headline news!

In 2000 we were unable to sit back after the election and reflect on a job well done. That election "drug on" and we are still feeling its effects. And then I try to get as much sleep as I can!

7

☐

☐

☐

The Role of Grassroots Organizing and the Political Party in Elections

MARK HOCH, POLITICAL DIRECTOR, REPUBLICAN PARTY
OF PALM BEACH COUNTY

The job of the political director is very broad based. I work on a variety of party activities, support Republican campaigns, interact with the public, and develop and enact party strategy. One of my main responsibilities is directing the grassroots efforts of the party in Palm Beach County. In fact, almost everything I do relates back in some way to the grassroots effort. Both political parties emphasize grassroots programs, which help to bring members and volunteers into the party. Although through the media the public sees and hears a lot about television advertising in campaigns, the media effort is only a small part of a campaign. There is no substitute for a grassroots approach to what is called "getting out the vote." The political party organizes through me a number of get-out-the-vote committees and initiatives from neighborhood walks to phone banks, which I will discuss further in a moment. So, the grass roots is where our focus is.

The Political Party in Elections

The county political parties are deeply involved in elections. Of course, elections are organized and administered by the county's elections office. But the parties monitor elections, familiarize ourselves with election law, the ballots, and voting systems, and seek to build support for our candidates in order to be successful on Election Day. All this requires a staff and financial resources. Our operating budget comes strictly from local donations. We get absolutely nothing from the state or national parties. This is a matter that has always been a bitter fight between local county parties and state parties, because a lot of times state parties will come into the county—especially a large and wealthy county like Palm Beach County—and take out a considerable amount of money, leaving little behind for the local party. This makes it difficult for us to do our job. But, at the same time, the national and state parties and their candidates are reliant on us to support their efforts and get out the vote locally. For as long as I have been working for local parties, I have seen and heard complaints by almost everyone involved in local parties about this problem. It is complex because we are all separate entities—the national, state, and local parties, but we all must work together.

Although there is a lot of coordinating that occurs between the three levels of the political party, in the end we are still separate entities and function as such in the area of fund-raising. The local party ends up working together more with the state party than the national party. The public sometimes does not understand this complex relationship and the fact that we are separate entities. For example, sometimes when we ask for donations here in Palm Beach County, party members will say that they already sent a check to the national party. We have to then try to explain the nature of what we do at the local level and that, as we are separate organizations, just because someone from Palm Beach County sent money to the national party, it does not mean that we in the county will see any portion of it.

The local Republican Party exists to serve not only party members but local Republican candidates for office. We accomplish this mission in a number of ways. Although we do not print campaign bumper stickers and buttons, we will help candidates generate volunteers, provide technical advice, and actually offer them services such as helping them get their yard signs placed around the county. For instance, prior to elections we develop a database of volunteers willing to help and people or businesses that are willing to have a sign placed in their window or yard. The local party will contact those willing to display party signs and will send volunteers out to put the signs in the yard. This may not sound like a necessary service, but it is a large logistical undertaking to find people willing to have signs installed, locate the property, and put up the sign.

If a candidate for office contacts us with a question, for example, on how to go about having bumper stickers made, we will help them identify a reputable vendor who manufactures bumper stickers. But we do not actually print up such materials. This responsibility rests with the candidates. The state party might offer such services because their financial resources are much larger than ours. But the local party is the best resource for energizing the party membership and getting out the vote.

The neighborhood walks and phone banks are good examples of how the party targets voters. It is not feasible from a time or cost perspective, or from the perspective of the proper usage of limited resources, to try to reach all voters. Television commercials, if shown enough and on enough different stations and shows, can reach a wide audience with a message. Even these are targeted in terms of the demographics of the viewers. But local party efforts are forced to target voters because of limited resources and, because we are the party organization in a specific county, we are ideally suited to target voters in that county. All of our efforts are targeted.

To assist us in targeting voters, we use election maps and election results available at the county elections office. Once I have sufficient data, I then break down the data as needed using spreadsheets and statistical analysis. This is a major part of my job and something I do before attempting to organize any get-out-the-vote activities. The information is free and available to the public.

Through the data, we can determine where Republicans performed well and where we did not do well. We can break down this information by precinct and by election. This is all part of targeting voters. We are not only interested in the largest precincts and those that support Republicans, but we also look at precincts that have been "on the bubble," which is to say that they are close, 50-50 races. This type of "swing" precinct could influence elections and is targeted. Safe Republican precincts will probably vote Republican, so the local party does not need to concentrate efforts on the attractiveness of the Republican message in those precincts. Rather, our work will be to assure that these individuals get out to vote.

GOTV

There are a number of approaches we use to get out the vote (GOTV). In fact, the task is so important to us that we organize committees around the different facets of getting out the vote. One thing to remember is that no matter how much a candidate knows about the issues, how eminently qualified the candidate may be, how electable or popular according to the polls, if the voters do not show and vote, the candidate will not win.

When party members show up to vote, it often benefits the entire party and all candidates from that party. It is always a good thing for democracy when people vote. But from a strategic perspective, because many people are loyal to the party and tend to vote for candidates of that party, if we get them out to vote it might benefit Republicans from the candidate for sheriff to the party's presidential nominee. A lot of people do use the political party as a reference as they get lower down the ticket. For example, candidates for local office such as city council or commission adopt the strategy of handing out palm cards or business cards outside the precinct on the day of the election. Or they will have volunteers stand outside the polling locations and do this. The public might not know who is on the ballot in those races and might not have a firm opinion on who it is they intend to vote for in local races. But if the voters receive a candidate's card as they enter the polling site, they might remember the name when voting. This works for voters with ties to that party and prevents them from simply not casting a vote in some local races. I have seen such local candidates win by six votes, and their affiliation with the Republican Party and strategy of handing out cards at the precincts probably gave them the victory.

At the top of the ticket—president, governor—most voters already have their minds made up by Election Day. So there is only so much in terms of advocacy for a candidate the local party can do. But there is much we can do for local candidates, and this is only one example of what we do. Strategically, it makes sense at times for the local party to work from the perspective of the top of the ticket, meaning the national office or highest offices in the election. It is a big priority for the party at all levels to try to get our candidates elected to these high offices. Also, if such candidates are popular—as Ronald Reagan was in 1980—they may have "coattails" and help candidates of their party further down the ticket get elected. However, many local candidates are inadequately funded and staffed and have little political experience. They have nowhere else to turn but to the local party. Candidates for state office have the state party, candidates for Congress have the Republican Congressional Campaign Committee. So we must work to elect our local candidates, even if strategically we are working from the top of the ticket. To find a balance, we might use the top of the ticket as a motivator. For instance, our message might be: We want you to vote and we are encouraging you to get out and support Governor Jeb Bush and the entire Republican ticket in this election. The top of the ticket works as a lead-in, but we are still supporting our local candidates.

Although the fundamentals of phone banking, neighborhood walks, and other GOTV activities are similar regardless of the election at hand, the activities and strategy of the local party do vary somewhat depending upon the election and candidate. For instance, there is a different approach to primary elections than to general elections. Because the party must represent all members and candidates of the party, we generally take a hands-off approach during the primary election. We do not want to show favoritism among our candidates for the same office, we do not want to create divisions within the office. Furthermore, a smaller role in the primary election will allow us to concentrate our efforts and save our resources for the general election, when we want to defeat the Democratic Party's candidate. In some state legislative races we might have three or four Republicans competing for the right to face the Democratic candidate in the upcoming general election. In this case, we would not endorse any of the candidates, but would inform them all of the services the local party makes available. An exception to this would be, for instance, if Governor Jeb Bush were running in the Republican primary and had an opponent. In this case, Governor Bush is the de facto party leader in the state and we are going to support him.

Phone Banking

The Republican Party of Palm Beach County does a lot of "phone banking." This is an effective way of getting out the vote. Our phone banking strategy is generally to let the individual candidates and campaigns work on gaining the support of independents. The county party focuses on turning out the vote of registered Republicans. Through phone banking and other efforts we can assure that the core group who vote Republican in elections get out to vote on Election Day.

The local party keeps records on registered Republicans and those expressing interest in voting for or volunteering for the party. We then identify these individuals and either call them on the phone, go door-to-door and pay them a visit, or provide them with literature. Our goal is to inform them of the pending vote, set forth our party's candidates and issues, and remind them of how important it is to get out and vote.

The phone bank calls typically start just after the primary election. This is how we did it during the 1998 and 2000 election cycles. Our goal is to phone every single Republican in the county, but for a county the size of Palm Beach County such a goal is extremely difficult to achieve. We have 235,000 registered Republicans in the county. It takes a lot of time and a lot of volunteers to reach that many people by phone. Some people change their phone numbers, others move, and people are not home all day every day. So we know we will not make contact with every single one.

A more realistic strategy is to begin targeting the most viable individuals. This involves rating or assessing the membership according to the criterion of whether the person votes in every single election. Our rating will categorize people as those who vote in every election, those who vote sometimes, those who rarely vote, and those who never vote. Armed with this knowledge, in our first round of phone banking we will probably not include those who always vote—nor those who never vote.

The phone banking will target those who sometimes vote. For instance, one tends to see a significant drop-off in voting turnout when it is not a presidential election. During the 2000 election—which, of course, was a presidential election year—Palm Beach County enjoyed an almost 70 percent turnout among registered voters. The turnout among Republicans in the county was almost 71 percent. That is extremely high. Palm Beach County generally has a voter turnout higher than the national average. Obviously, it would be nice to see a 100 percent turnout, but the 70 percent figure is also very high considering the turnout during a nonpresidential election. Such elections might produce a 10–15 percent turnout in a primary election but a whopping 50–60 percent turnout in a governor's race. Phone banking is an important part of turning out voters. Moreover, it is important for the Republican Party because the party is at a disadvantage in Palm Beach County. Through aggressive phone banking that targets the Republican base, we attempt to offset the majority advantage enjoyed by Democrats in the county. The goals of phone banking are to turn out voters, especially those who otherwise might not vote, to offset the numerical advantage of the Democrats, to at least hold the existing voter turnout rates, and to try to increase those rates.

In past elections, the county party has run three phone banks during such GOTV efforts. One phone bank targets the central part of the county, another the northern part, and the third one southern Palm Beach County. On average, ten to fifteen volunteers staff the phone banks, making the actual calls. A key is to make the calls when the public is most likely to be at home. We generally call from roughly 6:00 p.m. to 8:30 p.m. After 8:30 p.m., some people get a little upset if they are called at home, especially senior citizens. If we start much before 6:00 p.m., many people are not home from work yet. An exception to this phone bank schedule is that we sometimes use senior volunteers who come to the phone bank during the day to make calls. For such phone banks we target retired precincts for calls.

A two-and-one-half-hour phone bank is the norm. Also, the party office is centrally located in the county and easy to find. Some volunteers will prefer to make the phone calls from their home. While we do not want to turn away any volunteer and try to accommodate all their requests, we discourage this practice as a last resort. We also do not want to allow our phone bank lists out of our office for a variety of reasons. We would not have control over the nature and length of the call, nor could we verify whether the calls were made. Most campaigns have the same view on phone banking. Even though many of our phone banks are run out of the main party office in the county, we do try to set up phone banks throughout the county. This is done to accommodate the volunteers who might not want to drive to the main office if they live far from it. Palm Beach County is a geographically large county, so this is a possibility. When we set up phone banks around the county, we will target the south part of the county with a phone bank in south Palm Beach County and so on.

Another key to successful phone banking is to keep the phone call short. We do not want to take up a person's time. Nor do we want to get them upset by expecting them to talk to us for more than, say, two minutes. To account for such potential problems and to ensure that our message is accurate and consistent, we develop the phone script and provide it to all our phone bank volunteers. We also train the phone bank volunteers on how to handle problems and questions, and I am often available if something unusual arises during the call.

A final key to a successful phone bank is to accompany the message of getting out to vote with additional information. The call will look less like a political appeal and more like a helpful information service. And providing information to our members is something we try to do anyway. For instance, we will mention during the call that a new law on elections states that individuals do not need a reason for choosing to vote by absentee ballot. If the voter is interested in this, we will provide information on how to vote by absentee ballot and we will provide the phone number and address of the elections office and even offer to mail the voter an absentee ballot request form.

Volunteers

Whether we are doing phone banking or other GOTV initiatives, we rely on volunteers to accomplish our goals and mission as a party. The phone banks are staffed by volunteers. Campaigns are full of volunteers. In general, our volunteers are involved with the party either locally or nationally. We also use our executive committee members as volunteers, and they recruit more volunteers. Part of my job is to both recruit and maintain our team of volunteers. Volunteers often feel further connected to or vested in the party through volunteering and, in addition to being the basis of our grassroots efforts, the volunteers are also part of the Republican Party's face in the community. They are our representatives in the community.

We also try to have volunteers work in the community where they live. For example, with phone banks, we might assign the volunteer to call phone numbers in their community or participate in neighborhood walks in their neighborhood. The process is more effective in this way. The party also organizes activities and events around the county so as not to exclude any communities. Volunteers are giving up their time and many may have little experience working in politics. This being so, the party wants to make the experience of volunteering as easy and friendly as possible.

Neighborhood Walks

Another GOTV strategy is neighborhood walks. While it might not sound it, neighborhood walks are very detailed. It usually takes me a good two days to put together a neighborhood walk. The volunteers participating in the walk and the prospective voters we talk to never really see the planning aspect of the walks, so people are often surprised to find out how much work goes into the event. But that is how it should be. We do not want to take up any time beyond what is needed.

A day is designated for the walk, as is a meeting place such as the party headquarters or a satellite headquarters near the targeted neighborhood. Neighborhood walks are very targeted. We do not simply walk in any neighborhood. We pick neighborhoods strategically and try to conduct two walks before every election in each region of the county: two in the south, two in the central, and two in the north part of the county, as well as two in West Palm Beach, the largest city in the county. Because we have limited resources financially and in terms of volunteers, this is often the most walks we can conduct.

I break down the areas where we will conduct the walk by designated important precincts for the party. Important neighborhoods or precincts include the largest ones as well as those with the largest number of registered Republicans. With the election data available and our data files, we can further break down neighborhoods and precincts by street. For example, if we know a certain street has only two registered Republicans, we will not even bother walking on that street. We need to reach the most Republicans in the shortest period of time. During the walks, we will knock on doors, briefly discuss with the citizen the importance of voting Republican in the upcoming election, and provide them with information and literature on the election and Republican candidates. The whole process is very targeted.

Voter Education

The political parties also work to promote voter education. An informed electorate is an empowered electorate, and the parties can play a role in making this happen. Of course, we feel that our party's message and candidates are attractive and that the more the public knows about the party, the more it will support the party. But elections in general are complex events, and the voting public often knows little about how elections are run or their rights as citizens and voters. The local party tries to educate voters about such matters as when the election will be held, special referenda that will be on the ballot, and how to vote using an absentee ballot. For instance, I have encountered many people who do not know that they can vote by an absentee ballot, that they no longer need a reason for doing so, that all they need to do is to request one from the elections office, and that, once they receive their absentee ballot, they can no longer vote at the polling location unless they bring that ballot with them. By educating voters, we are helping them to vote and ensuring that the party does not lose potential votes.

The Republican Party of Palm Beach County also provides training for our candidates for office. For instance, we recently had the Republican National Committee come into the county and conduct training programs on our behalf. Many local candidates will have a lengthy list of questions about how campaigns and elections work. We are here to help them answer such questions. We also provide similar services to the voters. The party will generate volunteers for local candidates and, at the request of the state or national party, will help mobilize local volunteers for statewide and national campaigns. At the same time, this effort to develop a volunteer team provides political involvement for voters. In a way, we are doing both the candidate and the voter a service by bringing them together.

Some candidates solicit our help, while we reach out to others. Typically, the county party initiates the first contact with the candidate. We let them know who we are, what we do, and that we are here for them. It is then up to them to follow through. A similar approach occurs with the voters, although the party often makes more of an effort to stay in touch with voters after the initial contact for obvious reasons. The office also provides literature for the public on the Republican Party, its issues, and its candidates.

Election Day

Of course, many months are spent preparing for an election, but the work of a political party and the party's political director do not end before Election Day. The days leading up to the election are a very busy time. In the final stretch of the race, we will heavily bombard voters with our message and urge them to get out to vote. During this time we will increase neighborhood walks and phone banks and will make additional personal calls. We will call those individuals who have not yet returned their absentee ballots so we do not lose a potential vote.

The local party also helps get people to the polls. In addition to reminding people in the time leading up to Election Day, we call them on Election Day to make sure they voted and, if they have not yet done so, encourage them to get out and vote Republican. The party relies on many volunteers on Election Day. Some local party operations assist voters with rides to the polling site.

Election Day for party leaders starts early. The county headquarters usually opens around six a.m. on Election Day. My day will usually then run until about five the following morning. The first part of this long day is spent at the headquarters making phone calls to Republican voters to remind them again to get out and vote. But we also use our headquarters as a base of operations for the county. The party places poll watchers at precincts around the county. Their job is to monitor the voting to make sure it proceeds properly. If they discover a potential problem, they will call me and I will identify the problem and gather the necessary information and facts. I will then look into the matter and contact the supervisor of elections. We provide phone numbers and cell phones to our volunteers, and our phones are busy for most of the day. I also have access to the cell phone and pager for the supervisor of elections, because in the event of a problem it is hard to get through to her office.

It is legal for the parties to use poll watchers. The elections office requires that requests be made with them before the election, and there are forms we must fill out. A form for each individual must be submitted to the supervisor of elections. The elections office then provides those persons with official badges they must wear. Florida law permits the party to have one poll watcher per polling site. Our poll watchers spend much of the day at a particular precinct.

The local party recruits poll watchers. These individuals need to know what to look for, and we provide training for them. There are a number of things poll watchers will need to be looking for. For example, they keep an eye on the poll workers to make sure they are not acting in an illegal or partisan manner. Poll workers are assigned to provide assistance to voters requiring it, but only up to a certain point and for a short period of time. They can show the voters how to cast their votes, but they cannot vote for a person unless the person is disabled and accommodations have been made. Another potential problem, and one we have received phone calls about in the past, is people not being permitted to vote. If anything looks out of the ordinary, that is when they call me. If someone has not been allowed to vote, I will ask to talk to that person to identify whether the reason is legitimate or not. Basically, I am troubleshooting the whole day. But the party also has a group of attorneys available to provide assistance, and I will call them if need be.

The poll watchers have a second function—to observe the election for the party. They are part of the party's "get up and go" efforts, and they help us identify if voter turnout is light or heavy in each precinct. From this information, we can adjust our phone bank calls accordingly to precincts where turnout is light. We try to recruit poll watchers who are attorneys or who know a lot about elections. They are also individuals involved in the Republican Party, and many are part of our executive committee. We also have observers who have access to the elections office and the actual counting of the votes, but only one person per party is given access to the computer room where the votes are counted at the end of the day. I have fulfilled this duty in the past, and it has required me to stay at the elections office until the counting was finished at four or five the following morning.

During Election Day, the party also keeps tabs on Republican turnout. Oftentimes the candidates or media will contact us for this information. We also talk to other local and national party officials to see how we are doing overall in other races. For instance, I stay in touch with the chair of the Republican Party of Palm Beach County throughout the day, providing information on voter turnout and on any problems experienced at the precincts. The elections office makes information available on its Web site and we also monitor this. When the votes are being counted at the end of the day, we follow the results of each precinct with eagerness.

The 2000 Election

The 2000 election was a memorable one. A number of lessons were learned by all involved. Palm Beach County's elections office has now changed the voting machines, so the parties and voters of the county had to adjust to a new voting system for the 2002 election. The elections office tested the system around the county in an effort to introduce it to the voters and work the bugs out. None of us wanted another election like 2000 and no one wanted to discover that the ballot or machine used to record votes was a problem. The elections office had all the kinks worked out of the system by the November 2002 election, and everything went smoothly.

In any given election, problems will occur. There is always something and a reason for someone to contact me with questions or problems. The party attempts to train the poll watchers in what to watch out for, and this training will not only allow them to catch problems but will cut down on false accusations and unnecessary calls to my office. Even the best-trained poll watchers will not catch everything, nor can they be expected to know the details of election law. Given the controversy generated from the 2000 election, we are spending more time training poll watchers. And since the county purchased a new voting system, we have had to learn about the new technology and system. Many of the election laws were also changed. Florida no longer has primary runoff elections. The last one was in 2000. The state introduced the use of provisional ballots to guarantee that everyone would have the opportunity to vote, even if their eligibility was questioned.

One of the main controversies surrounding the 2000 election in Palm Beach County was the use of the "butterfly ballot." Everyone should know that the elections office showed us what the butterfly ballot would look like. It was sent to the party right after the runoff primary. So we knew what it was going to look like. Also, the elections office sent out sample ballots to voters. Such things are public information. The Democrats saw the ballot, all the political parties saw the ballot. At the time, nobody said anything about it. It did not create a problem, nor did it meet with resistance. If anyone had a problem with it, I am assuming they would have made a point of it within a few days of seeing the ballot. Nor was the old punch-card voting system necessarily problematic. It was used for years. Another aspect of the 2000 election that was seen as being a problem was the undervotes and overvotes. However, there are always undervotes and overvotes. I analyze previous election returns as part of my job, and I know they occur.

What happened was that the press made an issue out of things that were not unique to the 2000 election as if they had never occurred before. I remember in the days after the 2000 election watching the news and thinking to myself that all the concern over undervotes and overvotes was nothing new to me. I saw it in previous elections, in municipal elections, in primaries. It happens in every election. In fact, elections supervisors generally print reports of the results of elections. They do this in Palm Beach County for every election, and these reports list the number of undervotes on them. This issue is simply something that the press never really picked up on in previous elections. I have talked to a number of reporters who admitted they knew undervotes and overvotes existed because they had been covering elections—including elections in Palm Beach County—for years.

Even with the election reforms and new voting system, we will have undervotes in the next election. Whenever people are involved in the process, there will be mistakes. Some people make mistakes when voting. In the 2002 election the new voting system eliminated most of them. The touch-screen computer that is part of the new system will eliminate the problem of overvotes, because the computer will not permit the voter to record a second vote for a candidate once they cast a vote. The old punch-card system was somewhat flawed in that it could not prevent overvotes. But no system will prevent undervotes. In a recent election in the city of Wellington in Palm Beach County a controversy was stirred when undervotes were discovered. So it will remain with us and we are all certainly much more aware of such matters after the 2000 election.

One of the consequences of the 2000 election is that it raised the level of awareness about elections and voting for all of us. Everyone is now aware that one vote does count. This is an important lesson we learned. When one considers that George W. Bush won Florida—and thus the presidency—by fewer than ten votes per county, it is easy to see that every vote counts. I have seen local elections decided by one or two votes. This always disturbs me, because I think that if we had only knocked on one more door or made one more phone call before the election . . .

The 2000 election raised public awareness about voting. During our work since Election 2000 we have found that the public wants to talk about the election. An unprecedented number of Republicans have since signed up to be volunteers. I heard from many people that after the last election they realized just how important it is for them to get out there and volunteer and how much the party needed every person to get involved.

The 2000 election raised awareness within the Republican Party about the importance of grassroots initiatives. Accordingly, since 2000 we have worked even harder in developing our grassroots programs. In anticipation of the next election, the party is trying to recruit more volunteers so that we might increase our phone banks and neighborhood walks. We are also trying to raise more money to fund such initiatives. Those of us who work behind the scenes in campaigns and elections learned we need to be more vigilant in preparing for elections. Obviously, anything can happen. In this sense, the 2000 election was also a wake-up call for everybody, including political professionals. Lastly, it provided a real education for the country about democracy and our electoral system.

8

□

□

□

Candidates, Parties, and Local Election Politics

CATHY DUBIN, FORMER EXECUTIVE DIRECTOR,
DEMOCRATIC PARTY OF PALM BEACH COUNTY

There is never an election that is not partisan. This occurs on several fronts. Voters are often partisan. They have preferences regarding their party's issues that might be better reflected by a particular political party, and they prefer certain candidates to other candidates. Candidates run in elections as members of political parties. Many elections officials are elected or appointed by political leaders who appoint only individuals sharing their views and party affiliation. Also, there is always somebody who has a view of something, given the particular party that they belong to, and they want that belief or position carried forward in the public agenda—a woman's right to choose, whether there should be charter schools or not, whether there should be school vouchers, and so on. People realize that through political parties they might have a better chance of seeing that preference brought to reality. This is simply the way it is.

However, certain public offices such as those working with election administration should not be partisan positions. Whether or not that will change is doubtful. On the other hand, there are a number of other offices such as zoning and permitting, for example, where removing any partisan or political affiliation makes good sense. In fact, I would go as far as to say that even the city commission should not be partisan. The same goes for the county commission, although in Palm Beach County that office became highly partisan in 2000 as a direct result of both the personalities of those serving on the commission and the great controversy caused by the 2000 election.

The chair of the Republican Party of Palm Beach County happens to be the county commissioner I opposed in the 2002 election. There was some ill will created because of the controversies surrounding the way the election was run and the votes were counted in 2000. Some felt that this particular commissioner had a hard time determining where to draw the line between addressing an election crisis in an objective manner and acting from a position of partisan interest. The same has been suggested of Democratic commissioners, so the commission has become quite partisan.

There are, after all, possible conflicts of interest in that elected officials are overseeing an election at the same time they are functioning as agents of their party. These allegations have been leveled at various elections officials. In Palm Beach County the controversial supervisor of elections, Theresa LePore—who became well known for designing the flawed "butterfly ballot"—is now an independent, unaffiliated with any political party. However, even though an elections supervisor might be a member of a political party, this does not necessarily mean that the individual cannot set aside partisan interests and conduct a fair election. Even though Supervisor LePore has come under great fire, in her defense I have to say that she always treated everybody equally until the 2000 election.

Palm Beach County and the 2000 Election

Palm Beach County, the county's elections supervisor, and our infamous "butterfly ballot" did not come out well in the national media coverage of the 2000 presidential election. In fairness, the media focused on the negatives associated with the election and elections officials. This is not to say that the ballot design and other mistakes that occurred during the administration of that election were not contributing factors to the disputed results. Indeed, if one were to zero in on what really cost Democrat Al Gore the election, it would have to be that butterfly ballot.

There were other problems in the administration of Palm Beach County's election, but this appeared to be the decisive factor. For instance, during presidential elections, voting turnout is always high and in 2000 Palm Beach County had its highest turnout. It was a tightly contested election. However, the problem arose of undercounts in the votes, which made no sense. Why would people go out to vote in a presidential election in record numbers and then fail to cast a vote for president but register a vote for, say, tax collector? There were roughly 10,000 such undervotes in the county.

It is possible some people attempted to vote for president but were confused by the butterfly ballot. It is also possible that the "punch" system was difficult for senior voters. Palm Beach County has a large senior population. If enough punched "chads" remain in the voting machine, the buildup behind the ballot makes it difficult to punch the hole completely through, given the small hole and device used to mark one's vote. It is also possible that numerous voters attempting to cast a vote for Al Gore may have mistakenly voted for Patrick Buchanan, the Reform Party candidate. In a county like Palm Beach County, it is odd that 3,433 votes went to Pat Buchanan, which he himself has admitted he probably did not receive. Equally troubling were the 19,000 overvotes recorded. Many of these overvotes were by people who voted for the same candidate twice on the ballot. It appears that many voters, possibly confused by the butterfly ballot, punched a vote for Gore or one of the presidential candidates and then took the time to write in "Gore" on the ballot. These overvotes were discarded, which should not have been done for voters indicating their obvious preference for president by both punching Gore and writing in Gore's name. These voters made their preference known and such "spoiled ballots" should have been counted.

Many individuals who worked so hard for the party throughout the campaign, election, and then the recount process felt that their vote did not count. This is how I felt, even though I know I voted correctly. I also know that it was in fact hard to figure out the butterfly ballot. The press and comedians had a good time poking fun at Florida, calling the state "Flori-DUH!" However, I have a college degree magna cum laude and have worked on many campaigns and elections, yet I had trouble with the ballot, which I had taken home to vote two weeks prior to Election Day. I had to vote with an absentee ballot because I would be busy with the election all day on Election Day. Yet, even from the comfort of my home, I had to look at the ballot three times. For many people the ballot did not align properly in the voting machine. Gore's name was listed on the ballot second from the top, but the hole to punch to indicate a vote for Gore was the third hole from the top. So those who alleged that it was only the elderly or only a small number of African Americans who had trouble with the ballot are incorrect, although a number of seniors have come forward with complaints about the ballot.

I do not believe the officials or supervisor of elections in Palm Beach County purposely designed the butterfly ballot to be flawed, and I do not believe it was done to benefit the Republican candidate, George W. Bush, even though that is what ended up happening. Many commentators have pointed out that both the

Republican and Democratic Parties had to approve the ballot in order for it to be used. But this is not entirely true. It is true that a copy of the ballot was sent to the parties, but the copy we received in the mail did not need to be approved. It was simply sent to us. It had already been designed and readied for state approval. The approval was from Katherine Harris, Florida's secretary of state and head election official. The Democrats might be guilty of not identifying the problem beforehand.

There were a number of other problems, including African Americans being turned away from polling sites for a variety of suspect reasons. However, given my position, I do not feel it would be proper for me to comment further on these allegations. I can say that emotions in the county were very high after that election. For me, it was the most incredible election I had ever experienced. Emotions remain high to the present time, and will most likely carry over into future elections.

Lessons Learned from 2000

There are a number of lessons to be learned from the 2000 election, the most important being the need to educate the voters. Although it might seem like a minor or even unnecessary task, both the political parties and the elections office need to make sure that voters know how to use voting machines. Likewise, it is important to familiarize voters with the ballot, the voting process, and their rights as voters. If, for instance, voters need to take five minutes to vote, they are permitted to do so. If voters need additional time or have questions about the voting process, they are able to take the time and ask for assistance from the voter assistance officials at the polling site. This empowers voters and ultimately will cut down on instances of voting error such as undervotes, overvotes, and spoiled ballots. So it is worth the effort.

The parties and the elections office make information available to voters. All of these today have Web sites. Voters have a lot of information available to them, but they need to go out and get hold of this information. Why people have not done this in the past is beyond me. Perhaps they assumed elections were well run and without error. People had faith that the system would work well. Or they did not take elections seriously. I think after the 2000 election people no longer assume elections work well. People now know that every single vote that is cast matters, and it is also imperative that the public play a more active role in its government and its elections.

During the 2000 election, there were allegations of some voters being turned away from the polls in certain counties near the time that the polls closed. If voters are in line at 7 p.m. when the polling site closes, however, they are permitted to vote. If voters were armed with this knowledge, it might prevent such problems. There is a role for voters to make the effort to educate themselves. An example is that many voters would probably prefer the convenience of voting from their home but are not aware that they can do so. Some voters think that the only way they can vote with an absentee ballot is if there is a major crisis or illness, but that is not the case.

This is one of the many activities political parties can undertake prior to an election to help their members and the integrity of the election. The Palm Beach County Democratic Party did participate in voter education and an array of other similar services while I was an officer in the party. Now that everyone knows more about such problems and the extensiveness of spoiled ballots and voter uncertainty about the process, both parties will make it a priority. To be sure, voter education has become the party's main emphasis, especially in the areas of absentee ballots, voter's rights, and how to use the new computerized voting system.

Another task of the party is to increase the party's membership. In particular, the party needs to attract young voters. I try to get young people to register to vote. Often the responses from young people are along the lines of "Well, why should I vote?" or "It does not mean anything anyway if I vote." One of the lessons we learned from the 2000 election is that every vote counts. Everyone in Palm Beach County and in Florida now knows this. Young people now know how important their votes are. Just recently in the city of Wellington in Palm Beach County there was an election where a candidate lost by only four votes. Of course, in such a tight race and given what we know about how votes are cast and how they are counted, the party contested the election. Apparently some of the new voting machines did not work right.

The voting technology itself is only part of the solution and but one of the lessons that came out of the 2000 election. Regardless of the voting system used, voters really need to do their homework; they need to know who they are voting for and need to learn about the candidates and parties. Voters need to get involved in the political process beyond simply going to the polls once every two years, because it is so important to know what is going on in this country. For instance, now that the country is faced with a war on terror, there is an increase in patriotism, but at the same time our rights are being taken away. A great tool for educating the voter is the Internet. Any citizen can learn more about voting, the candidates, and the parties by using the Internet. The supervisor of elections for Palm Beach County has a helpful Web site. On this Web site, she provides all sorts of relevant information about voting and how to find out more about the new voting machines. The elections office has been taking the new voting machines around the county for individuals to see and practice voting. Also, individuals are invited to go into the supervisor's office and practice on the machines. Happily, the new voting technology worked well in the 2002 elections. But, there is a lawsuit against those machines, in part because there is no paper backup for the actual vote. If one takes that example of a candidate winning the recent election in Wellington by four votes, with the new computerized system there is no way to double-check the vote. The computer database will only tell you the same thing that the machine tells you. That is not good. There needs to be some sort of backup mechanism or paper trail to use in the event that a recount becomes necessary.

It is possible that the closeness of Election 2000 has made individuals aware that every single vote matters and that only a small number of votes might have swung the whole election. This awareness could function to increase voter turnout in future races. On the other hand, the 2000 election might have the opposite effect. If people feel disenfranchised, if they feel that perhaps the election was a sham, they might not bother to vote. The next elections in Palm Beach County will, in my opinion, be very different elections. The candidacy of Joseph Lieberman on the Democratic ticket energized the Jewish vote—a significant vote in the county. Also, voters are still angry at the way the election was administered. During the recount process, for example, the canvassing board did not get the votes in in time, so those votes were not counted. This leads me to believe future elections will be payback elections. Now, I do not necessarily agree with that, but I believe that is the state of mind of many voters. Afterward, I believe everything will go back to the norm.

The new computerized voting technology may or may not be part of the solution. Some types of voters are intimidated by technology and computers. It might deter them from voting. This is why an absentee ballot program would be beneficial. These voters could vote by using an absentee ballot from the comfort of their home. If I were still the executive director of the Democratic Party, this would be a priority for me. The party can organize a program to have voters complete an absentee ballot request form. Of course, the party cannot cast a vote for them. But the party can explain to voters how to use the form and can help them obtain the ballots. The Republican Party has an advantage here, something they used in 2000. They have the resources to have voters' names, addresses, and all the other information already placed on the forms, making it much easier and much more convenient for the voters, who have only to indicate their vote preference. The Republican Party naturally has a lot more money to spend on such a program because they are supported by big business and tend to raise a lot more than Democrats.

Regardless of the new technology and all the issues already mentioned, many elections come down to people and good old-fashioned grassroots politics—getting people out to knock on doors and earn votes. That takes volunteers, and that takes either youth or people with the time to spend. It is tiring work, and some senior volunteers are unable to do this type of campaigning anymore. Another thing that perhaps needs to happen is for Election Day to be a day off from work for everybody. Nobody then has any excuse not to go to the polls.

There are always going to be problems on Election Day. There will never be a perfect election. When I woke up on Election Day in 2000, I assumed there would be one or two problems—a polling place not working, a machine not working. But I never expected what happened that day. This election was a wake-up call to everyone. My desire is that something good will come out of it in terms of a new awareness of and interest in how elections are run. And maybe it provided some momentum for needed reforms—in particular, campaign finance reform that builds on what we have in place and better voter education, especially given the new technology and voting systems that will be in place as a result of 2000. The effect of 2000 has already been felt in terms of new and improved voting technology. This was necessary but is only part of the bigger picture. Lastly, perhaps the best "reform" would be simply if more people stepped up to the plate to run for office.

Elections from the Perspective of a Candidate

In 2002 I was a candidate for a seat on the county commission in District IV. There are seven county commissioners. The county is broken up into seven "single member districts," which cover the unincorporated areas as well as the cities, and the people of each district voting for their respective commissioner. The commissioners work with the mayors of the cities and for the entire county.

I decided to run for office for a variety of reasons. In truth, I never thought I would be a candidate. I always enjoyed politics and was involved in politics for much of my adult life, but always behind the scenes. However, looking at the problems in the county and problems with elected officials, I thought it was about time for me to step up and run. People should not be afraid to run for public office. A lot of good people are afraid to run because of the negativity in politics today and the threat of having their reputation smeared by dirty politics.

In order to pursue elected office, there are a number of steps a prospective candidate must take, formally and informally. One of the first steps I took as a candidate was to hold a press conference and formally announce my candidacy. Then I filed with the elections office. The filing process is not difficult. One simply needs to fill out the necessary paperwork with the local elections office and then pay a filing fee. Or, if the candidate can get enough signatures from the public, the fee is waived. To qualify, the candidate would have people sign cards on his or her behalf. After the 2000 census, the county was not exactly sure how many cards needed to be signed in my case, so they gave me a percentage of the district or the option of paying a filing fee of roughly $4,000. That might seem like a high amount, but it should not deter people from running for office, because there is always the option of getting the signatures to forgo the fee. The signatures typically constitute a percentage of the overall population in the area in which you are running for office.

If you are planning on running for office, you will need to get used to this type of activity. Getting people to sign cards to support your candidacy is like getting people to vote for you. The percentage of signatures required is small enough that it is not out of reach for the average person.

Running for office is a challenging task, and you must be sure you are ready for the undertaking. It takes a lot of reflection to determine why you want to run for office and what issues you feel passionately about. Another important step is to consult your family and learn their feelings about the candidacy. This was vital for me, as I am married and have a family. I wanted to talk to them about how I should go about running for office and whether they supported me. It was essential to me, for example, to have my husband be there 100 percent for me. Because we had a very good relationship, this was an essential part of my candidacy. I also needed to know I would have the support of my children. Candidates must make sacrifices. I knew I would not get to see my grandchildren as much as I would like to for a while, because they live in Chicago. Each candidate must make this type of decision. Fortunately, for me, my whole family was on board for my campaign.

Informally, one of my initial steps was to talk to the chair of the Democratic Party of Palm Beach County about my interest in the position. Then I talked to as many people in the party as possible, from those in leadership to grassroots volunteers. This helped me to get a feel for what it would be like to run and for the needs and interests of those in the party, and also allowed them to get a sense of who I was and what I was all about. When meeting people around the county, I was asked a number of questions. The public expects candidates to be well informed and to both listen and have some answers. Some of the typical questions I was asked included: Why are you running for office? What do you think you could offer? What are the problems that you see facing this county? They also wanted to know about my background and, especially in Palm Beach County, everyone wanted to talk about the 2000 election. When I was at the state Democratic Convention in Orlando, it was the dominant topic of concern. It remains fresh on the minds of voters.

The party can provide advice and assistance during the process of establishing your candidacy. However, the party's resources are limited, and if several individuals are pursuing the same office from the party, the party must be careful to not show favoritism. When approaching the county party leaders about my intended candidacy, I had specific questions and requests in mind. First of all, I wanted to get a feeling for the demographics of the area—basic population characteristics that would help me understand and reach voters. I also wanted to get a feeling for the issues. Fortunately, I had already been involved nationally, statewide, and countywide in politics, so I had learned an important lesson, one often associated with former Democratic speaker of the U.S. House of Representatives Tip O'Neill: All politics is local. People are concerned with issues at home. Palm Beach County is my home, and I shared the concerns of my neighbors.

Fortunately, I found probably 98 percent of the party leaders and members of my party receptive and supportive of my announcement to pursue elected office. Support from the party is important because they can do several things for you. They can help with "phone banking," the process of contacting party voters and donors. Without the party's help, it is difficult for the average person to make this type of contact. The party can provide candidates with information on how to set up a Web site. Perhaps most important, they can help you raise money.

Unfortunately, money is important in a campaign. A necessary evil. The candidate really has to raise a certain amount of money to be competitive. For me, this is the worst part of politics and the worst part of being a candidate. I wish there were another way, but it must be done. It is also the most difficult part of the campaign. Most people running for office share my sentiments and agree that asking for money is the hardest part of campaigning.

The system of financing campaigns is way out of whack, from the amount of money needed to run for many offices to how it is raised to the prevalence of what is called "soft money." Soft money means that companies can contribute to or underwrite their own campaigning and issue-advocacy on behalf of a candidate without anybody knowing where the money and message came from because, technically, it is not endorsed by the candidate. In my campaign, any advertising message from me was funded by hard money: money and a message that is approved by Cathy Dubin. This is stated in the actual political advertisement. Many people perceive that financing problems such as the use of soft money are found only in presidential or congressional campaigns, but they are everywhere, even at the local level.

Money is an important part of running for office because there are so many expenses in a campaign. In my case, this was especially true because I faced an incumbent who happened to be the chair of the Republican Party. Republicans tend to raise more money than Democrats, and incumbents tend to raise more money than challengers. So I faced a very tough race. I needed to raise money simply to help get my name out there. Name recognition is important, especially for a challenger. This means I had expenditures for printing campaign material such as bumper stickers and buttons, brochures and flyers, and for a media campaign. In order to reach a wide group of voters, candidates must use the media—newspapers, radio, television—for advertising. There is no substitute for grassroots campaigning such as knocking on doors in certain circumstances. However, in a large, urban, and competitive place like Palm Beach County, candidates will need a media campaign as well. Publicity and printing constitute a large segment of campaign finance.

Most of the people working on campaigns are volunteers, and that, of course, helps save the campaign money. But it is not always an easy task to get people to give up their time and put in the demanding work that goes into a campaign. Those working on my campaigns included a mixture of friends and active members of the county's Democratic Party, along with some individuals who simply for one reason or another came to me and volunteered their time. This is a good way for anyone to learn about politics and to begin to get involved in the democratic process.

A lot of work goes into a campaign and a lot of work by the candidate goes into preparing the last-minute details before Election Day. As a party officer I needed to know the intricacies of how elections are administered. The same goes, I found, as a candidate. Surprisingly, some candidates know little about election laws and the process of voting. This is an area where the party can provide assistance. Of course, the elections office is there for voters and candidates alike. One of the more detailed and confusing aspects of elections is election law. Another is campaign finance. Fortunately, my husband is proficient in finance, so he served as my treasurer. Every campaign must by law designate a treasurer. I liked the fact that I did not technically control the money in my campaign, yet the individual charged with that responsibility had my trust. Even if problems that arise in a campaign are not the candidate's fault, ultimately it will be the candidate whose name is associated with the problem. The elections office has officials who are available to assist candidates and campaigns with the details of election law. Also, the office of the supervisor of elections has a Web site that will provide answers to most questions related to elections. If I had specific problems, I also consulted an attorney. In general, candidates need to know about the voting process, the ballot, and so on.

The advertising strategy also changes in the days leading up to Election Day. At the outset of the campaign and through most of its length, a major focus is on raising money, meeting as many people as possible, and lining up support. The closer to the election, the more money I spent. The limited time in the final days meant I had to schedule shorter appearances and schedule them back-to-back. It also meant I needed to rely a lot on the media to get my message out. In the beginning of the campaign, I did not advertise at all. I simply handed out cards and brochures and made public appearances.

The strategy and actions leading up to Election Day also depend on the nature of the competition. My opponent raised more money to the tune of about ten-to-one, which made the campaign difficult and dictated my strategy. I obviously could not match her one-for-one in expensive media ads. Accordingly, the main ingredient of my campaign was grassroots. Knocking on doors, meeting community groups, visiting neighborhoods, being willing to go anywhere, anytime. The campaign contacted some groups, others called us requesting the appearance. Such appearances intensify the closer one gets to Election Day.

The candidate has a full day on Election Day. I ran from poll to poll to poll. I vote by absentee ballot because I am so busy on Election Day and did the same as a candidate. I planned on meeting as many voters that day as possible. I shook a lot of hands! I think it helps to show voters you care enough to try and meet them. Meeting voters at the polls is basically one of the only things left to get out the vote that has not already been done. The candidate and the candidate's staff will also identify supporters and call them on the phone to ask politely if they voted yet and, if not, if they are going to get out and vote. We would ask them to please vote for Cathy Dubin and remind them that the polls are open until 7 p.m.

Yet, on the other hand, if the candidate has not gotten the job done by Election Day, it is probably too late. I introduced myself to voters and many came up to ask me why they should vote for me. Also, after they vote I thanked everyone for simply voting, even if they did not vote for me. But candidates also need to make sure there are no problems with the vote and then check the early results. Candidates are permitted to go to the polling sites, though you are not allowed to actually campaign inside the site. Candidates are required by law to remain a certain distance away from the entrance to the polling place. The parties get permission to send approved elections observers to the polls.

Election Day is always a long day for candidates and party officials, and it comes at the end of a long campaign, where everyone involved is lacking sleep. In the end, I do not care so much who wins the race, as long as elections are fair and equitable.

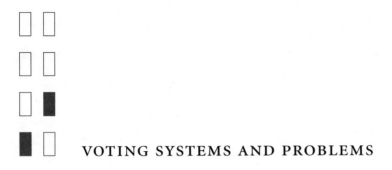

VOTING SYSTEMS AND PROBLEMS

9 ☐

☐

☐

Voting Technology and Voting Access in Twenty-first-century America

TERESA C. GREEN, RHONDA S. KINNEY, AND JASON MITCHELL,
EASTERN MICHIGAN UNIVERSITY

It goes without saying that the 2000 presidential election attracted a good deal of popular attention, political debate, and scholarly examination. Most of the focus has fallen on Florida and its vote counts—and failed recounts—because the outcome of the presidential election was ultimately decided by the results in Florida. This count has been called into question on a variety of grounds, including the use of different voting technologies and counting methodologies across communities. The sheer closeness of the presidential election highlighted a whole host of problems that in some cases have been neglected for decades: inadequate voting systems; lack of voter education; deficient election administration at both the state and local level; confusing and contradictory election laws; and fundamentally flawed legislative programs. Some suggest that confusing ballots, older voting technologies, political pressure, and numerous other problems resulted in the disenfranchisement of thousands of voters in Florida and elsewhere.

All debate points to the low priority that Florida's public policymakers placed on elections. At this point, a consensus seems to have emerged that the solution to problems of the kind encountered in the Florida election in particular is to improve voting technology, and that if state (or federal) governments would simply provide the funds for localities to purchase new, more advanced voting equipment, we would not have to face this type of situation again. The mantra has become "No more hanging or pregnant chads."

We began this study from a similar vantage point—looking at the level of voting technology available in several counties in the Detroit metropolitan area. As you will see, to some degree the data guided us to several conclusions about relationships between technology and the socioeconomic characteristics of any given voting population. However, our study also led us to conclude that the 2000 election story is really not unique and should not be viewed as such. Rather, the issues that emerged from this case study were illustrative representations of the historical record relating to voting rights access in the United States. What we suggest here is that the election must be placed in historical and political context. Once this is done, the story of the 2000 election gets clearer and the conclusions reached are quite distinct from those driven by concerns about technology.

Historical Evolution of Voting Rights and Access

A serious concern in examining the Florida count was that many of the problems appear to have occurred in less affluent counties with a high percentage of minority voters. In fact, it might be argued that this case merely highlights problems that are common throughout the United States. These issues are not unique to the Florida case and have recurred in many other states. In Cook County, Illinois, almost one of every six presidential ballots was tossed out in Chicago's minority precincts—a higher percentage than in Atlanta, St. Louis, even Florida, or just about anywhere else, according to an account in the *Wisconsin State Journal* on December 28, 2000. The two districts with the highest rates of uncounted ballots (7.9 percent) were in Chicago and Miami. Both are poor districts and both used punch cards. However, according to a July 9, 2001, report in the *New York Times,* we must be careful to note that socioeconomic conditions do not explain the entire picture. In the Seventh District in western Alabama, where 31 percent of the people live in poverty and 68 percent are minorities, one finds the lowest percentage of uncounted ballots of forty districts surveyed by Congress (only .03 percent). The Seventh District has modern voting technology.

Once one examines the historical development of voting rights in the United States, it becomes clear that the 2000 election represents the interplay of long-standing and familiar patterns. While the 2000 election shed new light on these issues, they were not born in relationship to this immediate case study. Since the nation's birth, analysts have described American political culture as the primary illustration of contemporary liberal democracy and as government by common consent providing equal rights for all. Its advocates fail to give due consideration to undemocratic ideologies and conditions that have molded American politics.[1] The presidential election of 2000 can serve as a tool to determine how technology issues fit along a historical continuum of inequity in U.S. voting access. History illustrates a clear pattern of enhancing voting access for some Americans while simultaneously suppressing voting access for others. Once one clearly sees this, the questions about voter access and technology must be viewed differently. The purchase of new technology becomes tangential to older, and far more vexing, issues of how voting access has been differentially provided based on race, gender, education, income, and class. Understanding the legacy of voting rights access also provides us with the tools needed to understand present and past behaviors as well as our reactions to them.

The history of voting access in the United State suggests that various means of disenfranchisement have always posed a problem for the ideal of a democratic egalitarian society. Turnout was generally high in the early decades of the country's history—reflecting in large part the restriction of voting rights to propertied males. As Michael S. Schudson writes in his history of American voting patterns, "voters in 18th century Virginia or New England would publicly announce their choice, often in the presence of the candidates themselves. The act of voting was essentially a gentlemanly affirmation of support for the status quo, an organic view that the polity has a single common good and that the leaders of locally prominent, wealthy and well-established families can be trusted to represent it."[2]

The political democracy that existed at the founding amid moderately propertied white men was enclosed by an array of other rigid systems of unequal status, all for the most part accepted by the American revolutionaries. It was considered appropriate for men to rule over women. White northern Europeans were considered superior culturally and presumably biologically to black Africans, Native Americans, and certainly any other race or civilization. Many British Americans also approached religion as an innate condition and regarded Protestants as created by God to be theologically, morally, and politically superior to Jews, Muslims, Catholics, and others.[3]

The use of such legal devices as poll taxes, white primaries, and grandfather clauses has always seriously called into question America's commitment to free and fair elections when addressing voting access for minorities.[4] The continued

Brooks - Cork Library
Shelton State
Community College

renewal of the Voting Rights Act of 1965 serves as a constant reminder of the United States' historical failure to protect the voting rights of all Americans. However, voting access has from the very beginning been a continual struggle to resist extending the franchise to many groups considered at the margins of the democratic process. Included in the list of the disenfranchised at various points in time were landless white men, women, Native Americans, and many immigrant groups.

Liberalizing efforts to expand voting rights have repeatedly been defeated by those inclined toward new biased forms of race- and class-based power structures. Those forces have sometimes effectively neutralized major voting victories, particularly in the half century following Reconstruction, and the fate of that era may be reverberating today. Charles Francis Adams Jr., great-grandson of a signer of the Declaration of Independence, grandson of an antislavery congressman, veteran of both the Union Army and the liberal reform movement—told a 1908 Virginia audience that the "glittering generalities" of the Declaration of Independence and the belief in racial equality during Reconstruction seemed "strangely remote, archaic even."[5] Sophisticated tenets of racial inequality were common in American universities and public opinion throughout U.S. history. With blacks, Native Americans, women, and others relegated to the status of narrowly accepted participants in the political process, America can easily seem a much more fully liberal democracy than it was or is.[6] These huge exceptions to our willingness to live up to our egalitarian ideals suggest our acceptance of many of the exclusionary policies that have prevailed during most of U.S. history.

It is difficult to define these divergences from the democratic ideal as "exceptions" when they occurred in various forms from the late eighteenth century to the twenty-first century. As the following set of illustrations suggests, the exceptions are not only numerous but far-reaching. The 1887 Dawes General Allotment Act reassigned tribal lands and gave U.S. citizenship to individual Native Americans, along with a twenty-five-year period of federal trusteeship before those individuals could have full land rights and therefore full rights as citizens.[7] The Supreme Court affirmed requirements that Chinese Americans obtain certificates of citizenship that were not a requirement for white Americans.[8] Further, officials were allowed to deport ethnic Chinese who were later determined by courts to be native-born U.S. citizens.[9]

Complicated eligibility and registration systems, poll taxes, and civics tests acted primarily as tools to exclude large segments of voters. While these methods on the surface seem to be impartial, they were intended to disfranchise black citizens in particular. Even progressives such as Carter Glass called openly for accomplishing racial disfranchisement by devious methods. He urged the 1901–1902 Virginia Constitutional Convention to adopt every "discrimination within the letter of the law" that promised "the elimination of every Negro voter who can be gotten rid of." These attempts succeeded. Louisiana provides an incredible example. In 1896, 95.6 percent of blacks were registered, with more than half (130,000) voting. After disfranchising measures were put in place, black registration decreased by 90 percent and by 1904 totaled only 1,342.[10] Although Puerto Ricans were granted citizenship in 1917, they were barred by law from participating in all the privileges of that citizenship. Provided fewer constitutional rights than other American citizens, they were not even given the right to fully participate in federal elections.[11]

Women took a significant step toward unlimited citizenship when they gained the vote with the passage of the Nineteenth Amendment in 1920. But they were little more privileged than nonwhites by Darwinists of the late nineteenth and early twentieth centuries.[12] Although the 1922 Cable Act permitted women to retain their American citizenship even if they married aliens, it excepted those who married men "ineligible by race for naturalization." Women, like blacks and Native Americans and most Asian Americans, stayed both lawfully equal citizens and officially subject to specific constraints based on their perceived biological and cultural inferiority. Accounts such as these reveal, intended or not, that these marginalized groups appear so irreparably aberrant and dangerous that they do not deserve equal standing in the political community. The aggregate effect of these continuous failures to explore the broad pattern of civic exclusion has been to make it far too easy for scholars to decide that democratic inclusiveness has been the standard.[13]

The approval of inegalitarian doctrines by prominent politically dissident females and the black male intelligentsia at the dawn of the twentieth century strongly implies that these ideas had widespread appeal. Distinguished academics such as Richard Epstein today maintain that the nation should abolish all race-based laws, even the 1964 Voting Rights Act, preferring programs of black self-help in the marketplace, exactly the assertion many nineteenth-century liberals utilized to defend abandoning Reconstruction.[14] Contemporary conservative African American leaders such as Justice Clarence Thomas, economist Thomas Sowell, Ward Connelly, and the present national security advisor, Condoleezza Rice, like Booker T. Washington before them, appear to agree with these "self-help" views.

We do not present the above discussion as a complete or exhaustive review of voting rights access in the United States. Instead we do so to suggest that if we accept that ideologies and institutions of a racial, gendered, and class hierarchy have shaped America in interaction with its liberal and democratic features, we can make more sense of a wide range of inegalitarian voting policies newly contrived after 1877 and perpetuated through much of the twentieth century. Those policies were dismantled only through great struggles, and it is not clear that these struggles have ended. We can better explain the nation's past by acknowledging how and why liberal democratic ideals have been challenged with repeated success. Furthermore, we will improve our understanding of the present and future of American politics if we do not conclude they are based on inherently liberal or democratic ideologies and conditions.[15]

Data Analysis

We propose that differences across communities in access to modern voting machine technology are related to a variety of socioeconomic variables. Specifically, we contend that educational attainment levels, income levels, and racial makeup of communities explain variations in the types of voting machines communities possess and their level of voting access. In this section, we examine these relationships in the context of three counties in southeastern Michigan—Macomb County, Oakland County, and Wayne County.

State Level Context

A study of voting technology issued recently by the Michigan Department of State suggests that there currently exists no single, ideal voting system. Each system offers a mix of advantages and drawbacks.[16]

- The punch card system is relatively inexpensive and portable. However, it does not alert voters to errors without a precinct tabulator. Recounts can be time consuming as well as difficult.
- The mechanical lever system, while durable, is bulky and expensive to store. It prevents voters from making errors, but it creates no paper trail. The required ballot layout often inspires voters to quit voting or "fall off" before reaching the end of the ballot.
- Paper ballots offer easy-to-follow voting procedures and are relatively inexpensive. However, they are labor intensive and time consuming to count. Paper ballots also provide no mechanism by which to alert voters to errors.

- Optical scan systems, the most widely used system in Michigan, do not alert voters to errors if communities use central count scanning devices. Additionally, the printing standards for these systems make production of ballots costly. Further, the counting equipment is sensitive, ballots are cumbersome to store, and recounts are time consuming.
- Direct Recording Electronic (DRE) systems are the most expensive used in Michigan. They are highly accurate, eliminate the need for ballot printing, and enable recounts to be performed instantaneously.

As recently as the 2000 election cycle, all of these voting systems were used in the state of Michigan. In all there were

- 693 precincts in the state using lever-style voting machines, one of the oldest voting systems still in use in the United States
- 1,443 precincts using a punch-card system
- 137 precincts using paper ballots
- 3,006 precincts using an optical scan system, one of the newest voting systems on the market
- 97 precincts using direct recording electronic voting machines, where the voter touches a screen or a button on a computer to record each vote

Along with an overview of technology employed throughout the state, it is useful to understand how ballots are actually counted in Michigan. While some states attempt to define voter intent in order to make determinations about what constitutes a valid, "countable" ballot, for the most part Michigan has declined to approach that slippery slope. In fact, when compared with other states, Michigan exceeds the average in promulgating rules and procedures to guide election officials and workers in evaluating validity. And unlike in the Florida case, statewide ballot count criteria are often quite specifically stated. For example, under standards developed in 1978, a valid punch-card vote is one in which the chad is completely removed or hanging by one or two corners. There are no exceptions to this rule.

Community Case Study

The three southeastern Michigan counties on which we focus our case study are all proximate to the Detroit metropolitan area, with the city itself contained in Wayne County. Wayne County houses a relatively large number of communities with low median incomes, substantial proportions of citizens classified by the U.S. Census Bureau as below the poverty line, and substantial minority-group populations. Wayne County was the only county in the case study that lost population between 1990 and 2000 (-2.4 percent), and this decline continues today. In contrast, Macomb County's population increased by 9.9 percent between 1990 and 2000. Oakland County's population increased 10.2 percent. Both of these counties outpaced the overall ten-year growth rate of Michigan (6.9 percent). The populations of both Macomb and Oakland Counties had higher median incomes than Wayne County. The median income for Oakland County was $59,677, compared to $49,601 for Macomb County and $35,357 for Wayne County. The largest city in Wayne County, Detroit, had a median income of only $18,742, or less than half of the median income for Oakland and Macomb Counties.

The racial composition of the counties demonstrated an uneven minority distribution as well. Macomb County had a black population of only 2.7 percent, compared to 10.1 percent in Oakland County and 42.2 percent in Wayne County. Michigan as a whole had a population that was 14.2 percent black. Educational attainment levels in the three counties followed similar patterns.

Along with the census data summarized above, we gathered information from each township or city in the three counties about the type of voting technology currently employed by that community. We were able to obtain data from each of the 111 communities in the three counties. Table 9.1 summarizes these findings.

Our analysis illustrates that in Macomb County voting equipment type ranges from the oldest to some of the newest, with a substantial majority of communities using optical scanner systems. In all, 62.5 percent of the cities or townships in the county used optical scanner systems, 20.8 percent used punch-card systems, and 16.6 percent used voting machines.

The communities of Oakland County—the wealthiest in Michigan—present a somewhat different summary profile. Here we already begin to see the relationship of socioeconomic factors to the possession of relatively advanced technology. In Oakland County we found that 90 percent of the cities or townships used optical scanner systems, 2 percent used punch-card systems, 4 percent used paper ballots, and 4 percent used voting machines.

Finally, in Wayne County, we again find a majority of communities using optical scanning technology, but also a substantial level of older machines in use. In the most populous county, we find that 62.5 percent of the cities or townships used optical scanner systems, 12.5 percent used punch-card systems.

Table 9.1. Voting Technology

County	Touch Screen	Optical Scan	Punch Card	Lever	Paper Ballot
Macomb	0.0%	62.5%	20.8%	16.6%	0.0%
Oakland	0.0%	90.0%	2.0%	4.0%	4.0%
Wayne	2.5%	62.5%	12.5%	22.5%	0.0%

These preliminary figures certainly suggest a differential pattern of access to modern technology across these counties. Newer technologies were present to a greater degree in areas of southeastern Michigan that had higher socioeconomic indicators while older, less advanced technologies were present in counties with low socioeconomic conditions. In order to examine these questions in a more systematic fashion by community, we performed an OLS regression analysis designed to identify variation across communities in voting machine type. The dependent variable in the analysis—voting machine type—is presented as a categorical variable with whole number values between 0 and 4, where 0 represents the least advanced form of voting technology (paper ballots) and 4 signifies the most technologically advanced form (optical scanning).

We include as independent variables the county where a community was located, the percentage of community residents below the poverty line, the percentage of residents with a high school education, and the percent who classified themselves as members of a nonwhite racial group. Some Michigan counties, including Oakland and Macomb in this analysis, have provided funding for technology. Specifically, Oakland County has provided a high level of support, Macomb a small amount of support, and Wayne virtually no support. We therefore hypothesize that communities located in Wayne County will most likely possess the least advanced technology, Macomb County communities will likely house the next highest levels, with Oakland County communities being the most likely to enjoy the most advanced voting technology. We expect negative relationships between voting technology and both the percentage of community residents below the poverty line and the percentage who identify themselves as nonwhite. We anticipate a positive relationship between the percentage of high-school-educated residents and access to more advanced voting technology. Table 9.2 presents the findings of this analysis.

As table 9.2 indicates, a significant relationship does exist between the county where a community is located and the type of voting technology present. Another clearly significant relationship found in our sample is between the percentage of a community's population living below the poverty line and the

Table 9.2. Explaining Voting Machine Access

	Coefficients	Standard Error	P-Value
Intercept	3.17	0.47	0.00
% minority population	0.02	0.01	0.20
% in poverty	-0.07	0.04	0.05
County	0.27	0.13	0.04
% high school grads	0.01	0.02	0.59

Regression Statistics

Multiple R	0.35
R square	0.12
Adjusted R square	0.09
Standard error	1.11
Observations	111.00

voting technology in the community. Both our race and education variables are not statistically significant in the regression analysis. However, this finding in particular must be interpreted carefully, because race, education, poverty, and county are significantly correlated with one another. This multicollinearity limits the degree to which one is likely to find statistical significance even when real relationships exist among variables. It is worth mentioning, however, that each of the observed relationships is in the expected direction. When viewed in their entirety, these results reinforced our proposition that socioeconomic factors are, in fact, significantly related to voting technology access in Michigan.

Current State of Voting Rights Access

This section examines whether our case study suggests anything about the broader picture of voting rights access in the United States. In order to properly contextualize our case study of voting technology access in Michigan, a number of other contemporary rule-based policies in the area of voting access across the United States are reviewed below. In particular, this section examines felony disenfranchisement, absentee voting procedures, and registration procedures, motor-voter laws in particular. We suggest that there are observable patterns found in the manner and degree to which states implement these procedures. In much the same way that technology access varies, these patterns are related to race and other socioeconomic variables.

Felony Disenfranchisement

In many states, access is limited on the basis of criminal convictions. This is related to geography and disproportionately impacts men of color. Southern states are far more likely to limit access on this basis. While a student at the University of Virginia, Vesla Weaver did a study of the 1996 presidential election returns in all fifty states, examining the correlation between voter turnout and race and between disenfranchisement and parolee/type—probationer, inmate, ex-convict, etc., as well as parolee race.[17] She found that the states, mostly in the South, with the smallest voter turnout rates among blacks were those states with permanent-disenfranchisement laws prohibiting felons from voting for life. States with the strongest restrictions also had a tendency to be those with the largest populations of African Americans. Subsequent research demonstrated that most voting restrictions established by state legislatures affecting state and federal elections were approved between 1890 and 1910.[18] Once Congress ratified the Fifteenth Amendment in 1870, giving black men the vote, many state legislatures, particularly in the South, sought new ways to prevent them from voting. It was not until 1965 when President Lyndon Johnson signed the federal Voting Rights Act that all of the discriminatory laws were struck down, except the felony conviction measures.

Most disenfranchised felons are not currently incarcerated, and most are not informed that even a probationary sentence in some states is grounds for losing the right to vote for life. Weaver's study showed that voting restrictions have disenfranchised 3.9 million Americans, or 2 percent of the voting population. In fourteen states, mostly in the South, convicted felons cannot vote in federal elections. More than 25 percent of the black male population is barred from voting in Alabama, Mississippi, Virginia, and Florida. A May 10, 2001, Ascribe Newswire essay stated: "In 1999, U.S. Rep. John Conyers (D-Mich) introduced legislation that would have required states to allow ex-felons with completed sentences to vote in federal elections, but the bill languished in committee because none of his fellow lawmakers wanted to appear soft on crime."[19]

In their 1998 report "Losing the Vote," Human Rights Watch and the Sentencing Project documented state by state the impact of disenfranchisement laws. Table 9.3 lists the twenty states with the highest disenfranchisement of black men. Although Michigan was not among the top states in terms of percentage, a rather substantial number—22,700, or 5.4 percent of the black male population—in the state were disenfranchised.

According to the *Record,* Florida is the main target for supporters of felon

Table 9.3. States with Highest Percentage of Blacks Disenfranchised for Felony

State	Total Felons	% of Total[a]	Disenfranchised Black Male Felons	% of Black Men[b]
Alabama	241,100	7.5	105,000	31.5
Florida	647,100	5.9	204,600	31.2
Mississippi	145,600	7.4	81,000	28.6
Wyoming	14,100	4.1	400	27.7
Iowa	42,300	2.0	4,800	26.5
Virginia	269,800	5.3	110,000	25.0
New Mexico	48,900	4.0	3,700	24.1
Washington	151,500	3.7	16,700	24.0
Texas	610,000	4.5	156,000	20.8
Delaware	20,500	3.7	8,700	20.0
Rhode Island	13,900	1.8	2,800	18.3
Wisconsin	48,500	1.3	14,900	18.2
Minnesota	56,000	1.6	7,200	17.8
New Jersey	138,300	2.3	65,200	17.7
Maryland	135,700	3.6	67,900	15.4
Tennessee	97,800	2.4	38,300	14.4
Oklahoma	37,200	1.5	9,800	12.3
Arizona	74,600	2.3	6,600	12.1
Missouri	58,800	1.5	20,100	11.3
Georgia	134,800	2.5	66,400	10.5

Sources: "Losing the Vote," Human Rights Watch and the Sentencing Project. See www.hrw.org/campaigns/elections/results.htm and www.hrw.org/press98/oct/vote_summ1022.htm.
[a]Percentage of adult population who are disenfranchised.
[b]Percentage of black men who are disenfranchised.

enfranchisement.[20] It is one of eleven states that usually disenfranchise all felons for life. Proponents of such restrictions feel felons have lost their rights and privileges as citizens. The problem in Florida and other southern states dates to the Reconstruction era. Florida's 1868 constitution gave blacks the vote as a condition of the state's readmission to the Union, but the document simultaneously disenfranchised felons and those guilty of larceny at a time when such charges were overwhelmingly against blacks. Florida allows ex-convicts to apply for a reinstatement of their voting rights, but it requires applicants to have no more than $1,000 in delinquent fines. Legally, this might be equivalent to a poll tax in cases where fines imposed are disproportionate to the jail time or offense, or where the state either fails to process records in a timely manner or imposes hurdles to reenfranchisement.

According to the Sentencing Project, state disenfranchisement laws have a dramatically disproportionate impact. Thirteen percent of all black men (1.4

million) are disenfranchised. This represents one-third of the total disenfranchised population in the United States and reflects a rate of disenfranchisement that is seven times the national average.[21] These numbers are especially troubling in light of what we know about the specific establishment of differential classification and sentencing guidelines for similar crimes set up in order to address perceived urban crime problems and other issues over time. Election voting statistics point to the political importance of black disenfranchisement: 1.4 million black men were disenfranchised and 4.6 million black men voted in 1996.[22] This sizable portion of the population has an impact on election results.

Ernie Preate Jr., a former Pennsylvania attorney general, wrote: "In Pennsylvania, felons were allowed to vote for centuries. It was changed in 1995 in the dead of night when a felon franchise clause was inserted into the 'motor voter' bill, officially called the Voter Registration Act."[23] The name of the bill proclaimed encouragement of people to vote, when in fact one provision disenfranchised 40,000 people. According to the Associated Press, the Commonwealth Court in Harrisburg, Pennsylvania, found "no rational basis" for barring convicts from registering to vote for five years after their release or allowing former felons who had been registered prior to their prison terms to vote.[24]

Absentee Voting

While access to voting is limited or nonexistent for felons in some states, other populations are selectively encouraged to vote through absentee voting and other mechanisms.[25] Levels of absentee voting are not entirely a function of state law, but also depend on attempts by political parties to encourage their supporters to vote by mail. Reducing legal barriers is essential for increasing absentee voters, but party mobilization efforts are also critical to expanding the absentee voter pool. This could shift the balance of electoral politics. For instance, given their party's greater mobilization efforts, Republican candidates appear to be benefiting disproportionately from absentee voting, particularly where turnout is otherwise low.[26]

Liberalizing absentee requirements has generated the anticipated effect of increasing turnout, but not by encouraging turnout among those groups less likely to vote like the young and less educated. The increased turnout is found only among certain populations, who find it easy and convenient to vote when pre-filled-out applications are mailed for them. In states where senior citizens automatically qualify for absentee ballots and where partisan lists are accessible, the parties are mobilizing seniors to vote by mail in greater numbers.[27] State Republican Party leaders are employing absentee mobilization with far more effectiveness than their Democratic counterparts. As a result, absentee voters tend to be wealthier, older, and more Republican than the average American voter. With turnout in off-year elections, special elections, and midterm elections often lower than 20 percent in some communities and states, the ability of the Republican Party to mobilize core supporters to vote by mail offers an advantage to Republican candidates.[28]

Registration and Motor-Voter Laws

As absentee voters enjoy more liberalized laws, other voters still face barriers. Voter registration laws may be among the most important barriers to voting for some Americans. To overcome what some see as undue difficulty in registering to vote, Congress passed the National Voter Registration Act in 1993. This was an attempt to streamline the registration process by allowing eligible voters to register when they obtained or renewed their driver's licenses. In an effort to reach the poor and other groups with historically low turnout levels, the law also required states to supply voter registration applications at offices providing public assistance. This provision faced strong opposition by Republicans until Democrats agreed to language ensuring that recipients of public benefits would not be pressured by agency officials to register for a particular party.[29] This stands in sharp contrast to the silence that surrounds the practice of providing pre-filled-out absentee ballots to voters in the military, dual residents, the elderly, and other typically partisan groups. Additionally, not all states fully implemented the terms of the motor-voter law, particularly those portions relating to registration in public service agencies.[30]

Conclusion

First and foremost, this study suggests that the widespread purchase of newer and more accurate voting technologies may not be the sole answer to the problems encountered by many voters in the 2000 presidential election. Voting technology represents only one potential obstacle to voter access in the United States. It must be understood that it is a representative problem, symptomatic of underlying patterns of limited access, rather than an isolated problem with an easy solution. The symptoms' underlying causes must be addressed if we are to prevent similar problems from plaguing future elections.

Historically, certain groups and classes of voters in the United States have had to surmount barriers to voting that were not encountered by other, more privileged voters. Whether states and communities have used poll taxes, grandfather clauses, felony convictions, property requirements, race or gender status, or other means to limit voting, it is clear these measures have been a force in elections throughout the country's history. Voting technology must be viewed as an extension of the pattern of correcting such problems. As was seen in metropolitan Detroit, the oldest voting technology was concentrated in areas with higher poverty rates, larger minority populations, and lower levels of educational attainment. This stands in stark contrast to those communities employing the latest, most accurate voting technology.

It might be cautioned that recent technological advances in voting may pose new challenges to equal voting access. The Internet has been suggested as a potential vehicle for enhancing voter participation. If implemented in the near future, this has the potential to be another example of a reform that appears neutral but in application would likely be unevenly distributed. Internet access has been linked to race, class, and income.[31] According to a recent study, 83 percent of Americans in the highest socioeconomic bracket have Internet access, compared with only 35 percent of the poorest Americans.[32] At the least, an emphasis on Internet voting would enhance voting opportunities among the privileged while ignoring the problems associated with voting in other groups.[33]

Despite the importance of voting technology in voter access, technology should be viewed as a secondary issue. We need to think about how to design our institutions and laws of access to encourage voting in an equal manner. In order that this might be accomplished, we must recognize that equality in voter access has been, and remains, an ever-changing target. The barriers that have been discredited in the past have all too often been replaced with more subtle obstacles that until recently were viewed as neutral vehicles to enhance voting. The historical progress in selectively enfranchising citizens should make us vigilant in assessing the impact of changes in voting laws, the administration of those laws, and voting technologies. If we do not remain aware of past practices, the electorate will suffer and doubt will be cast on the nation's commitment to equal voting access for all.

Notes

1. Smith, "Beyond Tocqueville, Myrdal, and Hartz."
2. Schudson, *The Good Citizen*.
3. Smith, "Beyond Tocqueville, Myrdal, and Hartz."
4. Schmidt, "Black Disfranchisement."
5. Smith, "Beyond Tocqueville, Myrdal, and Hartz."

6. Fields, "Slavery, Race and Ideology."

7. Wolfley, "Jim Crow, Indian Style."

8. *Fong Yue Ting v. United States,* 149 U.S. 698 (1893).

9. *United States v. Ju Toy,* 198 U.S. 253 (1905).

10. Kousser, *Shaping of Southern Politics.*

11. *Balzac v. Puerto Rico,* 258 U.S. 298 (1922).

12. Degler, *In Search of Human Nature*; Russett, *Sexual Science,* 11–12.

13. Smith, "Beyond Tocqueville, Myrdal, and Hartz."

14. Epstein, *Forbidden Grounds.*

15. Smith, "Beyond Tocqueville, Myrdal, and Hartz."

16. See http://www.sos.state.mi.us/pressrel/active/2001.

17. Weaver, "Racial Profiling at the Polling Place."

18. Kousser, *Shaping of Southern Politics.*

19. Ascribe News wire service, May 10, 2001.

20. *Record,* October 25, 2000.

21. Fellner and Mauer, "Losing the Vote."

22. U.S. Census Bureau, *Election of November 1996.*

23. Ibid.

24. Associated Press wire service, September 19, 2000.

25. Oliver, "Effects of Eligibility Restrictions."

26. Ibid.

27. Ibid.

28. Ibid.

29. Cooper, "Is America's Democracy in Trouble?"

30. Teixeira and Rogers, *America's Forgotten Majority.*

31. Koch, "The Digital Divide."

32. Joyce, "A High Speed Disconnection."

33. Piven and Cloward, *Why Americans Still Don't Vote.*

□

□

□

Balancing Competing Interests

Voting Equipment in Presidential Elections

MARTHA E. KROPF, UNIVERSITY OF MISSOURI–KANSAS CITY,
AND STEPHEN KNACK, WORLD BANK

Citizens in Palm Beach County, Florida, gathered at the polls to cast their votes on issues that merited national attention. They cast votes on whether the words *under God* needed to be in the Pledge of Allegiance, and on their favorite patriotic songs and landmarks. This momentous election was not held to make policy with the force of law. Rather, it was a mock election held as a test of new electronic touch-screen voting machines. Elections officials in Palm Beach County—home to the "butterfly" punch-card ballot said to have cost Gore so many votes—were testing new equipment nearly two years after the controversial 2000 presidential election. According to Palm Beach County elections officials, the strength of the tested equipment was that it made it impossible to overvote (selected more than the allowable number of choices) and it warned voters when they undervoted (selected no choices). Together, undervotes and overvotes made up the approximately two million "voided" presidential ballots from the 2000 election.[1] For the purpose of this chapter, we will refer to them as "voided" ballots.

Elections officials, and the public more generally, became aware of the problems inherent in voting equipment following the 2000 presidential election. Researchers showed that the now infamous punch-card ballot is associated with higher rates of invalidated presidential votes.[2] Some county officials moved toward newer "modern technology" such as optical scan and electronic touch-screen equipment, and many politicians called for standardization of voting equipment. However, the technology that is most appropriate for one jurisdiction may be inappropriate for another, because of differences in jurisdiction size and other reasons.[3] Still others have suggested that values other than accuracy of the vote counting are considered as well when policymakers address equipment problems.[4]

As elections officials change technology, they inevitably make trade-offs among competing values and goals.[5] Accuracy—reducing the rate of voided or invalidated ballots—is important, but a report by Caltech/MIT highlights three additional goals: auditability, management, and accessibility of voting. Cost, of course, is a consideration as well. In Florida in 2000, auditing the intent of the voter was difficult (recall media reports of endless checking of punch-card ballots) but possible (assuming it could be agreed upon whether a hanging "chad" was a vote). Other voting technologies such as most electronic machines and lever machines do not record the voter intent separately from what was recorded directly into the machine, so they lose on auditability. However, these machines score well for accuracy, as they can be programmed to prevent undervoting and overvoting, reducing the number of voided ballots. Management of ballots includes such issues as how fast the votes are counted. Hand-counted paper ballots provide a good example of trade-offs among some of these goals. They have the lowest error rates, but they take longer to count, which is why they are generally used only in small counties.[6] Accessibility—for instance, allowing disabled voters to vote without assistance—is also key, but electronic machines that provide for accessibility may be substantially more expensive.

Of course, the goal of accessibility also requires that all voters have an equal opportunity to cast their votes, and to cast them in private. Limitations of voting technology may deter many people, not only the disabled, from voting. For example, are people able to use the technology, or are there barriers such as long lines or equipment breakdowns that prevent them from voting? Equipment that allows voters to correct their ballots or signals that ballots are incomplete may lengthen the time it takes to vote. The cost of direct recording election (DRE) systems might prevent elections officials from being able to purchase a sufficient number of units. Older lever machines are prone to mechanical problems that are not easily fixed. These problems may cause longer lines at the polls.

This chapter considers the competing values of accuracy, or reducing the number of voided ballots, and of accessibility, not only for the disabled but in the broader sense of making it more convenient for anyone to vote. Fail-safe voting technologies, sometimes referred to as second-chance technology, reduce undervoting and prevent overvoting, thereby decreasing the rate of voided ballots. These technologies notify the voter of mistakes, either in the voting booth or when a voter checks his or her ballot after votes have been marked. We find that, collectively, the fail-safe technologies—lever machines, electronic machines, and precinct count optical scan equipment—decrease voided ballots significantly. We also address the issue of accessibility neglected in previous studies, analyzing the role of fail-safe technologies in deterring would-be voters who are discouraged from voting by long lines or other equipment problems. Our analysis shows that voter turnout in counties using this equipment was significantly lower in the 1996 election.

Research on Voting Technology

The study of "roll-off" has a relatively long history. Roll-off is commonly defined as the difference between the number of persons voting, or voting in a contest at the top of the ballot such as president or governor, and the number voting in a particular contest further down the ballot. As the American public came to find out, however, roll-off can occur for the contest at the top of the ballot, in this case defined as the difference between the number of voters who actually came to the polls and the number who cast valid votes in that contest.

The research on this phenomenon has had three focuses: intentional undervoting, equipment problems, and equal-protection issues.

First, roll-off may be intentional. Intentional undervoting may occur in cases such as fatigue, lack of choice, or lack of information about the candidates.[7] Indeed, much if not most of the roll-off in lower races on the ballot is deliberate, in the sense that the voter does not leave the polls thinking that he or she voted in a contest when no vote was actually recorded. About 2 percent of persons voting on Election Day do not cast a valid ballot in the presidential contest.[8] However, survey evidence indicates that the bulk of these undervotes are mistakes, as no more than three-fourths of a percent of voters nationwide report deliberately skipping the presidential contest on the ballot.[9]

A number of scholars argue that roll-off is influenced more by voter information about the various contests than by position on the ballot or by complicated ballots and voting machines.[10] Wattenberg and his colleagues show that roll-off from the 1994 gubernatorial vote in California was as high as 37 percent for judicial contests halfway down the ballot, but fell to as low as 2 percent for well-publicized referenda at the bottom of the ballot. Using National Election Studies data on self-reported voting in House and presidential contests, they find that roll-off is higher for persons living in their area less than one year, and lower for strong partisans and the more politically informed.

The second research approach offered an explanation more popular in the wake of the 2000 election—that roll-off may be accidental. This approach emphasizes faulty voting equipment, including the much maligned punch-card ballots.[11]

A study by the Caltech/MIT Voting Technology Project examined how differences in voting equipment contribute to variations in the rate of voided presidential ballots. Surprisingly, the study found that punch-card and DRE systems generate approximately the same rate of voided ballots, but that lever machines and optical scan systems perform better in this respect.[12] Other scholars disagree, finding that DRE, lever machines, optical scan, and paper ballots all produce significantly fewer residual votes (between a half and a full percentage point on average) than punch cards.[13] Our own research, controlling for a variety of county demographic factors and state-level factors, found that optical scan systems and lever machines performed significantly better than punch-card technology. The 1996 county-level data we used showed that lever machines had the lowest error rate (2.2 percent) of all the technologies. Optical scan machines had a comparable rate of 2.7 percent and electronic machines 3.1 percent.[14]

The study of faulty equipment did not begin with the 2000 election. Much of the early literature on voting equipment supports the idea that fail-safe equipment can reduce roll-off. It has been reported that the number of invalid ballots in West German federal elections dropped precipitously in 1961 when lever machines—which made overvoting impossible—replaced hand-counted paper ballots. This particular study found that invalid votes were more common among older voters and in rural areas, where lack of anonymity increased social pressures to show up at the polls, even for persons apathetic about the contests on the ballot.[15]

Mather's study of Iowa found that roll-off in the top contest was consistently lower in counties using lever machines than in counties using paper ballots. For all other contests, roll-off was higher using lever machines; Mather attributed this result to the intimidating ballot design of lever machines, which visually confronted voters with the entire range of choices simultaneously.[16]

Similarly, Thomas found higher roll-off in Michigan referenda in precincts using lever machines than in those using paper ballots.[17] Another study argued that "punch-card systems may present greater obstacles to voting than alternative ballot technologies and may result in more undervoting, overvoting and misvoting."[18] It was based on an experiment involving several hundred voters, randomly assigned to use different types of voting equipment, in a simulated election. Undervoting and overvoting were both significantly more frequent with punch cards than with paper ballots or electronic machines.

Nichols and Strizek showed that electronic voting machines used in twenty-nine wards in Columbus, Ohio, in the 1992 general election sharply reduced roll-off in contests further down the ballot, relative to the other forty-five wards where lever machines were used.[19] The feature of these machines that likely produced this difference was the presence of a flashing red light above each set of choices that stopped flashing only when a vote was recorded for that contest. Five demographic variables collectively explained from 15 percent to 44 percent of the variation in roll-off in various races. Adding the voting equipment dummy, the explained variance increased dramatically, ranging from 83 percent to 93 percent across items on the ballot.

The third approach to the problem of voided ballots builds on the first two: researchers who have taken either or both of these approaches have emphasized the role of race and equal representation. A related line of research examines whether variations in voting equipment in use across the country contribute to the political underrepresentation of certain demographic groups, such as the poor or minorities. One way this could occur is if these groups were more likely to reside in areas using punch cards or other equipment that tends to generate high rates of invalid votes. Our research found little support for that hypothesis: nationally, there was very little difference in the likelihood that whites and blacks, or poor and nonpoor, lived in counties using punch-card technology.[20] Counties with punch-card systems tend to have higher incomes per capita, higher tax revenues, and larger populations than do counties with modern voting equipment.

Not only our research, but other recent studies show that counties and precincts with more African Americans have higher levels of voided ballots.[21] However, in counties with equipment that can be programmed to prevent overvoting (lever machines and DRE) or that allow voters to check their ballots before submitting them (precinct-count optical scan equipment), that relationship disappears.

The weight of this evidence suggests that certain technologies, namely lever machines, electronic voting machines, and certain optical scan equipment can reduce the rate of voided ballots. However, few studies have examined whether these technologies may cause other problems, such as reduced voter turnout. These technologies may reduce turnout if there are longer lines on election day because of breakdowns in old lever machines, or because many people are checking their ballots or revoting. Among nonvoters who were registered to vote in the November 1996 Current Population Survey (Voting and Registration Supplement), 1.2 percent blamed long lines or waits at the polls for their failure to vote. Voting studies have not examined whether lower turnout is related to the type of equipment in use. Thus, this chapter takes the second approach to the study of roll-off—studying voting equipment to ascertain whether or not fail-safe technology will reduce the rate of voided ballots, but also examining the competing value of accessibility of the equipment to voters on election day.

Types of Voting Equipment

In most states, decisions about which type of voting equipment is used are made at the county level. Voting equipment data are collected after each general election by Election Data Services (EDS) and these data are used for this analysis. Each county is classified as using one of the six basic types of equipment in use, which are reviewed briefly in Appendix B. In states where municipalities determine voting equipment in use, there is variation within some counties. These "mixed systems," commonly a mix of paper ballots and either lever machines or optical scanning, constitute a seventh category.

Some types of technology may be more likely to prevent overvotes and undervotes—the fail-safe technologies. In certain optical scan systems, voters can check their ballots at the precinct, feeding them into a special reader that will register their choices and, in the case of an undervote or overvote, offer the option of correcting the ballot. These are "precinct-count" optical scan machines. With other types of optical scan equipment, votes from all precincts are collected and counted in a central location. These "central-count" optical scan systems do not allow the voter to correct the ballot.

Lever machines may also be programmed to prevent overvoting, with interlocks that prevent voting for more than one candidate. However, in the five boroughs of New York City, "sensor latches" intended to prevent accidental undervoting were disabled, producing far higher rates of voided ballots than in other lever machine jurisdictions. Thus, some technologies may decrease the incidence of ballots that are voided accidentally, that is, decrease the chance a voter believes he or she has cast a vote although none has actually been recorded.

Data and Methodology

We merged the voting equipment data from EDS with demographic data obtained from *USA Counties 1998,* available from the U.S. Census Bureau, as well as several state-level variables, such as whether the state held a gubernatorial election in 1996. EDS also surveys states and counties to obtain information on the total number of voters who came to the polls and the number of valid votes cast in the presidential contest. From these data, the rate of voided ballots is calculated as the percentage of all people who voted for whom no valid vote in the presidential contest was recorded. These data also allow us to compute voter turnout, defined as the total number who came to the polls divided by the voting-age population of the county. Since decisions on voting technology are made in most states on the county level, our unit of analysis will be counties.

The EDS file does not contain information on the voting equipment used by absentee voters, or by "early" voters, which often differs from technology used by election-day voters. In Los Angeles County in 2000, for example, the small number of voters who cast ballots in the early voting period prior to Election Day used DRE equipment, while Election Day voters used Votomatic-style punch cards. In classifying all voters in a county by the equipment used on Election Day, a certain amount of measurement error is introduced. Early voters and absentee voters were far less numerous nationwide in 1996 than in 2000, however, so this problem is less severe for our analysis than it would be if we were to replicate it for the most recent election.

We discovered some errors in the election returns data reported by county officials from which the rate of voided ballots is constructed. In most cases, it is the turnout number that is suspect rather than the number of presidential votes cast. For example, the maximum roll-off rate is 29.9 percent, for Warren County, Indiana, which reported only 3,647 votes for president but a total turnout of 5,201. With a voting-age population of only about 6,300 and only 5,424 names on the registration rolls, the total turnout figure appears implausibly high, particularly when compared to neighboring counties. Counties with implausibly high roll-off numbers are deleted, as are those counties with negative roll-offs.

In this study, we first compared the mean values of the rate of voided ballots and voter turnout between counties using fail-safe technology and those using punch cards or other technologies that do not prevent overvoting and that typically do not allow the voter to check his or her ballot for errors. Second, we examined whether these results were sensitive to the addition of several controls shown to be important factors in the rate of voided ballots. For the turnout analysis, we include demographic factors used in standard voter turnout models such as income, education, age, and stability of the community.[22]

Results

Compared to all other voting technologies, fail-safe technologies significantly reduce the incidence of voided ballots. Our findings demonstrated that counties with fail-safe technologies have a 2.5 percent rate of voided ballots, compared to 2.8 percent for all other counties. Voter turnout is also significantly lower on average in these counties (51 percent compared to 58 percent), consistent with anecdotal evidence that certain types of equipment such as lever machines can deter some people from voting by creating longer lines. These differences are statistically significant.

Table 10.1 examines the possibility that these differences in voided ballots and voter turnout may be attributed to some other county- or state-level variables. We control for other factors that may affect the rate of voided ballots as identified in our previous work in this area. First, one must consider sources of accidental under- or overvoting such as the number of younger voters and the change in turnout rate from 1992–1996, as rough measures of the number of inexperienced voters. Older voters who suffer from poorer vision, reduced manual dexterity, or inexperience with modern technologies may also cause accidental undervoting. Finally, education level in the community serves as a proxy for ability to understand and follow instructions correctly. Factors associated with intentional undervoting are also important, including whether there is a senate or gubernatorial race on the ballot, whether a "none of the above" option exists on the ballot—an option that actually only exists in Nevada—the number of candidates on the ballot, and residential stability of the county. The number of candidates on the ballot offers the voter more options probably causing fewer intentional undervotes. However, beyond a certain point, the number of candidates becomes more confusing, increasing the number of voided ballots. Thus, we also include a variable to represent this relation-

Table 10.1. The Effects of Fail-Safe Technologies

On Invalidated Votes

Intercept	9.421	(1.343)
Fail-safe technology	-0.524[b]	(0.232)
Change in turnout rate, 1992–96	-7.092[c]	(1.900)
Senate contest on ballot	0.024	(0.265)
Gubernatorial contest on ballot	0.168	(0.391)
Nevada—"None of the Above" Voting Option	-0.823[c]	(0.450)
Number of presidential candidates on ballot	-1.289[c]	(0.271)
Number of candidates on ballot squared	0.070[c]	(0.018)
% lived in county 5 years or more (1990)	0.285	(0.992)
% of Voting Age Population over 65	2.706	(1.844)
% of Voting Age Population under 25	2.715[a]	(1.520)
$ with high school diploma	-2.570[b]	(1.101)
Log of population	-0.169[b]	(0.072)
% African American (1996)	1.953[b]	(0.851)
% Latino (1996)	1.400[c]	(0.885)
% below poverty line	1.161	(1.554)
R squared	0.209	(1913)
Sample size	1,913.	

On Voter Turnout

Intercept	-0.214	(0.175)
Fail-safe technology	-0.015[b]	(0.007)
Log of per capita income	0.050[b]	(0.022)
% with high school diploma	0.471[c]	(0.017)
% of Voting Age Population over 65	0.182[b]	(0.084)
% of Voting Age Population under 25	-0.343[c]	(0.059)
% African American (1996)	-0.010	(0.051)
% Latino (1996)	-0.073	(0.044)
% lived in county 5 years or more (1990)	0.193[c]	(0.062)
Log of population	-0.030[c]	(0.003)
Senate contest on ballot	0.005	(0.010)
Gubernatorial contest on ballot	-0.008	(0.013)
Number of candidates on ballot	0.027	(0.017)
Number of candidates on ballot squared	0.001	(0.001)
R Squared n	0.640	(1,883)
Sample size	1,883.	

Note: Standard errors are corrected for heteroskedasticity and nonindependence of errors within states.

[a]Indicates significance at .10 for 2-tailed test.

[b]Indicates significance at .05 for 2-tailed test.

[c]Indicates significance at .01 for 2-tailed test.

ship statistically—the number of candidates squared—suggesting a curvilinear relationship. Finally, we include demographic measures to capture equal protection issues: percent of county residents who are African American and Latino, and percentage who are poor.

The table illustrates that fail-safe technologies are associated with a significantly lower rate of voided ballots, even when controlling for these additional variables. Other things equal, fail-safe technology is associated with a reduction of more than 0.5 percentage points in the rate of voided presidential ballots.

Results support the hypothesized curvilinear effect of the number of presidential candidates listed on the state ballot. A larger number reduces the rate of voided ballots up to a threshold of nine, beyond which further increases in the number of candidates increase the rate. Table 10.1 also indicates that having the choice of "none of the above" in Nevada decreases the rate of voided ballots. Counties with more African Americans and Latinos have higher rates of voided ballots. More highly populated counties, and those with higher percentages of high school graduates, also have fewer voided ballots. Larger increases in turnout between 1992 and 1996 are, surprisingly, associated with decreases rather than increases in the rate of voided ballots.

The table further examines the possibility that the relationship between voter turnout and fail-safe technology may be attributable to some other county- or state-level variables. Guidance on appropriate control variables is provided by voter turnout studies, which have established a number of empirical regularities. For example, income and education are strongly related to voting.[23] Older individuals are more likely than the young to vote as well.[24] We also controlled for ethnicity, although when controlling for education and income, minorities are often found to be as likely to vote as whites.[25]

Those who have lived in a community longer are more likely to be embedded in their communities and therefore more likely to vote.[26] Certain factors may be expected to increase interest in voting, increasing turnout. For example, having a senatorial or gubernatorial race on the ballot may generate greater interest at the state level. Having more candidates on the ballot for the presidential race may offer the voter more choices, and thus increase his or her chances of going to the polls. However, after a certain level, more choices have diminishing marginal returns.

Thus, on a county level, it makes sense to study such factors as per capita income, percentage of individuals with a high school diploma, percentage of people over sixty-five, percentage of people under twenty-five, percentage of

African Americans and Latinos, percentage of people who have lived in the county for five or more years, as well as the size of the county measured by the log of the 1996 population. The analysis also includes the number of candidates and whether there is a statewide race on the ballot.

Table 10.1 also indicates that counties with fail-safe technologies have significantly lower voter turnout statistically, controlling for the demographic profile of the county- and state-level factors. The model is also consistent with other analyses of voter turnout. Counties with more individuals with a high school diploma, greater per capita income, more older individuals, and fewer young individuals have a higher rate of voter turnout. More populous counties also have lower turnout.

Discussion

The agenda-setting effect of the election of 2000 as well as a variety of studies has shown national, state, and local policymakers that some changes in voting equipment are in order. Indeed, despite terrorism and war that took the spotlight off the 2000 election, on October 29, 2002, President Bush signed the "Help America Vote Act" (HAVA) into law. The legislation authorized close to four billion dollars over three years for a number of electoral reforms at the state level. A key part of the legislation provides funding for states to replace outdated voting equipment, in particular, punchcard and lever machines, though it does not mandate that states rid themselves of older technologies. While it is not entirely clear whether the entire four billion dollars will be appropriated to the states, many jurisdictions and states will face tough decisions about what sort of technology they should adopt. States such as Florida and Georgia have already decided to modernize their equipment, with Georgia adopting touchscreen machines all over the state and Florida adopting a mix of optical scan systems and touchscreen systems.

As with any policy decision, competing goals affect the decision to adopt new voting technology. The relative priority, for the media and the public, of accuracy and speed in reporting results was dramatically altered by the 2000 election, which also increased awareness of registration problems that can prevent people from voting. However, policymakers should be aware that maximizing accuracy of measuring voting intent may affect other goals. This chapter suggests that the type of voting equipment in use may influence voter turnout rates. This finding does not imply that more accurate but slower equipment should never be used, but merely highlights the inevitability of trade-offs and the fact that accuracy is only one of several worthy goals to be considered in election administration, despite the intense media focus on "uncounted votes" following the 2000 election.

This study notes that if policymakers choose more accurate voting equipment, it may come at a price in terms of accessibility at the polling place. Our analysis finds that equipment that can be programmed to prevent overvoting, or to allow voters to double-check their ballots, are associated with lower rates of voided ballots. However, for those counties, turnout is also significantly lower, controlling for county-level factors that have been shown to affect turnout. One could argue that our conclusions are limited somewhat because the fail-safe technologies in 1996 were dominated by lever machines, which are no longer manufactured in the United States (although replacement parts are available). But it has been one of the most important fail-safe technologies to this point.

It should be noted that rates of voided ballots do not capture the complete nature of the problem in places such as Palm Beach County, Florida, in the 2000 election, where votes were mistakenly cast for the wrong candidate—in particular by many Gore supporters who apparently voted by mistake for Buchanan. Nevertheless, changing to the fail-safe technologies may help solve this problem. For example, the Caltech/MIT study shows that DRE systems have produced the same roll-off rate as punch-card or other systems on average over the last several elections (although DRE performed better in 2000). However, DRE systems might generate far fewer mistaken votes, particularly the newer touch-screen systems that review a summary of choices made by the voter before the ballot is submitted.[27]

As noted in other studies, it is too simplistic to believe that the "best" type of voting technology will not vary over time and across jurisdictions, depending on factors such as the number of ballots that must be counted and the number of contests that must be fit on the ballot and other goals, as outlined in the Caltech/MIT report from 2001. Uniform equipment will not necessarily lead to uniform results, and past performance does not necessarily predict future performance. The Caltech/MIT study found that hand-counted paper ballots performed best of all, but obviously this finding, based on the experience of small counties, cannot necessarily be generalized to large counties, where vote counters may have far less time to examine each ballot. The number and variety (in content and language) of ballots required for a county as large as Los Angeles can make optical scan systems impractical. The same models of DRE equipment that generate roll-off rates of 3–4 percent in Kentucky and New Mexico produce rates below 2 percent in other states, and below 1 percent in Tennessee. Punch cards are likely to perform far better in the next few elections than in the past, as voters remembering the Florida fiasco will take extra care to insert the cards correctly, punch their choices forcefully, and remove any hanging chad.

Although both houses of Congress passed legislation in 2001 that would help states buy new technology, conferees were still trying to work out differences in the legislation more than a year later. It may be that future elections will again renew calls for standardization of technology and the use of technology that will allow voters to check their ballots before casting their votes.

Notes

1. Caltech/MIT Voting Technology Project, "Residual Votes."
2. Knack and Kropf, "Voided Ballots"; Knack and Kropf, "Who Uses Inferior Voting Technology?"; Kimball, Owens, and McAndrew, "Who's Afraid of an Undervote?"; Caltech/MIT, "Residual Votes."
3. Brady et al., "Counting All the Votes"; Brady, Verba, and Schlozman, "Beyond SES"; Knack and Kropf, "Roll-Off at the Top."
4. Caltech/MIT, "Voting," 23–25.
5. Ibid.
6. Caltech/MIT, "Voting"; Knack and Kropf, "Who Uses Inferior Voting Technology?" 511.
7. Bullock and Dunn, "Election Roll-Off"; Burnham, "American Political Universe"; Engstrom and Caridas, "Voting for Judges"; Vanderleeuw and Utter, "Voter Roll-Off"; Wattenberg, McAllister, and Salvanto, "SAT Test."
8. Caltech/MIT, "Voting."
9. Knack and Kropf, "Roll-Off at the Top."
10. Wattenberg, McAllister, and Salvanto, "SAT Test."
11. Brady et al., "Counting All the Votes"; Caltech/MIT, "Voting"; Darcy and Schneider, "Confusing Ballots"; Knack and Kropf, "Voided Ballots"; Mather, *Voting Machines*; Nichols and Strizek, "Electronic Voting Machines"; Rusk, "Australian Ballot Reform"; Shocket, Heighberger, and Brown, "Effect of Voting Technology"; Stiefbold, "West German Elections"; Thomas, "Voting Machines and Voter Participation"; Walker, "Ballot Forms and Voter Fatigue."
12. Caltech/MIT, "Residual Votes"; Caltech/MIT, "Voting."
13. Brady et al., "Counting All the Votes."
14. Knack and Kropf, "Who Uses Inferior Voting Technology?"; Knack and Kropf,

"Voided Ballots."

15. Stiefbold, "West German Elections."

16. Mather, *Voting Machines.*

17. Thomas, "Voting Machines and Voter Participation."

18. Shocket, Heighberger, and Brown, "Effect of Voting Technology," 522.

19. Nichols and Strizek, "Electronic Voting Machines."

20. Knack and Kropf, "Voided Ballots."

21. Ibid.; Kimball, Owens, and McAndrew, "Unrecorded Votes" (chapter); Tomz and Van Houweling, "Racial Gap."

22. Wolfinger and Rosenstone, *Who Votes?*

23. Ibid.; Brady, Veba, and Schlozman, "Beyond SES."

24. Wolfinger and Rosenstone, *Who Votes?*

25. Tate, *From Protest to Politics.*

26. Knack and Kropf, "For Shame!"

27. Fischer, "Voting Technology."

Unrecorded Votes and Political Representation

DAVID C. KIMBALL, UNIVERSITY OF MISSOURI–ST. LOUIS; CHRIS T.
OWENS, TEXAS A&M UNIVERSITY; AND KATHERINE MCANDREW
KEENEY, SOUTHERN ILLINOIS UNIVERSITY–CARBONDALE

Through the controversy involving the 2000 presidential election and the Florida recount, the nation learned of the difficulties some voters have in casting a valid ballot. Roughly two million voters—almost one in every fifty to cast a ballot—failed to record a choice for president in the 2000 elections.[1] These were the result of "undervotes" (where voters make no selection) and "overvotes" (where too many selections are recorded). For example, the confusing "butterfly" ballot in Palm Beach County, Florida, in which candidates were listed on two facing pages, generated unusually high levels of invalidated ballots, mostly overvotes, and of votes for Pat Buchanan, mostly from citizens intending to vote for Al Gore.[2] In Florida, where George W. Bush's official margin of victory over Al Gore was a mere 537 votes, more than 175,000 ballots failed to record a vote for president. Not surprisingly, the handling of unrecorded votes was at the center of the legal and political disputes surrounding the Florida recount. In at least five other states—Iowa, New Hampshire, New Mexico, Oregon, and Wisconsin—the number of unrecorded votes was larger than the vote margin between Bush and Gore. So it is possible that the election results in some states, and thus the winner of the presidential election, could have been different if unrecorded votes had been cast properly and counted as intended.

How did this problem occur, and what can be done to minimize the number of unrecorded votes in future elections? We examine election results in 2,895 counties across the United States and in more than 5,600 Florida precincts to examine the likely causes of unrecorded votes in the 2000 election. We identify changes in election administration that may reduce the number of unrecorded votes in future elections.

In the wake of the 2000 election controversy, several blue-ribbon commissions, government investigators, and academic panels have proposed election reforms designed to reduce the number of unrecorded votes. In 2002, Congress passed, and President Bush signed into law, the Help America Vote Act (HAVA), which mandates several election reforms and authorizes almost $4 billion in federal grants to improve the election process. Finally, state legislatures are considering many changes in election administration in response to HAVA and the difficulties presented by the 2000 election. Many of the reform laws and proposals focus heavily on voting equipment, especially the replacement of punch-card voting machines. Like others conducting studies, we find that voting technology as well as demographic characteristics influenced the frequency of unrecorded votes in the 2000 election. However, election laws and administrative decisions that determine ballot design and the options available on the ballot strongly influence the number of unrecorded votes. In many cases, other election administration rules or features—ballot design, the availability of straight-party voting, laws regarding write-in votes—have a greater effect on unrecorded votes and are less expensive to change than voting technology. By focusing so much attention on voting technology, the election reform movement may be missing other cost-effective methods to reduce the number of unrecorded votes in future elections.

Why Are There Unrecorded Votes?

Since elections in most states are administered at the county level, where decisions about voting methods are often made, we start by examining unrecorded votes in American counties. We collected data on the number of ballots cast, the presidential vote totals, voting technology, ballot features, and demographic characteristics for 2,895 counties in the 2000 election. While this sample covers 92 percent of all counties and 95 percent of votes cast for president in the 2000 election, we could not get complete data for every county.[3] Not all states require elections officials to count or report the number of unrecorded votes or the total number of ballots cast in an election. In addition, a few jurisdictions reported erroneous totals, as when the number of presidential votes exceeded the number of ballots cast. (Thus, any election reform law should require election administrators to report the number of overvotes, undervotes, and ballots cast, in addition to the vote totals for each candidate.)

We simply compute the difference between the number of ballots cast and the number of votes cast for president to calculate the percentage of unrecorded votes in each county. Among the counties in our sample, 1,853,267 unrecorded votes were cast in the presidential contest, or 1.8 percent of ballots cast. The distribution of unrecorded presidential votes across counties is heavily skewed. Most counties have relatively low rates of unrecorded votes, but some counties have high rates. The percentage of unrecorded votes ranges from 0.02 percent to 15.0 percent, with a median of 1.7 percent, a mean of 2.3 percent, and a standard deviation of 1.9 percent. In one out of every four counties, more than 3 percent of the ballots failed to record a vote for president. The next section examines why unrecorded votes were more common in some counties than in others.

Ballot Layout and Options Can Produce Unrecorded Votes

There is some concern that voter confusion may cause unrecorded votes. Voters may fail to select a candidate or make too many selections when they are confused by voting technology, ballot instructions, or ballot design. In addition, it is an axiom of politics that many voters are ill informed about the full range of candidates and issues that confront them on a ballot. Consequently, voters use an array of decision-making shortcuts to simplify the voting process.[4] Party affiliation may be the strongest voting aid, and ballot designs that accentuate partisanship tend to produce lower rates of unrecorded votes. For example, in the 2000 presidential election only fifteen states included a straight-party voting option on the ballot. The straight-party option, which typically appears at the top of the ballot with each party's name and logo, allows people to cast a vote for the same party in every contest on the ballot. This makes party affiliation more salient and affords the voter a very simple and almost error-free method of completing the ballot.

Our analysis reveals that the straight-party ballot device reduces the number of unrecorded votes. Table 11.1 indicates the frequency of unrecorded votes in the 2000 presidential election as a percentage of all ballots cast. In states with a straight-party option on the ballot, 1.3 percent of the ballots cast failed to record a vote for president. In states without straight-party voting, the figure was 2.0 percent, or more than half again as much.[5] While these numbers may seem small, this is a substantial difference. In a national electorate of roughly 100 million voters, every percent of increase means an additional million unrecorded votes. Unrecorded votes would be less common if other states adopted the straight-party voting option. In addition, this evidence is consistent with other studies showing that unrecorded votes are less common when the ballot design minimizes voter confusion.[6]

Some Unrecorded Votes Are Probably Intentional

The straight-party option is not the only ballot characteristic that influences unrecorded votes. It may be that some voters intentionally leave the ballot blank if they do not like any of the listed candidates. As table 11.1 indicates, there was a substantially higher rate of unrecorded votes in the seven states where Ralph Nader was left off the ballot.[7] This suggests that voters who preferred Nader may have abstained from the presidential contest if his name was not on the ballot.

Of course, a write-in vote is an alternative for voters who want to register disapproval of the available choices on the ballot. As it turns out, however, many states severely limit write-in voting. Ten states simply did not include space on the ballot for write-in votes in the 2000 presidential election. Another twenty-five states allowed write-in votes but counted write-ins only for candidates who had filed a declaration of candidacy, something very few write-in candidates bother to do. Thus some voters in these states made write-in selections that were not counted as valid votes. For example, Arizona is one of the states that counted

Table 11.1. Unrecorded Presidential Votes in 2000

By Ballot Form

Ballot Format	Unrecorded Votes
Straight-party punch	1.3%
(15 states, 1,011 counties, 28% of ballots)	
No straight-party punch	2.0%
(35 states, 1,884 counties, 72% of ballots)	
Nader on the ballot	1.7%
(43 states, 2,346 counties, 90% of ballots)	
Nader not on the ballot	2.8%
(7 states, 549 counties, 10% of ballots)	
Write-ins not allowed	2.0%
(10 states, 551 counties, 9% of ballots)	
Write-ins counted only for declared candidates	2.0%
(25 states, 1,691 counties, 67% of ballots)	
All write-ins counted	1.1%
(14 states, 636 counties, 23% of ballots)	
"None of these candidates" option	0.6%
(Nevada only, 17 counties, <1% of ballots)	

By Voting Technology

Voting Technology	Description	Unrecorded Votes
Votomatic/punch card (507 counties/29% of ballots)	Punch card inserted behind booklet w/ballot choices, voter punches out holes, ballots counted by card reader machine	2.8%
Datavote/punch card (44 counties/3% of ballots)	Ballot choices printed on card, voter punches out holes, ballots counted by card reader machine	1.2%
Lever machine (370 counties/15% of ballots)	Candidates listed next to levers on machine, voter pulls down lever for candidate, lever machine records/ counts votes	1.6%
Paper ballot (221 counties/<1% of ballots)	Candidates listed on sheet of paper, voter marks box next to candidate, ballots counted by hand	1.9%
Optical Scan-Central Count (857 counties/15% of ballots)	Voter darkens an oval or arrow next to candidate on paper ballot, ballots counted by computer scanner at a central location	1.8%
Optical Scan-Precinct Count (513 counties/23% of ballots)	Voter darkens an oval or arrow next to candidate on paper ballot, ballots counted by computer scanner at the precinct	0.9%
Electronic (DRE) (312 counties/12% of ballots)	Candidates listed on computer screen, voter pushes button or touches screen next to candidate, electronic machine counts the votes	1.7%
Mixed (71 counties/4% of ballots)	More than one voting technology used	1.1%

write-in votes only for candidates who filed the required paperwork. If all write-in votes in Maricopa County, which includes Phoenix, were counted as valid votes, the number of unrecorded votes would have been 1.4 percent instead of the 1.7 percent indicated by official records. Only fourteen states allow and count all write-in votes for president. Finally, Nevada deserves mention as the only state to include a ballot line for "none of these candidates" in federal and statewide races, certainly a more conspicuous outlet for a protest vote than the write-in option. In fact, "none of these candidates" received more than three thousand votes for president in 2000, more votes than three of the candidates listed on the ballot in Nevada.

As table 11.1 also shows, unrecorded votes are roughly twice as common in states that restrict write-in votes by not allowing write-ins or by counting write-in votes only for qualified candidates. In addition, Nevada had an extremely low rate of unrecorded votes, one of the lowest in the country. This suggests that some of the unrecorded votes in the 2000 presidential election would have been write-in selections rather than votes for any of the candidates listed on the ballot. Other states interested in reducing the number of unrecorded votes may want to follow Nevada's lead or loosen restrictions on write-in voting.

Requiem for Votomatic Punch-Card Machines

We also examine voting machines to see whether particular technologies are associated with higher rates of unrecorded votes. Voting methods vary around the country. There are six basic methods of voting in the United States: paper ballots, lever machines, Votomatic punch-card machines, Datavote punch cards, optical scan ballots, and direct recording electronic (DRE) machines. The newest technologies, electronic machines and optical scan systems, are seeing increased use as jurisdictions replace the older methods of paper ballots, lever machines, and punch cards. Optical scan systems can also be divided into those where ballots are counted at a central location (county courthouse) or at the voting precinct. One advantage of the precinct-count optical scan systems is that they give voters a chance to discover and correct mistakes (overvotes and undervotes). The central-count optical scan systems do not have such an error-correction feature. A small number of counties, almost entirely in states where elections are administered by townships, used more than one type of voting technology in the 2000 general election.

Table 11.1 also provides summary data on the prevalence of each type of voting technology, a short description of the technology, and corresponding rates of unrecorded votes in the 2000 election. Votomatic punch cards and optical scan systems are by far the most commonly used voting technologies, while paper ballots and Datavote punch cards are the least common voting methods. As several studies have found, and as table 11.1 shows, Votomatic punch-card machines—source of the infamous "hanging chad"—produce substantially higher rates of unrecorded votes than any other system.[8] Beyond that, however, the differences between most other voting methods in terms of unrecorded votes are fairly small. In comparing newer technologies, precinct-based optical scan systems performed better than central-count optical scan systems and electronic machines.[9] Only the precinct-based optical scan systems performed better than lever machines and paper ballots.

It is worth noting the performance of Datavote punch cards, which often are lumped with their distant cousin, Votomatic machines. In Votomatic machines, the voter must properly insert a punch-card ballot into a booklet listing the offices and candidates. In contrast, the Datavote method is arguably less confusing because the candidates are listed directly on the punch-card ballot, removing the step of aligning the punch card with the ballot booklet. Datavote machines performed better, on average, than Votomatic punch cards and as well as any other method. Thus, if the overall frequency of unrecorded votes is the main concern of election administrators, counties using lever machines, paper ballots, or Datavote punch cards may not need to rush to buy new voting equipment, unless they can afford a precinct-count optical scan system.

The Demographic Basis of Unrecorded Votes

Several studies indicate that unrecorded votes are partly a function of socioeconomic characteristics. Unrecorded votes are more common in counties or precincts with large populations of racial and ethnic minorities, low-income residents, less-educated citizens, or elderly voters.[10] It may be that each of these groups faces a higher degree of confusion during the voting process, due to language difficulties, low levels of education, or disabilities, for example. Alternatively, many of these groups may be alienated from the political process and thus less interested in many of the contests on the ballot.

Table 11.2 breaks down the rate of unrecorded votes by the racial and ethnic composition of American counties. As many studies have found, it is evident

Table 11.2. Unrecorded Presidential Votes in 2000

Composition of County	Unrecorded Votes
By Race and Ethnicity	
Less than 10% black (2160 counties/61% of ballots)	1.5%
Between 10% and 30% black (424 counties/29% of ballots)	2.0%
Over 30% black (311 counties/10% of ballots)	3.1%
Less than 10% Hispanic (2515 counties/66% of ballots)	1.7%
Between 10% and 30% Hispanic (260 counties/24% of ballots)	2.0%
Over 30% Hispanic (120 counties/10% of ballots)	2.1%
By Median Income	
Less than $25,000 (359 counties/3% of ballots)	3.4%
$25,000–$32,499 (1226 counties/18% of ballots)	2.2%
$32,500–$40,000 (865 counties/39% of ballots)	2.1%
Over $40,000 (445 counties/41% of ballots)	1.2%
By County Size (Ballots Cast)	
Less than 5,000 ballots (758 counties/2% of ballots)	2.7%
5,000–9,999 ballots (696 counties/5% of ballots)	2.6%
10,000–50,000 ballots (1040 counties/22% of ballots)	1.9%
Over 50,000 ballots (401 counties/71% of ballots)	1.7%

that the frequency of unrecorded votes in the 2000 presidential election is related to the size of the African American population. Counties with larger concentrations of black voters tend to have higher rates of unrecorded votes. In contrast, the effect of ethnicity is weaker, although counties with larger concentrations of Hispanic voters tend to have slightly higher rates of unrecorded votes.

Table 11.2 further indicates that higher rates of unrecorded votes tend to occur in low-income counties and small counties. In contrast, large and wealthy counties tend to have relatively low levels of unrecorded votes. The findings with respect to income, race, and ethnicity indicate a socioeconomic disparity in unrecorded votes, suggesting that unrecorded votes are disproportionately cast by low-income and minority voters. It is not entirely clear why unrecorded votes are more common in small counties. Part of the explanation is that income levels are correlated with county size—small counties tend to have low median incomes and large counties tend to have high median income levels. It is also possible that larger urban counties have a more professional government apparatus, including election administration, than smaller rural counties, thus reducing voting errors.

It remains to be determined whether the effects of the demographic measures are the result of intentional undervoting by disaffected groups or the result of greater voter confusion and unintentional errors among disadvantaged groups. Some studies indicate that the elevated rate of unrecorded votes associated with confusing ballots and voting technology, such as Votomatic punch cards, falls disproportionately on racial and ethnic minorities and the poor.[11] Thus, it appears that disadvantaged groups are more confused by certain voting methods, a factor responsible for much of the socioeconomic divergence in unrecorded votes.

We find similar evidence in the 2000 presidential election. In particular, there is reason to believe that lever machines and electronic machines reduce the racial and economic disparity in unrecorded votes because they have features that reduce voting errors. First, both machines prevent overvoting—they do not allow voters to cast votes for more than one candidate. Second, lever machines and especially electronic machines conspicuously indicate to voters when they have undervoted, or not selected any candidate. Third, lever and electronic machines allow voters to correct mistakes without having to get a new ballot from poll workers.[12] Other voting methods—including optical scan ballots, which have quickly become the most popular in the country—do not have these features.

Table 11.3 presents the rate of unrecorded votes by race and income for the four most common voting methods used in the United States. The first two columns of the table show an apparent racial disparity in unrecorded votes in counties that used Votomatic machines and central-count optical scan ballots in the 2000 election. The percentage of unrecorded votes in counties with relatively large African American populations is substantially higher than in counties with relatively few African Americans. However, apparent racial differences in unrecorded votes are much smaller in counties using lever machines and precinct-count optical scan systems and vanish altogether in counties using electronic machines. In addition, table 11.3 suggests that the economic distribution of unrecorded votes is more equitable in counties using precinct-count optical scan systems and electronic voting machines. While low-income counties still have a higher rate of unrecorded votes than high-income counties, the gap between rich and poor counties is substantially smaller where electronic voting machines and precinct-count optical scan machines are used.

The straight-party voting option is another mechanism that helps voters avoid confusion and mistakes. Thus the racial and economic disparity in unrecorded votes may be confined to those states that do not have a straight-party option on the ballot. Table 11.4 provides some evidence to support this belief. In states without straight-party voting we see a familiar pattern, with unrecorded votes more common in counties with relatively large concentrations of black

Table 11.3. Racial and Economic Disparity in Unrecorded Votes by Voting Machine

Composition of County	Votomatic Punch Cards	Optical Scan Central Count	Optical Scan Precinct Count	Lever Machines	Electronic Machines
By Race					
Less than 10% black	2.2%	1.3%	0.9%	1.1%	1.7%
Between 10% and 30% black	3.1%	2.3%	0.7%	1.7%	1.7%
Over 30% black	5.6%	5.2%	1.9%	2.3%	1.7%
By Median Income					
Less than $25,000	4.5%	4.4%	1.1%	3.4%	2.7%
Between $25,000 and 32,499	3.2%	2.1%	1.3%	2.0%	2.2%
Between $32,500 and $40,000	3.0%	1.7%	1.0%	1.7%	1.7%
Over $40,000	2.2%	1.0%	0.8%	1.1%	1.3%

Table 11.4. Effect of Straight Party Voting on Unrecorded Votes

Composition of County	No SPV	SPV
By Race		
Less than 10% black	1.5%	1.4%
10%–30% black	2.3%	1.1%
Over 30% black	3.7%	1.3%
By Median Income		
Less than $25,000	4.4%	2.0%
$25,000–$32,499	2.6%	1.5%
$32,500–$40,000	2.3%	1.5%
Over $40,000	1.3%	1.1%

voters. But in states with straight-party voting there is no apparent racial disparity in unrecorded votes. Similarly, the discrepancy in unrecorded votes between rich and poor counties is much smaller in states with a straight-party voting option on the ballot.

National data thus indicate that changes in voting technology (replacing Votomatic punch-card voting machines) and ballot design (including straight-party and write-in options) would reduce unrecorded votes. While the national data give an indication of the sources of unrecorded votes, the main controversy over uncounted ballots focused on the state of Florida. Did the same factors produce unrecorded votes in Florida? For the most part, they did.

What Happened in Florida?

The 2000 presidential election in Florida produced a "perfect storm" in terms of unrecorded votes. The state's demographic and election-administration features suggest a high rate of unrecorded votes compared to other states. For example, Florida ranks above the national average in its population of low-income residents, nonwhite residents, and elderly citizens, all factors associated with higher levels of unrecorded votes. At the same time, Florida does not have a straight-party option on the ballot and it counts write-in votes only for declared candidates. Furthermore, the largest counties in Florida used Votomatic punch cards in the 2000 election. To top it all off, ten presidential candidates qualified for the Florida ballot in 2000, prompting several counties to list presidential candidates in multiple columns or pages. This created further confusion for voters. The combination of all of these forces produced more than 175,000 unrecorded votes for president, or roughly 2.9 percent of ballots cast in Florida

—one of the highest rates in the country. Throw in an extremely close presidential election that hinged on a razor-thin margin of victory in Florida, and the result was an explosive controversy over unrecorded votes.

We examined a database of unrecorded votes in the 2000 presidential election, including overvotes and undervotes, from each Florida voting precinct.[13] Most of the unrecorded votes for president in Florida, roughly 65 percent, were overvotes, a much higher share of overvotes than in other states that reported such data. This suggests that voter confusion was a more important factor in the Florida election. As in our county analysis, we find that punch-card voting machines were a source of unrecorded votes in Florida. Twenty-four counties, including the state's most populated ones, used punch-card machines in the 2000 general election, while most other counties used optical scan ballots. As expected, unrecorded votes were more common in counties using punch cards.

However, ballot design was the most critical source of unrecorded votes in Florida.[14] Because of a change in state law that eased ballot access requirements for minor parties, ten presidential candidates qualified for the ballot in Florida. As elections officials will attest, fitting ten candidates on the same column or page of a ballot is not always an easy task. Nineteen counties in Florida listed the presidential candidates in more than one column. For example, the "butterfly" ballot in Palm Beach County listed the candidates on two facing pages. In Duval County, the presidential candidates were listed on two nonfacing pages. In other counties, candidates were listed in more than one column on the same page. If voters mistakenly thought new columns represented a new contest, they may have overvoted by selecting a candidate from each column.

Table 11.5 shows the consequences of what may seem like a mundane decision about the way presidential candidates are listed on ballots. In counties where candidates were listed in one column, 2.1 percent of ballots contained unrecorded votes for president. In counties where candidates were listed in more than one column, unrecorded votes for president jumped to 7.6 percent. Overvotes were far more common in counties with the confusing ballot design, while undervotes were relatively uncommon regardless of the ballot design. This result supports a theory that listing candidates in multiple columns increases the likelihood of inadvertent mistakes by voters.

As in the national data, we also find an interaction between ballot design and race and income. In Florida counties with the confusing presidential ballot design, high rates of overvotes and unrecorded votes were concentrated in precincts with large black or low-income populations. As table 11.5 further indicates, in counties that adopted the confusing ballot design, well over one of

Table 11.5. Unrecorded Presidential Votes in Florida

	Unrecorded	Overvotes	Undervotes
Ballot Design			
Straightforward: candidates listed in 1 column (47 counties, 4,684 precincts, 82% of ballots)	2.1%	1.2%	0.8%
Confusing: candidates listed in 2 columns (18 counties, 1,077 precincts, 17% of ballots)	7.6%	5.9%	1.7%

Table 11.6. Racial and Economic Disparity in Unrecorded Votes by Ballot Design

Composition of Precinct	Confusing Ballot Design		Straightforward Ballot Design	
By Race	Unrecorded Votes	Overvotes	Unrecorded Votes	Overvotes
Less than 10% black	5.9%	4.2%	1.7%	0.9%
Between 10% and 30% black	8.0%	6.5%	2.1%	2.1%
Over 30% black	16.0%	14.3%	5.5%	
By Poverty (household income under $15,000)				
Less than 10%	5.8%	3.9%	5.5%	3.7%
Between 10% and 25%	7.7%	6.1%	2.1%	1.2%
Over 25%	13.3%	12.3%	3.9%	2.4%

every ten voters in heavily poor or black precincts mistakenly voted for more than one presidential candidate. In contrast, in counties that listed presidential candidates in a single column, overvotes remained below 4 percent even in precincts with the largest populations of poor or black residents.

These results raise concerns about unequal treatment and representation of voters in American elections, especially in light of the "equal protection" rationale used by the Supreme Court to decide the 2000 presidential election in the *Bush v. Gore* case.[15] In fact, the American Civil Liberties Union relied heavily on an equal protection claim when it filed lawsuits in several states to replace punch-card voting machines. There is some debate as to whether the racial and economic disparity in unrecorded votes indicates discrimination against minority and low-income voters.[16] Politically speaking, Democrats should be more concerned than Republicans about ensuring the valid votes of poor and minority voters, and that is the way recent debates about election administration and reform have often played out. The jury is still out, however, on the charge of voter discrimination. On the one hand, it does not appear that older voting methods, particularly punch cards, are targeted to counties with large minority or low-income populations.[17] The cumbersome administrative process of replacing voting technology would make that difficult. In addition, most of the Florida counties that adopted the confusing presidential ballot design had Democratic election supervisors.

On the other hand, there is a long history of partisan manipulation of the straight party line on the ballot. For example, Republican-controlled legislatures in Michigan and Illinois recently eliminated the straight-party option from state ballots over the unified objections of Democratic lawmakers. In both cases, the impact of the change on minority voters was a major point of contention.[18] Regardless of the largely partisan debate about voter discrimination, however, improved voter education efforts, especially in areas with concentrated low-income and minority residents, are worth pursuing to reduce the number of unrecorded votes in future elections.

Conclusion

An analysis of the 2000 presidential election results nationwide and in Florida indicate that ballot design and voting methods influence the frequency as well as the racial and economic distribution of unrecorded votes. While voters probably intend some unrecorded votes, it is clear that many unrecorded votes are the product of confusion and mistakes by voters.

In the wake of the 2000 elections, many counties are considering new voting technology, and there is intense competition between manufacturers of electronic voting machines and optical scan systems to replace older voting methods. In some quarters, optical scan voting methods are touted as the best available equipment in terms of minimizing the number of unrecorded votes.[19] This recommendation may need to be qualified, particularly since central-count scan systems appear to perform no better than any alternatives to punch cards. If one is interested in reducing the disproportionate racial and economic impact of unrecorded votes, our evidence suggests that precinct-count optical scan systems and electronic voting machines perform better than central-count optical scan methods. At a minimum, the evaluation of different voting technologies merits closer analysis, especially an experimental study to see how voters interact with each voting method.

The 2002 elections reinforced the belief that new voting technology reduces the number of unrecorded votes cast in major elections. In Florida, all counties were forced to use electronic voting machines or precinct-count optical scan systems in time for the 2002 elections. While these changes did not prevent widespread voting difficulties in the Florida primary election in September of 2002, they did reduce the number of unrecorded votes in subsequent elections.[20] Only 0.8 percent of ballots cast in Florida's gubernatorial election of 2002 failed to record a valid vote, a significant decline from the 2000 presidential election in Florida. In Georgia, the entire state upgraded to electronic touch-screen voting machines for the 2002 general election. Only 1 percent of ballots cast in the state's gubernatorial election of 2002 failed to record a valid vote, a dramatic drop from the 3.5 percent unrecorded votes in the 2000 presidential election in Georgia. In addition, Georgia avoided many of the Election Day difficulties that plagued Florida's 2002 primary election. This was likely due to a massive effort to educate voters and train election workers on the new voting machines. Georgia election officials toured the state demonstrating the new voting equipment, and election judges were required to complete 12 hours of training before the 2002 election (far more than is typically required in other states).

However, it is important to keep these improvements in perspective. Voter turnout was much lower in the midterm elections of 2002, which usually means less stress for election judges and the system. In addition, the midterm electorate tends to be dominated by committed partisans who are less likely to make voting errors. Furthermore, the gubernatorial elections in Florida and Georgia featured only three candidates, thus limited the ballot design problems seen in the 2000 presidential contest. Finally, election improvements in these two states came after significant expenditures on election administration. For example, the new touch-screen voting machines cost the state of Georgia $54 million.[21] While appropriations arising from the recent federal election reform law will help state and local governments pay for election improvements, in the economic downturn of the early 2000s many states may not be able to afford the changes made in Florida and Georgia.

In the march to election reform it is important to look beyond voting technology. Switching to a new voting technology can be very costly, while relatively inexpensive changes in ballot design may have a bigger effect in reducing the number of unrecorded votes in future elections. Adding ballot lines such as the straight-party and write-in options that help voters complete an error-free ballot, and avoiding designs that create confusion, may go a long way toward minimizing the number of unrecorded votes, which will improve the health of elections.

Notes

1. In contests farther down the ballot, such as races for county offices, the number of unrecorded votes is typically even higher. See Bullock and Dunn, "Election Roll-Off"; Nichols and Strizek, "Electronic Voting Machines"; Caltech/MIT Voting Technology Project, "Voting."

2. Wand et al., "The Butterfly Did It."

3. This represents a more complete data set than other studies of unrecorded votes in the 2000 election. In states where elections are administered by townships rather than counties (Maine, Massachusetts, Michigan, New Hampshire, Vermont, and Wisconsin), we aggregated the vote totals and voting technology data to the county level. In addition, some cities (including Kansas City, Chicago, and Washington, D.C.) have separate election administration authorities. We treat such cities' data as county equivalents and adjust the figures for the county from which they come. See also Kimball, Owens, and McAndrew, "Who's Afraid of an Undervote?"

4. Popkin, *The Reasoning Voter;* Lupia and McCubbins, *The Democratic Dilemma.*

5. The differences in rates of unrecorded votes presented in the table remain statistically significant in a multivariate analysis that controls for voting technology and several demographic and election administration factors. See Kimball, Owens, and McAndrew, "Who's Afraid of an Undervote?"

6. Wand et al., "The Butterfly Did It"; Cauchon, "Ballots, Not Machines"; Darcy and Schneider, "Confusing Ballots, Roll-Off, and the Black Vote."

7. Nader did not qualify for the ballot in Georgia, Idaho, Indiana, North Carolina, Oklahoma, South Dakota, and Wyoming. These states have some of the toughest ballot access laws in terms of petition signatures needed for minor-party candidates. See Winger, "Nader Wins Illinois."

8. Asher, Schussler, and Rosenfield, "Effect of Voting Systems"; Shocket, Heighenberger, and Brown, "Effect of Voting Technology"; Saltman, *Accuracy, Integrity, and Security;* Dugger, "Annals of Democracy," 40–108; Caltech/MIT, "Voting"; Brady et al., "Counting All the Votes."

9. Several counties with precinct-count optical scan systems did not activate the feature that alerts voters if they have made an error. We coded these counties as being equivalent to central-count systems. More recent research indicates that the latest generation of touch-screen electronic machines perform better than older full-face electronic machines. Touch-screen machines perform about as well as precinct-count optical scan systems. See David C. Kimball, "Voting Methods Two Years After Florida." (Paper presented at the annual MPSA conference, April 2003.)

10. Walker, "Ballot Forms and Voter Fatigue"; Darcy and Schneider, "Confusing Ballots"; Bullock and Dunn, "Election Roll-Off"; Nichols and Strizek, "Electronic Voting Machines"; Nichols, "State Referendum Voting"; Kimball and Owens, "Where's the Party?"; Brady et al., "Counting All the Votes"; Herron and Sekhon, "Overvoting and Representation."

11. Darcy and Schneider, "Confusing Ballots"; Knack and Kropf, "Invalidated Ballots"; Tomz and Van Houweling, "Racial Gap"; Hansen, "Demographic Analysis of Double-Punching."

12. For a more detailed comparison of voting methods, see Tomz and Van Houweling, "Racial Gap," 2–8.

13. We downloaded the Florida precinct data from November 7, 2001, from http://www.usatoday.com/news/politics/nov01/ballots-usat.htm. The precinct figures compiled by the newspaper consortium did not include data for Glades County, a small county in southern Florida. There also was a disparity between official election results and the newspaper data for Martin County (the newspaper data indicated no unrecorded votes in the county). Therefore we exclude Martin County from our analysis.

14. In a multivariate analysis of unrecorded votes in Florida that controlled for a host of demographic and election administration factors, the two-column ballot design was the biggest source of unrecorded votes. Results are available from the authors. Also see Cauchon, "Ballots, Not Machines."

15. For a compilation of the relevant court decisions and discussion of the legal issues in the 2000 presidential election, see Issacharoff, Karlan, and Pildes, *When Elections Go Bad*.

16. The debate includes many other issues, such as voter registration and voting rights for convicted felons. See United States Commission on Civil Rights, *Voting Irregularities in Florida During the 2000 General Election;* Lichtman, "Report on the Racial Impact of the Rejection of Ballots Cast in the 2000 Presidential Election in the State of Florida"; Lott Jr. "Non-Voted Ballots and Discrimination in Florida."

17. Knack and Kropf, "Who Uses Inferior Voting Technology?"

18. For other examples, see Darcy and Schneider, "Confusing Ballots"; Hamilton and Ladd, "Biased Ballots?"

19. Caltech/MIT, "Voting," 21–22; Caltech/MIT, "Residual Votes."

20. Caltech Media Relations, "Caltech-MIT Team Finds 35% Improvement in Florida's Voting Technology," September 19, 2002: <http://pr.caltech.edu/media/press_releases/pr12284.html>

21. Georgia Secretary of State, "Georgia Counts: Frequently Asked Questions," 2002: <http://www.georgiacounts.com/faqs.htm>

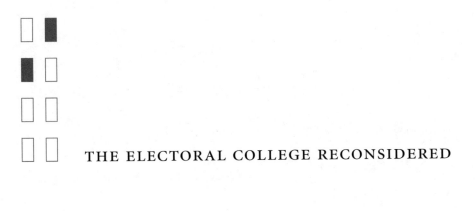

THE ELECTORAL COLLEGE RECONSIDERED

12 □

□

□

The 2000 Presidential Election

Is There a Better Way of Determining the Election Outcome?

JAMES COREY, HIGH POINT UNIVERSITY

George W. Bush won the 2000 presidential election by one vote—by one vote in the Electoral College and by one vote in the U.S. Supreme Court. Never before in the nation's history had the U.S. Supreme Court intervened in a presidential election and essentially decided the outcome of the election. This is precisely what happened more than one month after the popular vote in 2000. Seven justices found that the lack of standards used in counting ballots in Florida amounted to a violation of the Equal Protection Clause of the Fourteenth Amendment. There was disagreement only on a remedy. Two justices felt the counting should continue until December 18. Five justices of the U.S. Supreme Court reversed the recount decision of the Florida Supreme Court and remanded the case to the Florida court for further proceedings not inconsistent with the high court's opinion.[1]

The Florida Supreme Court threw in the towel and decided to take no further action. The vote recount stopped and George W. Bush won Florida by 537 votes and all Florida's twenty-five electoral votes, which gave him 271 electoral votes, or exactly one vote over the necessary 270 electoral votes. A subsequent recount of undervotes and other disputed votes in Miami-Dade County and other South Florida counties sponsored by the *Miami Herald* showed that Bush still carried Florida, by a "whopping" 147 votes.[2] However, the *Palm Beach Post* reported that the ballot confusion resulting in overvotes cost Gore 6,607 votes, or more than ten times the official winning margin of Bush.[3] The *Miami Herald* and another group of newspapers completed an examination of all of Florida's sixty-seven counties, looking at undervotes and overvotes. The net result of the count/recount/reexamination is that George W. Bush still carried the state of Florida by 152 votes.[4]

The outcome of all this? Even after the election, some Democrats (and others) still have not accepted the idea that George W. Bush is a legitimate president (although many of them expressed satisfaction with Bush after 9/11). Republicans tend to feel that the election was legitimate and the recounts were not necessary. However, as political commentator Rhodes Cook noted: "There have been a lot of words used to describe the election of 2000, but one rarely heard is the word 'great.'"[5]

Winning by one vote in the Electoral College had occurred before in the nation's history. In the disputed 1876 election, Rutherford Hayes won by one electoral vote over Samuel Tilden. This was also the second presidential election where the winning candidate did not get the largest popular vote. In 1824 John Quincy Adams had won a controversial election. It would happen again in 1888 when Benjamin Harrison's narrow Electoral College victory interrupted the presidency of Grover Cleveland. And in the election of 1800 there was actually a tie vote between Thomas Jefferson and Aaron Burr, which led to the passage of the Twelfth Amendment to the U.S. Constitution, changing the system by which presidents were elected.

Thus when the losing candidate in 2000, Vice President Al Gore, won about 550,000 more popular votes than George W. Bush, he became simply the latest candidate to have lost the U.S. presidential election in spite of winning more popular votes than the victor. But then, the other elections had been back in the nineteenth century. Because such a discrepancy had not occurred in more than a hundred years, a certain degree of complacency appeared to exist that it would not happen again. Not so.

A *New York Times* editorial noted: "The balloting breakdowns the country witnessed in November [2000] demonstrated that a complete overhaul is needed in the way Americans vote."[6] The editorial further noted that it was not only Florida that had problems with the election, spoiled ballots, overvotes, and so on: Oregon took nine days to determine its winner and New Mexico did not do so until November 30. Calls for the overhaul ranged from abolishing the Electoral College by constitutional amendment—a few bills were proposed—

to a series of fifteen reforms advocated by a National Association of Secretaries of State panel, which essentially advocated more voter education and poll worker training.[7]

This chapter provides a historical overview of the advent of the Electoral College and proposes a compromise reform position, one in between the two aforementioned proposals. It would retain the Electoral College but provide an alternative method for the allocating electoral votes by the states. The chapter also projects what the 2000 presidential election outcome would have been if using this alternative system of counting electoral votes had been used.

Background

Article II, section 1, of the Constitution allows each state to prescribe the manner in which its electors are chosen. In the early days of the country, presidential electors were selected by state legislatures. Initially there was a dispute as to how to count the votes of the people: by a statewide unit rule (state winner takes all), by local districts (the district plan), or by party and state (proportional plan).[8] By the late 1830s most states had popular election of presidential electors with a winner-take-all system. In 1863 South Carolina became the last state to drop the old method of having the state legislature select presidential electors.[9]

In the winner-take-all system, the presidential candidate who receives the most popular votes in a state wins all the electoral votes of the state. The loser comes up empty-handed. Lucius Wilmerding argued that such a system will "make the president the man of the states, but not a man of the people.... Judged by the popular principle, the general ticket can only be pronounced as unfair."[10]

A System for Electing the President

At the time it was established, relatively few people recognized the uniqueness of the office of president. Even today few people are aware of how novel the office was at its inception. At the time of the Constitutional Convention, a president headed no country in the world. If such an executive office was unparalleled, the Electoral College was even more so. Both were inventions springing from the best political minds of that time, and from great debate and compromise.

To understand why the United States has the Electoral College, it is useful to review what other alternatives were considered. First it was decided that the new nation would not be ruled by a monarchy but rather by a president.[11] There were many ideas floated as to how this new office would be filled. These can be condensed into three main ideas: (1) election by the national legislature, (2) election by state legislatures, and (3) direct or popular election.

Proposals and Debates

Roger Sherman was an advocate of the first idea and argued that the executive "ought to be appointed by and accountable to the legislative only, which is the depository of the supreme will of the society."[12] In essence, if the people trusted the members of Congress enough to elect them, why should they not trust these same officials to elect the president? However, opponents countered that a president elected by the national legislature would soon become nothing more than a puppet of the legislature. Elbridge Gerry of Massachusetts argued that "election by the legislature would not only lessen executive independence, but would give birth to intrigue and corruption between the executive and legislature previous to the election and partiality in the executive branch afterwards to those who elected him."[13] Gouverneur Morris suggested "that if the legislature elected the president, it would be like the election of a pope by a conclave of cardinals; real merit will rarely be the title of the appointment."[14] The opponents carried that argument, and election of the president by the national legislature was discarded.

Proponents of state election of the president believed this idea would promote harmony between the national and state legislatures. One proposal gave every state one vote for president. Opponents counted that it would cause more rivalry than harmony and would weaken the national government.

Finally, there was strong support for the direct election of the president by the people. Suffrage qualifications would be required, but basically voters would be white, landed males over age twenty-one. Popular election of the president was discussed at the Constitutional Convention by the likes of James Madison. One supporter of this proposal argued: "If the President is to be the guardian of the people, let him be appointed by the people."[15] James Wilson of Pennsylvania supported the direct election not only of the president but of both branches of Congress as well.[16] But the idea of popular election was strongly opposed by such leading figures as Alexander Hamilton and Thomas Jefferson. Direct election of the president was seen as having many problems, including (1) voter ignorance, (2) inadequate transportation and communication systems, (3) a lack of political parties, (4) sectionalism, (5) divergence between the interests of large and small states, and (6) north-south divisions.

Opponents of direct election of the president argued that the average citizen was not competent. Alexander Hamilton and others had a low perception of the American people's ability to elect the right person. There was no public schooling, and the literacy rate of the American population was very low at the time. To this end, Jefferson referred to the popular electorate as "the well meaning but uninformed people."[17] The famous statement of George Mason reinforces this point: "It would be as unnatural to refer the choice of a proper character for chief Magistrate to the people, as it would, to refer a trial of colours to a blind man. The extent of the Country renders it impossible that the People can have the requisite capacity to judge of the respective pretensions of the Candidates."[18]

In addition to the low esteem in which the electorate was held by the Framers, there were practical considerations. In Revolutionary times, transportation was limited to ships and dirt roads amounting to little more than horse or wagon trails. Communications consisted mostly of posted letters and a few papers printed in the largest cities. Under these circumstances, how would a popular election of the president be carried out?

Nor were there any established political parties.[19] This situation would change soon after ratification of the new Constitution when Federalist and anti-Federalist forces coalesced into the Federalist and Democrat-Republican national political parties. But the absence of these national parties compounded concerns over sectionalism in voting. While the Framers assumed George Washington of Virginia would be the nation's first president (he remains the only person ever to have been unanimously elected president by the Electoral College), there were long-term questions about who would follow. The concern of many was that each state or region would promote a favorite son and there would be no national consensus.

Compromise followed: The large-versus-small-state issue was defined by concerns over population and power. If the president were elected by popular vote, then states with large populations would overwhelm smaller states and determine the election outcome. Small states would be lesser stars in the constitutional galaxy.

The North-versus-South issue was another debate over population and power, but also reflected fundamental differences over such issues as slavery and commerce. The South was relatively underpopulated with eligible voters (white males over twenty-one) compared to the North. If slaves were counted as part of the South's population, the overall population between North and South was not that different. But southerners never contemplated that slaves would vote for president, so the disparity in eligible voters tipped very strongly in favor of the North. Southerners therefore feared that no southerner could be elected president, nor would their votes be as influential as northerners' in selecting the president.

Neither popular election nor any other of the ideas for electing the new president achieved majority support during the regular meetings of the Constitutional Convention, so the matter was deferred to a "committee on postponed matters." It was from this committee that the idea of an electoral college emerged. The convention adopted the idea with one change. The proposal called for the Senate to decide the election when a presidential candidate did not win a majority in the Electoral College. The convention changed the body to the U.S. House of Representatives.

Connecticut Compromise

Understanding the evolution of the Electoral College requires an understanding of the Connecticut Compromise that shaped the legislative branch. It is no coincidence that the numerical composition of the Electoral College is a perfect reflection of the legislative branch: each state has electoral votes equivalent to the number of individuals it sends to Congress. There were two principal clashes that were resolved by the Connecticut Compromise: large versus small states and free versus slave states.

Small states were worried about a loss of influence if population determined representation. Accordingly, each state was given two equal votes in the Senate, satisfying the smaller states. In the House, representation was determined by state population, satisfying larger, more populous states. But what population would count in determining representation? Southern slave states wanted to count their slaves as part of their state population, but northern free states thought the idea ridiculous. The infamous Three-fifths Compromise was reached, whereby slaves and Native Americans would each count as three-fifths of a person in determining House members and also in determining the number of state electors.

These same concerns were present in the origin of the Electoral College. Would each state receive one vote for president? Small states supported such a notion, larger states opposed it. Would presidential votes be determined by population? Large states and slave states supported such a plan, small states and free opposed it. So the principles of the Connecticut Compromise were borrowed for the Electoral College. Each state received two presidential electoral votes regardless of its size. State population determined the rest of the state's electoral votes. No one was completely satisfied, but each side could claim a partial victory—the essence of compromise.

The election of George Washington as president demonstrated the rationale of the Electoral College in picking the best person for the position. But soon after, political parties entered the scene, and the election of the president by wise men faded as partisan electors resorted to voting strictly according to party affiliation. The search for the wisest and best candidate in the nation was shunted to the side.[20]

Calls for Reform

Over the decades, there have been many calls for the reform of the Electoral College. In fact, proposals to reform or abolish the Electoral College far outnumber any other suggested changes to the Constitution. "Between 1889 and 1946, there were 109 Constitutional amendments proposed. From 1947 to 1968, another 265 proposals were made."[21] In 1969 the most serious attempt to eliminate the Electoral College through constitutional amendment took place. The bill passed the House 339–70 but was filibustered in the Senate, where it died. Opposition was lead by southern and small-state senators.[22] No other proposal to eliminate the Electoral College has made it this far.

The Twelfth Amendment to the Constitution, passed in 1804, changed the method of casting and counting electoral votes. If no candidate received a majority of electoral votes, a procedure was established that the House of Representatives would elect the president with each state having a single vote. In 1971 the Twenty-third Amendment added three electoral votes for the District of Columbia. Other than these amendments, the Electoral College remains intact. And it might well stay that way, as, with the exception of Australia, the United States has the most difficult amendment process in the world.[23]

The many calls for electoral reform can be organized into three major proposals: (1) Replace the Electoral College by popular election of the president. This is most often called "direct election." (2) Retain the Electoral College, but apportion state electoral votes according to the popular vote received by each presidential candidate. This is called the "proportional plan." (3) Retain the Electoral College, but award two electoral votes to the presidential candidate with the largest popular vote in the state and award one electoral vote to the presidential candidate with the largest popular vote in each congressional district. This is called the "district plan."

Stephen Wayne has analyzed presidential elections from 1960 to 1996 using all three methods. While direct popular election of the president would not have produced any different electoral outcomes in that time frame, Wayne finds that the proportional plan would have thrown the presidential elections of 1960, 1968, 1992, and 1996 into the House of Representatives, since no presidential candidate would have won a majority of Electoral College votes. The district plan would have resulted in the election of Richard Nixon over John F. Kennedy in 1960 and in an electoral tie between Gerald Ford and Jimmy Carter in 1976.[24]

A proportional voting system could encourage third parties that have never won an electoral vote. In fact, if third-party candidates could gather enough votes, they could deprive major-party candidates of a majority in the Electoral College, forcing the election to be decided by the U.S. House. As Wayne has demonstrated, this would have happened in four elections between 1960 and 1996. For this reason, the major political parties have never given this system even a cursory look.

The "single-member district" system has been used or is used by some states. Maine has had a split electoral voting procedure from the time it entered the Union in 1820. The only time Maine split its electoral vote was in the 1828 election, when John Quincy Adams took eight of nine electoral votes and Andrew Jackson took the other. Jackson went on to win the election in the Electoral College 178–83.[25]

In 1892 the U.S. Supreme Court upheld a Michigan law allocating electoral votes by congressional district. Michigan's vote in 1892 was split, with nine votes to Harrison and five votes to Cleveland. Shortly after, the law was repealed.[26] Nebraska's district system of voting was passed in 1991 and became effective in the 1992 presidential election.[27] But the district system has never resulted in a split of the state's electoral votes: in the 1992, 1996, and 2000 elections, the Republican candidate for president received all five of Nebraska's electoral votes.

The 2000 Election

Table 12.1 shows the results of the 2000 electoral voting in Maine and Nebraska. Even though these states could have split their electoral votes, the popular election results did not result in any electoral vote splitting. Maine was clearly Vice President Gore's state. He won 49 percent of the popular vote and was ahead in both of Maine's congressional districts. Therefore, he won all four electors from Maine.

Table 12.1. Maine/Nebraska 2000 Presidential Election

Maine

Cong. Dist.	Bush	Gore	Nader
1	148,618	176,293	20,297
2	137,998	143,658	16,830

Nebraska

Cong. Dist.	Bush	Gore	Nader
1	142,562	86,946	10,085
2	131,485	88,975	8,495
3	159,815	55,859	5,960

Sources: Maine Department of State (http://state.me.us/sos/cec/elec/2000g/gen00p-c.htm); Nebraska Department of State (http://www.sos.state.ne.us/Canvass2000/prescongdist.pdf).

In Nebraska, the opposite occurred. George W. Bush won more than 62 percent of the popular statewide vote and also won in each of Nebraska's congressional districts. Thus he won all of Nebraska's five electoral votes. It is also clear that in Nebraska the candidacy of Ralph Nader made absolutely no difference in the election outcome.

Table 12.2 provides information on the distribution of the electoral votes in 2000 if all states had used split-electoral-vote procedures similar to those in Maine and Nebraska. The effect of this "district plan" would have been 287 electoral votes for Bush. Gore would have received only 251. Bush would have had a margin of 36 electoral votes instead of the 4-vote margin between the two candidates in the actual Electoral College outcome.

With the district plan in place of the winner-take-all electoral system, we see that in the case of the largest state, California, Gore would have received only 35 electoral votes instead of all 54, and Bush would have received 19 instead of none. In Texas, Gore would have won 10 electoral votes, with Bush receiving only 22 instead of all 32 electoral votes in his home state. In Massachusetts, by some measures the most Democratic state in the nation, Democratic candidates won all ten congressional seats while Gore carried the state's twelve electoral votes; thus the effect of a district system would have been the same in Massachusetts. In Pennsylvania and Illinois, Bush would have picked up ten and nine electoral votes respectively. In losses embarrassing to the Democratic Party in Arkansas and Tennessee, home states of Bill Clinton and Al Gore, under the district plan Gore would have picked up two electoral votes in Arkansas and three in Tennessee instead of nothing in either state.

Table 12.2. 2000 Presidential Election by Congressional District

State	House Districts		Senate Seats		District System		Current System	
	Gore	Bush	Gore	Bush	Gore	Bush	Gore	Bush
Alabama	1	6	0	2	1	8	0	9
Alaska	0	1	0	2	0	3	0	3
Arizona	1	5	0	2	1	7	0	8
Arkansas	2	2	0	2	2	4	0	6
California	33	19	2	0	35	19	54	0
Colorado	2	4	0	2	2	6	0	8
Connecticut	6	0	2	0	8	0	8	0
Delaware	1	0	2	0	3	0	3	0
D.C.[a]	1	0	2	0	3	0	3	0
Florida	10	13	0	2	10	15	0	25
Georgia	2	9	0	2	2	11	0	13
Hawaii	2	0	2	0	4	0	4	0
Idaho	0	2	0	2	0	4	0	4
Illinois	11	9	2	0	13	9	22	0
Indiana	2	8	0	2	2	10	0	12
Iowa	2	3	2	0	4	3	7	0
Kansas	0	4	0	2	0	6	0	6
Kentucky	1	5	0	2	1	7	0	8
Louisiana	1	6	0	2	1	8	0	9
Maine	2	0	2	0	4	0	4	0
Maryland	5	3	2	0	7	3	10	0
Massachusetts	10	0	2	0	12	0	12	0
Michigan	9	7	2	0	11	7	18	0
Minnesota	3	5	2	0	5	5	10	0
Mississippi	1	4	0	2	1	6	0	7
Missouri	3	6	0	2	3	8	0	11
Montana	0	1	0	2	0	3	0	3
Nebraska	0	3	0	2	0	5	0	5
Nevada	1	1	0	2	1	3	0	4
New Hampshire	1	1	0	2	1	3	0	4
New Jersey	11	2	2	0	13	2	15	0
New Mexico	2	1	2	0	4	1	5	0
New York	27	4	2	0	29	4	33	0
North Carolina	3	9	0	2	3	11	0	14
North Dakota	0	1	0	2	0	3	0	3
Ohio	8	11	0	2	8	13	0	21
Oklahoma	0	6	0	2	0	8	0	8
Oregon	2	3	2	0	4	3	7	0
Pennsylvania	11	10	2	0	13	10	23	0
Rhode Island	2	0	2	0	4	0	4	0
South Carolina	1	5	0	2	1	7	0	8

State	House Districts		Senate Seats		District System		Current System	
	Gore	Bush	Gore	Bush	Gore	Bush	Gore	Bush
South Dakota	0	1	0	2	0	3	0	3
Tennessee	3	6	0	2	3	8	0	11
Texas	10	20	0	2	10	22	0	32
Utah	0	3	0	2	0	5	0	5
Vermont	1	0	2	0	3	0	3	0
Virginia	3	8	0	2	3	10	0	13
Washington	6	3	2	0	8	3	11	0
West Virginia	1	2	0	2	1	4	0	5
Wisconsin	5	4	2	0	7	4	11	0
Wyoming	0	1	0	2	0	3	0	3
Total	209	227	42	60	251	287	267	271

Source: The Almanac of American Politics, 2002 and author's compilation and calculation.
a. For Electoral College purposes, D.C. is treated as though it had two Senate seats and one congressional district.

Table 12.3. Sweep States in District Plan, 2000

Gore	Bush
Connecticut (8)	Alaska (3)
Delaware (3)	Idaho (4)
D.C. (3)	Kansas (6)
Hawaii (4)	Montana (3)
Maine (4)	Nebraska (5)
Massachusetts (12)	North Dakota (3)
Rhode Island (4)	Oklahoma (8)
Vermont (3)	South Dakota (3)
	Utah (5)
	Wyoming (3)
Total 8 states (41)	10 states (43)

The district plan would have produced no changes from the winner-take-all vote of the present Electoral College in about one-third of the states. Of course, seven states (plus the District of Columbia) have only one congressional district and must always deliver their three electoral votes as a package. But in an additional ten states, as table 12.3 shows, the electoral vote (in parenthesis) all went to one candidate. While slightly more states were solidly Republican, most were small in number of electoral votes. Thus the difference between the two candidates in all the straight-party states (and D.C.) produced a difference of only two electoral votes. There was solid evidence of split-ticket voting in that, in about 18 percent of congressional districts, voters elected a congressman of a different party than their presidential choice.

Retention of the Electoral College

There are many who believe that the Electoral College has outlived its usefulness. For example, Carolyn Jefferson-Jenkins as president of the League of Women Voters noted: "The Electoral College, a curious vestige of the eighteenth century, violates the principle of one man, one vote. The time has come to abolish it."[28] The rationale for establishing the Electoral College is no longer operative today. While this seems to argue for the elimination of the Electoral College, one also has to face reality. It is doubtful that a bill to eliminate the Electoral College would receive a two-thirds vote in both the House and Senate, and even less likely that three-fourths of the states would ratify such an amendment.

Why would Republicans want to eliminate the Electoral College, which gave the 2000 election to George W. Bush even though Gore had more popular votes? While the Democrats are probably not enamored of the Electoral College, they lack a two-thirds advantage in Congress. Many smaller states still feel more comfortable with the Electoral College, as it gives every state, regardless of population, two equal electoral Senate votes. Smaller states apparently believe that, with popular election of the U.S. president, only populous states would be important. Therefore, smaller states would be reluctant to ratify any amendment to abolish the Electoral College and reduce their self-perceived importance.

It has been argued that implementing reforms while keeping the Electoral College in place would be a prudent improvement over the current system by ensuring that every state would be in play, thereby creating an incentive for even greater grassroots activity.[29] Here are some of the arguments:

1. *Double Vote.* With the proposed district electoral vote counting system, a voter would have a double motivation to vote.[30] First, his or her vote would count in the state total for two electoral votes. This individual vote, at present, is diluted by being one of many in the aggregate voter pool. But this same vote would be counted in a congressional district where an individual vote would have more weight. This vote is essential to elect one elector, and every vote counts.

2. *Increased Voter Turnout.* The current electoral system actually depresses

voter turnout. States would be penalized in a popular election for the president if voter turnout were low, but with the winner-take-all feature of the current system, states are not penalized for low voter turnout. Under the present Electoral College system, states have no incentive to increase their voter turnout. With a district plan and greater voter motivation, we might reasonably expect greater voter turnout. It is recognized that other measures could be taken to increase voter interest and turnout, such as a national voting holiday or more free media coverage of elections. But surely a district plan that motivated party voters and independents in congressional districts would be a step forward in increased voter turnout.

3. *Major-Party Voters Whose Candidate Lost.* With the winner-take-all feature of the current Electoral College system, major-party voters who vote for the losing candidate come up empty-handed. They feel their vote did not count —or, worse, that it got converted into a vote for the opposition. Under a district plan, some of these voters might actually see that their votes count. As we previously saw, Republican voters in New York and California would have selected some electors for Bush, while Democratic voters in Texas, Tennessee, and Arkansas would have selected some electors for Gore. The district plan is not perfect—in some "safe" districts within "safe" states, such as Massachusetts, the voter for the underdog party may have no chance of making a difference—but it is far better than the present system in that respect.

4. *Minority Voters.* It has been noted that "[a]mong states that have a black population more than one percent above the national average, blacks are more concentrated in states (principally in the South) that are less favored by the quirks of the Electoral College."[31] In the current Electoral College, black and Hispanic votes are lumped together into the aggregate state total for the winner-take-all electors. Furthermore, these disadvantages are likely to increase with the increase of minority voters. Where minority voters are concentrated in certain congressional districts, a district plan would permit the voters in these districts to select electors of their political persuasion. This would likely result in heavily black districts selecting Democratic electors, as would some Hispanic districts. Other Hispanic districts—Cuban-American districts in Miami—might choose Republican electors. But with a district plan, at least many minority voters would see their vote actually make a difference, whereas in the current system their vote is marginalized.

5. *State/Local Party Rejuvenation.* With the current strategy to win a threshold of states in a national presidential election, state and local parties take a backseat in a national presidential campaign. A district plan to elect the presi-

dent would "spread out the election contest, increasing competition in more states and in more districts within states."[32] Further, a "case could be made, for example, that the district system could potentially energize local and state parties in areas of current weakness, with the added bonus of increased voter participation."[33] With contests in all 435 congressional districts (and D.C.), national presidential candidates would have to rely on local and state parties to help get out the vote for their candidacy. Suddenly these local and state parties would have a important role to play in national elections. Such a scenario could contribute to greater citizen participation.

6. *Election Irregularity.* In the event of irregularities in the vote, the reformed system would afford a remedy more easily than the existing system. Instead of a whole state's electoral vote hanging in the balance, only two electoral votes could be contested at the statewide level. Other electoral votes would be contested in a much smaller geographical area and on a one-to-one basis. (For example, this author is not aware of any congressional district election in 2000 that was contested.) This would likely prevent lagged results in any presidential election. Contested elections would usually have no material effect on the election outcome.

With the Florida 2000 election as an example, assume the state's two Senate electoral votes were contested, along with perhaps three or four House district results. This new total of six electoral votes, even if they were awarded to Gore, would not have changed the election outcome under the proposed counting method (but the popular majority would still have felt robbed).

7. *Unified Government.* With the proposed change in electoral vote allocation, a president would have to carry either a majority of House districts or a majority of states, if not both, to achieve Electoral College victory. This would likely result in the executive and legislative branches being controlled by the same political party, meaning a reduction in divided government and a greater resemblance to the European parliamentary model of democracy, where there is a close electoral relationship between the executive and legislative parts of the government.

In sum, if we concede that direct popular election of the president is not a realistic prospect, there appear to be three alternatives: (1) keep the present Electoral College as is; (2) keep the Electoral College, but count the electoral votes by the district plan; and (3) keep the Electoral College, but count the electoral votes by a proportional plan. No plan is perfect; there does not appear to be any electoral scheme without some defect. Analysis must consider the

Table 12.4. Comparing Electoral Plans

Electoral College	Direct Popular Election	District Plan
Comparative Advantages		
· Status quo. No change required · Historical tradition	· Popular democracy · Victory to candidate with most votes—"first past the post" · Stimulation of voting · Popular mandate	· No constitutional amendment required · Elections localized · State/local political parties emphasized · Each citizen = 2 votes · Citizen interest heightened
Comparative Disadvantages		
· Four misfires to date · Unfaithful electors · Anachronism · Indirect election · Antimajoritarian	· Plurality winner · Constitutional amendment required	· State-by-state implementation · Possible misfires (1960, 2000) · Possible election by Congress (1976) · Possible influence on redistricting
Features That Cut Both Ways		
· Conservative support · Winner-take-all · Small-state advantage	· Democrat/liberal support · Third parties encouraged · Small-state disadvantage	· Republican support · Small-state advantage retained

advantages of each plan and the sum gain of the plans. Table 12.4 presents a summary of these.

Conclusion

There are essentially two ways the district plan could be implemented. More states could adopt the district plan on their own and act as "laboratories of democracy." Any unintended consequences could be observed and noted. If the plan proved successful, it would eventually be adopted by all states.

The second method would involve federal government action. Regardless of which reforms were undertaken, state governments would want federal funds to upgrade election systems. The federal government could make the provision of federal funds conditional upon certain base-level reforms. For example, if the state adopted district-based presidential election voting, the federal funds for election system upgrade would support such a plan, if that is what federal officials preferred; if a state opposed change, no federal funds would be provided for equipment upgrade. It is possible that a large number of states would make the necessary changes in electoral vote counting to receive federal funds for equipment upgrades. Of course, the states would complain of heavy-handedness by the White House or Congress and it is doubtful the White House would act accordingly.

Maine and Nebraska have shown there is an alternative way of counting electoral votes, even though in practice their electoral vote outcome was no different because of it. The citizens of these states seem reasonably content with this system. If additional states adopted the same method, splitting of state electoral votes would likely occur and alter the presidential election system. The current Electoral College has served our country reasonably well for 225-plus years, but not without an occasional problem.

Notes

1. *George W. Bush et al., Petitioners, v. Albert Gore Jr. et al.,* 531 U.S. 949 (2000).
2. *Miami Herald,* special feature, March 11, 2001.
3. Ibid.
4. Ibid.
5. www.rhodescook.com/analysis/2001/stalemate.html.
6. *New York Times,* February 5, 2000.
7. Ibid.
8. Best, *Case Against Direct Election,* 16–17.
9. See *Congressional Quarterly,* December 8, 2000, 989.
10. Wilmerding, *The Electoral College,* 8.
11. Ibid., 4. See also Lutz et al., "Historical and Philosophical Perspective."
12. Peirce, *The People's President,* 40.
13. Ibid.
14. Ibid., 41.
15. Wilmerding, *The Electoral College,* 10.
16. Peirce, *The People's President,* 41.
17. Wilmerding, *The Electoral College,* 4.
18. Ibid. 5.
19. See *Congressional Digest,* January 2001, 1.
20. Schumaker, "Electoral College and Its Alternatives," 28. The Founders supposed that electors would be prominent citizens who would vote for a number of prominent individuals best suited for the office of president. With the introduction of parties, prominent citizens were replaced by party loyalists.

21. *Congressional Digest,* January 2001, 15. See also Lutz et al., "Historical and Philosophical Perspective," 35. More than a thousand proposed amendments to alter the process of presidential selection have been submitted to Congress.

22. Best, *Case Against Direct Election,* 20.

23. Lutz et al., "Historical and Philosophical Perspective," 46.

24. See Wayne in the December 8, 2000, issue of *CQ Researcher.*

25. Melissa Packard, assistant director of elections, Maine, e-mail to author, February 26, 2001.

26. See *Congressional Quarterly,* December 8, 2000, 989.

27. Neal Erickson, assistant secretary of state for elections, Nebraska, e-mail to author, February 10, 2001.

28. Carolyn Jefferson-Jenkins, "League of Women Voters."

29. Gans, "Electoral College Reform," 12.

30. Ibid., 32.

31. Lineberry et al., "Social Cleavages," 165, citing Longley and Braun, *Electoral College Reform,* 158; italics omitted.

32. Haider-Markel et al., "Role of Federalism," 65.

33. Cigler et al., "Changing the Electoral College," 97.

13 □

□

□

The Electoral College

Political Advantage, the Small States, and Implications for Reform

GLENN W. RAINEY JR. AND JANE G. RAINEY,
EASTERN KENTUCKY UNIVERSITY

By almost any standard, the presidential election of 2000 was unusual, dramatic, controversial, and revealing. The drama, however, focused on balloting irregularities in Florida, largely ignoring other matters with broader implications for representational processes and long-term coalition behavior, and for the models and priorities with which political scientists study these phenomena. Foremost among the missing was the role of the Electoral College. To remedy the omission, this chapter defends four basic assertions: (1) Contrary to assumptions in much political science literature, the small states have the advantage in the Electoral College. This was an intentional outcome of the Constitutional Convention, under pressure from the small states themselves. (2) The design of the Electoral College was at least as important as balloting irregularities in determining the outcome of the 2000 election in ways that have potential long-term implications for representative government. (3) Coalitional behavior among states, whether by chance or by design, is a key determinant of electoral outcomes, and coalitions in the 2000 election demonstrate the potential for enduring minority advantage in a geosocially divided nation. (4) A simple and obvious option is available for Electoral College reform to minimize the small state advantage but has been studiously ignored.

The Founders and the Electoral College

As was discussed in the previous chapter, there are a few reasons commonly cited for the Founders' creation of the Electoral College. First was their desire for a strong executive, and their fear that the public of 1787 was not well suited to select one. This was Alexander Hamilton's major justification for the Electoral College in *Federalist 68*, where he argued that it would ensure a "constant probability of seeing the station filled by characters pre-eminent for ability and virtue."[1] The "enlightened elector" idea is routinely cited by Electoral College opponents, who argue that the people are no longer isolated, uninformed, or uneducated, and/or that the system in fact never worked "as it was intended."

The second reason given is checks and balances, presumably secured by an independently elected executive.[2] But the Electoral College was not part of a grand blueprint of checks and balances, although the idea has served its supporters nicely in retrospect. In fact, the convention agonized over a variety of alternatives, including selection of the chief executive by popular vote and selection by the legislature, provoking warnings each time it moved toward the latter. In the words of Gouverneur Morris, the work of the legislature would be that "of intrigue, of cabal, and of faction"[3] and the president should not be hostage to the same. This distrust promoted support for electors who held no public office, and led to the Electoral College.

The third and most problematic reason given is the "federal principle"—placing the Electoral College in a Madisonian master plan to establish a balance between the national government, the states, and the people.[4] The difficulty with this argument is not that federalism is injected into the contemporary debate but that the issue of how to elect the president—so hotly debated and constantly rehashed at the Convention—is elevated to an overarching principle. In reality, there is so little Madisonian thought embedded in the origins of the Electoral College that Charles C. Thach Jr. noted in his study of the creation of the presidency, "Madison has with much justice been called the father of the Constitution. But the claims entered for his paternity do not extend to the fundamentals of Article II."[5]

In actuality, the Electoral College was a product of the large-state/small-state struggle for power and dominance—the same struggle that produced the Connecticut Compromise, the core of the federal idea. That victory only whetted the small states' appetites for power, and they escalated their demands. Gunning Bedford of Delaware even threatened to invite foreign intervention: "The large states dare not dissolve the Confederation. If they do, the smaller ones will find some foreign ally of more honor and good faith, who will take them by the hand

and do them justice."[6] Roger Sherman of Connecticut, fearing that larger states would not only control the national legislature but also dominate the selection of president, set for himself the antimajoritarian goal of reducing the advantage of their numbers.[7] He rationalized his position with such elitist statements as: "The small States have more vigor in their Govts than the large ones, the more influence therefore the large ones have, the weaker will be the Govt."[8]

The Electoral College was one of the small states' great payoffs, but its originator, ironically, was a large-state delegate, James Wilson of Pennsylvania. Wilson first called for popular election to underpin his concept of a national executive flowing from the people. Sentiment against this was strong, so he then proposed an electoral college with an elector from each district of the lower house chosen by the voters of that district.[9] This idea was soundly defeated, with only Maryland and Pennsylvania endorsing it. Thach observed, "The Maryland vote was determined by a belief that the small states stood a better chance in an electoral college than in the legislature. This is purely inferential, but at a later time the other small states saw the matter in the same light."[10]

The delegates debated multiple proposals for choosing a president—election by the people, by state governors, by a group from Congress, or by independently selected electors—and rejected all of them. Whether states would be given equal votes or proportional votes added further divisiveness over several proposals. The plan finally adopted after weeks of debate and appointment of an ad hoc committee was an electoral college of independent electors selected by states based on the sum of each state's representatives and its two senators (the "constant two") plus a contingency plan: if no candidate received a majority, selection would be by the House with one vote per state.[11]

The delegates were struggling to some degree with the unknown in finding the means to nominate and elect candidates for national office. They had to find consensus to produce a document with enough attractions for all to make it play well in the states. Concessions to the small states were only some of the expedient arrangements necessary to gain acceptance of the new constitution.[12] Since modern representative democracy did not exist, the small-state bias probably seemed unremarkable.[13] Moreover, the delegates were confined by circumstances. Sent to the Constitutional Convention by states to revise the Articles of Confederation, they voted in the convention by states, and states would have to approve their work. In short, federalism was an inescapable political fact of life. The Electoral College was a practical instrument to help facilitate agreement at the convention. The "federal principle" was nothing more than a golden calf begat by a huge cow of political expediency, and not a grand design for the Constitution.

Although convention delegates were proud of their electoral creation, it soon became controversial.[14] By 1796, with "slates" of electors already appearing, criticism erupted in New York against a Federalist elector who decided to vote for Thomas Jefferson instead of John Adams.[15] Controversy next centered on the disruption, conflict, and connivance caused when no candidate received a majority of the electoral vote in the elections of 1800 and 1824. As political parties developed, the Electoral College also evolved, as states adopted the "unit vote" or winner-take-all system in which all of a state's electoral votes went to the electors pledged to the candidate winning the most votes in that state.[16] The intent was to maximize a state's impact on the overall results. This plus the eventual universal selection of electors by popular vote raised new representational issues. One involved the "misfired election," in which a president would win in the Electoral College but lose the popular vote. This can happen in at least two ways: (1) The unit vote creates a "magnifier" or "multiplier" effect.[17] Winning enough states with low turnouts confers victory even if an opponent wins states with fewer electors but higher turnouts, since victory is determined by the number of electors, not by popular vote. Large states, of course, are particularly able to provide large blocs of electors on the basis of relatively low popular pluralities. The winning candidate can have less than a majority of a low turnout, and still win all of a state's electors. (2) The "constant two" allows a candidate to win the election by winning large numbers of small states with their disproportionate advantage in electoral votes, while the loser wins the popular vote but carries fewer but larger states.

Another representational issue, more common than the misfired election, involves proportion in victory. A candidate may win the popular vote by a modest plurality, but do so in many states, thereby carrying all of the electoral votes in those states and winning by a large margin in the Electoral College without a popular majority. During the post–Civil War period, this occurred in 1892, 1912, 1916, 1948, almost certainly 1960, 1968, 1992, and 1996.[18] Perhaps most dramatic was 1912, when Theodore Roosevelt and William Howard Taft together won more popular votes than Woodrow Wilson, but Wilson won the electoral vote 435 to 96. Disparities in the Electoral College representation grew with westward expansion and urbanization, since the ratio of representation between the largest and smallest states in the Electoral College grew correspondingly. In 1792 the largest state, Virginia, chose twenty-one electors, while the smallest states, Vermont and Delaware, chose three each, a ratio of seven to one. In 2000 California chose fifty-four electors, compared to three each for seven other states and the District of Columbia, a ratio of eighteen to one in favor of California compared to each smaller state. Yet demographic change has not erased the constant-two advantage for small states and may have amplified it. Based on 1990 census data, which governed the 2000 election, the largest nine states contained 128,859,757 people, or 52 percent of the total U.S. population of 248,709,073, but elected only 243 or 45 percent of the 538 electors.[19] The 453,588 people of Wyoming had three electors—one for every 151,196 people. California's 29,760,021 inhabitants chose fifty-four electors, one for every 551,111 people. With 100 Senate-based electors, if a candidate wins by more than 100 electoral votes, the constant-two advantage makes no difference, but the constant-two advantage gives small states a decisive influence in a close election if many small states vote for the same candidate.

Small-State Advantage

Assessing the effects of this advantage requires a means of comparing election outcomes with and without these bonus votes. This can be done by comparing the 2000 Electoral College apportionment to one without the constant-two votes—that is, to assume a number of electors based on a state's House membership only (retaining the unit vote). Such an Electoral College would, like the House itself, be largely but not entirely based on population. Since the Constitution guarantees each state at least one representative, states with total populations smaller than an average House district will be somewhat overrepresented. Rounding for population differences among states causes some states to be slightly over- or underrepresented.

Table 13.1 shows the different outcomes in four elections with close electoral votes, using the two approaches. In the controversial election of 1876, Rutherford B. Hayes "won" twenty-one states and 185 electoral votes (four states were contested but were later awarded to Hayes by a highly partisan commission). Samuel J. Tilden won only 184 electoral votes from seventeen states, while winning the popular vote 4,300,590 to 4,036,298. Without the "constant two," Tilden would have won 150 electoral votes to 143 for Hayes, changing the outcome of the election (unless the Republican Party had stolen another state for Hayes).

In the 1888 election, Grover Cleveland won the popular vote 5,540,309 to 5,439,853, but lost the electoral vote with 168 to Benjamin Harrison's 233. The states were almost evenly divided, with Harrison winning twenty to Cleveland's

Table 13.1. Impact of "Constant Two" Rule on Four Close Elections

Year	Candidate	Popular Vote	States Won	Electoral Votes	Electoral Votes Minus 2/State	Outcome Affected?
1876	Hayes	4,036,298	21	185	143	Yes
	Tilden	4,300,590	17	184	150	Yes
1888	Harrison	5,439,853	20	233	193	No
	Cleveland	5,540,309	18	168	132	No
1916	Wilson	9,129,606	31	277	215	Yes
	Hughes	8,538,221	18	254	218	Yes
2000	Bush	50,456,062	30	271	211	Yes
	Gore	50,996,582	21[a]	267	225	Yes

Source: National Archives and Records Administration, http://www.archives.gov/federal_register/electoral_college/scores.html.
[a]Includes D.C.

eighteen. Removal of the Senate-based electors would therefore leave Harrison with 193 and Cleveland with 132, producing no change in the outcome. In a third close race, in 1916, Woodrow Wilson won the popular vote over Charles Evans Hughes 9,129,606 to 8,538,221, and won 277 electoral votes to 254 for Hughes, but Wilson also won thirty-one states compared to eighteen for Hughes. Removal of the Senate-based electors in this case would have left Wilson with 215 electoral votes to 218 for Hughes, creating a "misfired" election and making Hughes a minority president by a very slim margin. The influence of the small-state advantage was evident, nonetheless: Hughes won the three largest states in the Union at the time—New York, Illinois, and Pennsylvania—and still lost the election.

Apart from these exceptions, the post–Civil War Electoral College showed great consistency. The victor typically won at least a plurality of the popular vote and a substantial majority in the Electoral College. States often voted in regional blocs, but it was not until 2000 that the nation split between one bloc of predominantly large states and another of predominantly smaller ones, the two blocs appearing as well to reflect national social and economic cleavages.

In recent decades, political scientists have taken representational differences and anomalies in Electoral College outcomes as the point of departure to analyze relative advantages of large and small states. In doing so, they have tended to equate small-state advantage with the constant-two provision, while the argument for large-state advantage focused primarily on the "magnifier effect" resulting from the unit-vote system and on anecdotal references to campaign priorities. *Large* here refers to the nine states that, by the 1990 census, contain a majority of the population; *small* means the remainder, which may benefit from the constant-two rule.

There has been a substantial body of argument that the largest states and their voters enjoy a sizable advantage over the smaller states. This view is supported in part by inferences from campaign practices—campaigns spending more time and effort on large states—and in part by mathematical models such as "voting power" analysis. Applying game theory and simplifying assumptions, voting power analysis generates a normalized index used to compare the ability of a citizen *within* a state to play a pivotal role in a presidential election. The index is based on (1) the chance that *each* state has of casting the deciding block of electoral votes in a fifty-one person "game" (fifty states plus D.C.), and (2) the proportion of voting combinations within *each* state in which a citizen can alter the outcome in *that* state. The results have been used to argue that citizens of large states have substantially greater power over outcomes than citizens of smaller states—except for the very smallest states, in which the overrepresentation in the Electoral College is presumably so great that their voters can throw their three electors back and forth with exceptional impact. Such analysis suggests that states of intermediate size, having about four to fourteen electoral votes, are really the most disadvantaged of all.[20]

In the presidential election of 2000, however, it was the small states that clearly enjoyed a decisive advantage. For the first time since 1888, the popular-vote winner lost the electoral vote. This election also witnessed a dramatic confluence of social, political, economic, and geographical divisions in the vote for president that put the small states in the spotlight. Al Gore lost the election because George W. Bush won more small states, which were proportionately overrepresented in the Electoral College. If the Senate-based electors had been removed from the count, reducing the electoral vote of every state and the District of Columbia by two, Gore would have received 225 and Bush 211, as shown in table 13.3.[21] Note that if any one of the smallest Bush states had shifted its three electoral votes to Gore, Gore would have won the election under the current system.

Voting Power Analysis Reconsidered

The unmistakable collective power of the small states in the 2000 election has encouraged reexamination of their presumed disadvantage. Graphic regional alignments in the election have led to speculation about a potentially enduring convergence of geographic regions with political and cultural attitudes—an emergent geosocial cleavage in America.

The evidence from voting power analysis must be reconsidered in light of the severe shortcomings in the underlying model. The technique's creators warned from the beginning that it incorporates assumptions that "the players [the states] all be independent agents, free from prior commitments and uninfluenced by considerations outside the stated objectives of the game."[22] Coalition behavior is neglected. Rather, the influence of each state is measured independently of other states. Given past history, this is an unrealistic assumption. Moreover, interstate coalitions may emerge spontaneously from mutual interests or because political leaders recognize such real or potential combinations and seek to orchestrate them. Voting power analysis has suffered from superficial conceptual and operational specification.[23] For example, population has been incorporated as a key variable in two different locations in the model: (1) one in determining the relative influence of a voter in a state, and (2) again when states are compared in terms of their electoral vote blocks. But the approach then assumes that population has no independent effect on election outcomes —that a state's advantage is entirely reflected in its ability to move a block of electors from one candidate to another.

State populations will in fact have powerful, direct effects on campaigns and election outcomes under almost any moderately equitable system of representation, and the political importance of large state populations is not just an artifact of the unit vote or magnifier effect. If direct popular election were used, a candidate who won by a given margin in a single state with ten million voters would gain more ground on opponents than if he or she won by the same margin in nine smaller states with one million voters each. So-called proportional reforms and district-based reforms mimic direct reliance on the popular vote by allocating electoral votes on the basis of popular vote or among districts within states, thus implicitly overcoming the presumed advantage that big states reap from the unit vote by forcing them to divide their electors between candidates. The equity promised is largely a sham, since (1) all but two of the states use the unit vote and would lose some of its effects; (2) it is usually proposed that the "constant two" be kept as part of the proportional allocation or given to the candidate that wins a state under a district system (a unit vote rule); and (3) the smallest states would continue under some of these proposals to award their House-based elector entirely to the popular vote winner (also a unit vote rule). The varied nuances in the design of these plans such as rounding rules, use of the "constant two," or voting by congressional districts are too complex to be examined here but the fundamental principles are solid: Unless a system of lopsided minority privilege is adopted, states with large populations will have large shares of representation and presidential candidates will know it. But if the small states act as a coalition under the present system, they have an undemocratic advantage against the large ones.

These weaknesses in voting power analysis have resulted in unstable findings and interpretations. For example, Mann and Shapely concluded that the "bias in favor of bigness" was "definitely visible" in their findings, but was "not large enough to be very significant as a practical matter." They further concluded that it was not "a significant counteragent" to the small-state advantage.[24] But Longley and Peirce later argued that "voters in the nine largest states have a disproportionately large relative voting power"[25] and "the advantage that citizens in the most populous state enjoy solely because of their place of residence is as great as 72 percent"—presumably a 72 percent higher voting power index.[26]

The election of 2000 spurred reexamination of voting power analysis and its assumptions. Gelman and Katz extended mathematical modeling to some aspects of coalition behavior.[27] But their approach continues the strained assumption that voting must be treated as an exclusively individual attribute —the voter's individual potential to cast the decisive vote in an election. Participation in coalitions is essentially an additive phenomenon in this approach, and the conditions that modify individual voting power include the closeness of elections and the likelihood that the voter's own state will be decisive. For example, Gelman and Katz say that in the 2000 election voters in California, Texas, and New York "had little chance of influencing the outcome" because the elections in those states were not close, and the chance that any one individual might have cast a decisive vote was therefore small.[28] This logic ignores the fact that the winning voters in those states had ensured the delivery of large blocks of electoral votes by forming large coalitions. It assumes instead that voters who form large, decisive coalitions are weaker for having done so. Nonetheless, results from the modified model led Gelman and Katz to essentially vacate the small-state advantage.

Attributions of large-state advantages based on candidate behavior also reflect simplistic modeling of cause and effect. For example, large states have been said to be advantaged because candidates spend disproportionate amounts of time campaigning in them, pay more attention to the parochial interests of large states, and ignore states that are already "decided."[29] But states with large populations attract candidates anyway because, of course, they have large shares of

representation. Politicians always couch political appeals heavily in local interests. And basic political strategy emphasizes investment of resources in undecided areas and the capture of swing votes, in any type of election. It is unclear
how the Electoral College might have amplified these behaviors, but it certainly
did not create them.

Evidence of a Voting Cleavage

Coalitions among states were also dramatically evident in the 2000 election.
Table 13.2 compares the outcomes across six regions of the United States as
divided by *Congressional Quarterly* on the basis of "shared background, economy, and tradition."[30] Bush carried all Southern and Plains states and all but one
Mountain state. Gore carried all states in the East but New Hampshire, and all
Pacific states. Only the Midwest was significantly divided, with Gore carrying
five states and Bush three.

The media dramatized Election 2000 as a potential watershed in regional
political and social cleavage. A widely circulated map of county-by-county
presidential vote results showing Bush's victories in red and Gore's in blue
pointedly demonstrated Bush's geographic electoral dominance, with victories
in thirty states, sweeping down from Montana to Texas, and then east through
the entire South from Kentucky down to (and eventually including) Florida,
forming a rough L-shape. Gore's blue areas appear as minor splotches concentrated in the Northeast, the Midwest, and the West Coast, including only twenty
states and the District of Columbia.[31] In fact, these splotches include most of the

Table 13.2. *Congressional Quarterly* Regions in 2000 Presidential Election

"South"	Alabama, Arkansas, Florida, Georgia, Kentucky, Louisiana, Mississippi, North Carolina, Oklahoma, South Carolina, Tennessee, Texas, Virginia, West Virginia
"East"	CONNECTICUT, DELAWARE, D.C., MAINE, MARYLAND, MASSACHUSETTS, New Hampshire, NEW JERSEY, NEW YORK, PENNSYLVANIA, RHODE ISLAND, VERMONT
"Midwest"	ILLINOIS, Indiana, IOWA, MICHIGAN, MINNESOTA, Missouri, Ohio, WISCONSIN
"Plains"	Kansas, Nebraska, North Dakota, South Dakota
"Mountain"	Alaska, Arizona, Colorado, Idaho, Montana, Nevada, NEW MEXICO, Utah, Wyoming
"Pacific"	CALIFORNIA, HAWAII, OREGON, WASHINGTON

Note: States in caps were won by Gore; all others were won by Bush.

metropolitan centers in which most Americans live, which is why Gore won the popular vote by more than 500,000 votes. Without Ralph Nader in the race, Gore would probably have achieved an even larger margin, perhaps winning the Electoral College.

The press found that these geographic divisions closely followed lines of social and economic stratification in society, suggesting "two separate Americas, each suspicious of the other, each protecting its way of life."[32] Gore's supporters were more likely than Bush's to be drawn from certain groups: low income, urban, working class, black, less educated, pro-abortion rights, pro-gun control. The "L" that is Bush country was dramatically obvious in 2000, but it had been gradually emerging in races for Congress and state governorships.[33]

Political scientists have reported their own findings of sustained regional cleavages in attitudes and behavior. Sears and Valentino concluded that the Republican political base is strongly supplemented by fundamentalist religious attitudes and also, especially in the South, by symbolic racism.[34] In a comparative analysis, Andersen and Heath argued that region is a more meaningful unit of analysis than country, in part because voting behavior is shaped by regional conditions.[35] If such attitudinal cleavages align systematically with political advantages, including the small-state advantages in the Senate and Electoral College, and therefore with regions and states, they may become the basis for a sustained confrontation between a majority and a minority faction, with the "L" cleavage dividing the United States socially, geographically, and politically. Since this cleavage also tends to pit the small Mountain, Plains, and Southern states against the large East and West Coast states, the Electoral College might become a significant weapon for the small states in a confrontation.

Whether the election of 2000 represents a major escalation of the "era of ill feelings"[36] from "razor-thin margins" in elections and associated partisan bitterness into a sustained regional confrontation remains to be seen. The election of 2000 was not a wholesale takeover of the United States; the executive was seized by a minority coalition, aided by an Electoral College advantage. The immediate impact has been to confer additional control over specific policies on the minority coalition.

Republicans have justified the outcome on the basis that the Electoral College is the way it is, and have offered some transparently strained arguments to defend their victory.[37] The media refer matter-of-factly to a red-zone/blue-zone dimension in executive policy and to its tendency to benefit red-zone states.[38] However, a sustained regional confrontation would require durable red-zone/

blue-zone coalitions and sustained, politically salient differences between them.

Legitimacy and reform are still important issues, of course. Bias in the Electoral College affects both the legitimacy with which executive authority is conferred and the conditions for interstate relations and potential regional confrontation. Moreover, the resulting sense of grievance may be exacerbated when an executive who is elected by questionable means imposes policies and dispenses favors notably different from those that would be expected of a losing candidate with a more legitimate claim.

The Bush administration has developed a policy profile that includes a rather obvious commitment to serving the interests of business and wealthy individuals, construed in self-aggrandizing terms. Examples have included de-emphasis on regulation or enforced responsibility in areas ranging from the environment to financial markets and corporate governance, as well as tax benefits and subsidies targeted at wealthy interests and large businesses. These have been linked to pre-9/11 rejection of specific cooperative efforts in foreign relations, among them the global warming treaty. The critical media commentary on these policies appears to have a basis in fact.[39] While it is not possible to know with certainty exactly how a Gore administration would have differed, Democratic presidents have historically not been so openly supportive of antiregulatory policies, upper-class tax benefits, and unilateralism in foreign policy.

Evidence for enduring red-zone/blue-zone coalitions and policy confrontation must inevitably be very speculative at this time. As Andersen and Heath observed, attitudes are not always reflected in votes, and therefore may not influence specific policies.[40] To further explore red-zone/blue-zone differences that might be expected to generate a sustained cleavage, the Bush states and the Gore states were compared on basic dimensions of social, environmental, and fiscal problems and policy. Dimensions of social policies and problems chosen for comparison included their willingness to contribute to social assistance programs, their spending on intellectual capital such as education, arts, and libraries, and their contributions to environmental problems. Economic and fiscal policies were examined in terms of economic productivity, relative tax effort and contributions, and relative draw-down on federal funding.

The social dimensions were operationalized as: state versus federal share of welfare and Medicaid costs; spending on education, the arts, and libraries; per capita toxic chemical releases; number of hazardous waste sites; and relative amount of pollution discharge into air and water. As shown in table 13.3, the Bush states included twenty-two (73 percent) in which federal funds provided

Table 13.3. Attributes of States Won by Gore and by Bush

Social Policy Attributes

	Gore	Bush	Total
Federal share of welfare and Medicaid, FY 2000, number of states > 60%	6 (29%)	23 (77%)	29
State and local education spending as % of personal income, FY 1999, number of states > median of 6.9%	9 (43%)	16 (53%)	25
Per capita spending on arts, FY 1998, number of states > median of $0.78	13 (62%)	12 (40%)	25
Total library operating expenditure per capita, FY 1998, number of states > median of $19.70	15 (71%)	11 (37%)	26
Toxic chemical release per capita, FY 1999, number of states > median of 16.3 pounds	4 (19%)	21 (70%)	25
Hazardous waste sites per million population, FY 2000, number of states > U.S. average of 4.77	13 (62%)	11 (37%)	24
Air pollution emissions per capita, FY 1999, number of states > U.S. average of 0.7 short tons	6 (29%)	22 (73%)	28
Surface water pollution discharge, FY 1997, number of states in top 25[a]	6 (30%)	16 (55%)	22

Wealth/Federal Contributors/Receipts

State Attributes	Gore	Bush	Total
Total of gross state products in trillions, 1999	$5.051	$4.258	$9.309
Federal personal income tax liability (in $ billions, 1999)	$523.66	$387.85	$911.51
Patents issued/100,000 pop., states > U.S. average, 2000	14 (67%)	5 (17%)	19
States w/ net gain in fed. spending over taxes paid, 2000	9 (43%)	22 (73%)	31
State/local revenue as % of personal income, 1999, number of states > U.S. average	15 (71%)	9 (30%)	24
State/local "tax effort" as % of national average tax rate, 1996, number of states > 100%	14 (67%)	2 (7%)	16

"Pork Fund" Rankings

Candidate Attributes	Gore States	Bush States
# in top 25 (2000)	6 (29%)	19 (63%)
# in top 25 (2001)	7 (33%)	18 (60%)

Sources: Wealth/Federal Contributors/Receipts: Hovey and Hovey, *CQ's State Fact Finder, 1999* and *CQ's State Fact Finder, 2002.* "Pork Fund" Rankings: Citizens Against Government Waste, http://publications.cagw.org/publications/pigbook/pigbook.php3?pigyear=00 and http://publications.cagw.org/publications/pigbook/pigbook.php3?pigyear=01.

a. Data unavailable for Kansas (won by Bush) and District of Columbia (won by Gore).

60 percent or more of the funding for welfare and Medicaid, compared to six (29 percent) of those won by Gore. Fewer Gore states were above the median in percent of personal income spent on education, but proportionately more were above the median in spending on the arts and on libraries. Many more Bush states showed high levels of toxic chemical release and of air and water pollution emissions; however, the number of states with hazardous waste sites tended in the opposite direction—thirteen (62 percent of his total) won by Gore compared to eleven (37 percent of his total) for Bush.[41]

State wealth and contributions to the federal system were operationalized as state gross product, relative output in patents, federal personal income taxes paid, net gain or loss in federal spending in a state versus federal taxes paid, state and local tax effort expressed as a percentage of a national index average of tax rates, state and local tax revenue as a percentage of personal income, and whether a state was highly ranked as a recipient of federal special projects ("pork" spending), as measured by the self-styled watchdog group Citizens Against Government Waste. The results are also shown in table 13.3.

Of the total gross state products of $9.309 trillion produced in 1999, the twenty states and the District of Columbia won by Gore produced $5.051 trillion, while the thirty states won by Bush produced $4.258 trillion. Of the $911.51 billion in federal personal income taxes paid in 1999, the Gore states and the District of Columbia paid $523.66 billion, while the Bush states paid $387.85 billion. A much larger proportion of the Gore states (67 percent) than of the Bush states (17 percent) are high producers of patents, implying technological and productivity advantages in the Gore states. Yet the states won by Bush are disproportionately the beneficiaries of federal spending. When federal spending in the states is expressed as the ratio of dollars spent to dollars of federal taxes paid, a ratio greater than one indicates that a state has been experiencing a net gain. In 2000, twenty-two of the thirty Bush states had such ratios, compared to nine of the twenty Gore states and D.C. In the aggregate, the relative federal draw-down by the Bush states is matched to lower state and local tax efforts. Fifteen of the Gore states (71 percent) were above the median in taxes collected as a percentage of personal income, compared to nine (30 percent) of the Bush states. Comparison on the basis of a "tax effort" index was even more lopsided, with fourteen of the Gore states being above the national benchmark in tax effort, compared to two of the Bush states.[42] Moreover, Bush states benefited disproportionately from "pork" spending. As table 13.3 indicates, at least 60 percent of the (mostly smaller) states won by Bush ranked in the top twenty-five jurisdictions in receipts of pork in both fiscal years 2000 and 2001.

Results and Reforms

These tentative comparisons suggest extensive differences in policy orienta-
tions between the Bush and Gore states. The two groups differ dramatically on
nearly all dimensions explored. Whatever the reasons for the pronounced disparities—whether enlightened national response to social and economic disadvantage in rural states or hypocritical looting of the federal treasury by self-
styled small-government conservatives—there is substantial evidence that the
Bush states draw down on wealth generated in the Gore states. James Madison
warned that conflict over property is the most virulent source of the vices of
faction. The interstate cleavage of the 2000 election, if lasting, might lead to
regional confrontation, fueled by the small states' ability to repeatedly exploit
their Electoral College advantage against the interests of the large states.

Should such a sustained expression of minority advantage actually emerge
through a small-state coalition, it would be hard to offset, since it would be
based on bias in the Constitution itself and could be corrected only by amending the Constitution or circumventing it. Madison defended the Constitution
in *Federalist 10* by arguing that minority factions would be inherently untenable in the face of the republican principle of popular elections.[43] Tyranny by
a majority, a more vexing problem, would be remedied by a large republic, in
which multiple social and regional divisions would make stable and enduring
majorities untenable as well. The election of 2000 reminds us that the application of the republican principle in the Constitution may be flawed. Unless
it can be shown that relatively large, stable minorities are also untenable, the
danger of a minority tyranny may loom rather larger than Madison suggested.

It is certainly possible that the particular coalition that elected George W.
Bush in 2000 will not endure. It is composed of multiple interests among
which there are significant fault lines—working-class moral and religious
conservatives, wealthy and middle-class business interests, self-styled "rug-
ged independents," and antigovernment ideologues, to name a few. The geographical, political, cultural, and economic dimensions of the coalition are
hardly isomorphic. Even so, a misfired election is surrounded by the penumbra
of leaders and policies illegitimately imposed, and hints at the tyranny Madison
hoped to avert. The controversies over the election of 2000 have, to some extent,
reactivated discussion over Electoral College reform. So far, there has only been
discussion and there is little evidence of serious reform. Were such to emerge,
it would probably fail in part because reform raises daunting issues of democratic values and institutional constraints.

For example, values cited as desirable in an electoral system include: (1) simplicity (does it make sense to the voters?), (2) fair representation (does it meet the "one person, one vote" criterion?), (3) legitimacy (does it result in a winner who is recognized as the rightful leader?), (4) the federal principle (does it preserve a special role for the states?), (5) stability (does it prevent the rise of "splinter parties" with their risk of legislative obstructionism?), (6) majority rule (can the winner claim a majoritarian mandate?), (7) original intent (is the system faithful to the views of the Framers?), (8) minority rights (does it give a fair voice to minority views?), (9) practicality (will it add cost or length to the process?), and (10) voter-friendliness (will it encourage voter turnout?). It is hard to dismiss any of these as inappropriate considerations; it is impossible to construct an electoral system that gives equal weight to them all.[44]

Advocates of reform often base their preferences on questionable assumptions. The federal principle is one such "matter of faith." However, other countries with federal systems have not seen the need to copy the Electoral College. Another nondebatable issue for some is the sanctity of the two-party system and avoidance of any reform that might promote a multiparty system. Yet a multiparty system can be as defensible as a two-party system as a vehicle for allowing adequate representation. Finally, for some, quantifiably fair representation is a given. While it is hard to disagree with the ideal of fairness, mathematical equality does not guarantee it and proposals to implement fairness often run into practical roadblocks.

Proposed reforms fall into two categories—those that involve amending the Constitution and those that do not. The latter are probably more feasible, since the Constitution requires action by three-fourths of the states to ratify amendments. Enough states would find self-interest in maintaining the present system that ratification would be difficult or impossible. Some internal reforms, not needing a constitutional amendment, can be made by individual states, but states are not likely to jump on the bandwagon of change (assuming there is one), and starting a bandwagon is harder, unless they see themselves disadvantaged by not doing so. Proponents of reform have tried to assess possible effects on party development, campaigning, and other parts of the political process, but no one can predict these with certainty. That in itself is no reason to avoid change. Some scholars have gone to great imaginative length to think of every possible worst-case scenario under the present system, including many that have never happened.[45] Others have cataloged the potential ills of proposed changes.[46] Still the Constitution is an organic whole, and change in one part may lead to pressure to change other parts.[47]

Among the most popular proposals to correct the disadvantages variously attributed to the Electoral College is direct election of the president, of which there are several variations. This is the most popular replacement for the Electoral College, despite its abandonment of the federal principle. It was the preference of 61 percent of Americans in a November 2001 poll.[48] It looks democratic and easy to understand. Every vote counts equally, and the winner of the popular vote would always be president. Its proponents argue that it would promote more campaign attention to small states. However, to attract candidates, a small state would have to promise the potential of a larger winning margin than a large state would provide.[49] Would a candidate really forsake California to campaign in Alaska? The fact is that in the 2000 election, direct popular vote would have helped the large states elect Al Gore.

Modern elections typically produce plurality victories—the popular-vote winner receives the most but less than a majority of the votes, meaning that more than half the population voted for the opposition. In a direct popular vote election, this might cause legitimacy problems. The following variations have tried to address some of these issues: (1) A direct popular vote with a runoff if there is no majority on the first ballot offers a clear winner with a majority of votes cast. However, runoffs generally have lower voter turnouts and lengthen an already long and costly campaign. (2) A popular vote with only a 40 percent victory needed to avoid a runoff makes a runoff election less likely. Yet there is no particular rationale for 40 percent, the threshold most often mentioned. A 41 percent victor wins with closer to a third than a majority of votes, raising questions of legitimacy, representational fairness, and majority rule. (3) In the "instant runoff" voting method, voters rank candidates, and votes are redistributed if there is no majority winner. This avoids a runoff while insuring majority support, but its critics say, perhaps unfairly, that it is too complex for American voters to grasp.

Proposals to keep but reform the Electoral College all share an attempt to link the electoral vote more closely to the popular vote and to attack the presumed large-state advantage of the unit vote. All avoid the issue of small-state electoral power and, as the following overview shows, none is without flaws: (1) The "automatic plan" would eliminate electors but retain the electoral vote, assigning each state's votes directly to the candidate on the basis of the popular vote. Elections would look more population-based, and worries about a "faithless elector" who chooses not to vote for his or her state's popular-vote winner would be eliminated. However, inequitable representation of state populations is retained, and the "faithless elector" has not been a real threat.[50] 2) The "proportional plan" mentioned earlier divides each state's electoral vote among the candidates in proportion to their shares of the popular vote, to create a closer approximation of the popular will. However, it requires decisions about how to round off and distribute electoral votes. Moreover, manipulating the Electoral College to assure near-certain victory for the popular-vote winner reduces the Electoral College to a mere smoke screen and offers no rational justification for this plan over a direct popular vote.[51] 3) The "national bonus plan" keeps the Electoral College but awards 102 "bonus" votes to the popular-vote winner, making a misfired election next to impossible. Seemingly designed for people who rationally reject the Electoral College but emotionally cannot let go of it, this plan looks even more contrived than the proportional plan.[52] 4) In the "district plan," voters in each House district choose one elector on a winner-take-all basis; the constant-two votes go to the winner of the popular vote statewide. This lets people feel closer to "their" elector. It does not eliminate the current antidemocratic bias. Also, presidential outcomes could be affected by the politics affecting decennial redrawing of congressional districts by state legislatures.

One reform possibility has been conspicuously absent from the debate— James Wilson's proposal at the Constitutional Convention. Elimination of the "constant two," leaving an Electoral College based on House seats alone, might offer a compromise between Electoral College supporters and popular-vote advocates. The persistent refusal to address the constant-two bias in reform proposals is noteworthy because the problem is so obvious and, at least in a constitutional sense, easy to reform. Yet our research has uncovered no public proposal to eliminate this bias until Representative Frank Horton of New York in 1969 included it as part of a version of the proportional plan that, apparently, received little support.[53]

Therefore, we offer for consideration what we shall call the "neo-Wilson plan." It is "neo" because it would retain the traditional and current practice of slates of electors pledged to the popular-vote winners within states, whereas Wilson's proposal was in the context of unpledged electors. It is not the Horton plan, which would have divided the electoral votes on the basis of the popular vote. The neo-Wilson plan has many positive attributes. The change required in the Constitution is simple. A proposed amendment could read: "The Electors appointed by each state to elect the President shall be equal to the whole Number of Representatives to which the State may be entitled in the House of Representatives." The plan would add no new complexities. It would keep the unit vote and the magnifier effect. It would provide symbolic legitimacy with an electoral college based almost exclusively on population, while guaranteeing the smallest states one elector each, in service to the federal principle. It would still require a majority of votes (219) to win, and would produce fewer elections in which the winner lost the popular vote. It would deliver clear "mandates" through decisive electoral college victories, but they would be much less exaggerated than in the current system.[54] A misfired election would be possible, but less likely.

The neo-Wilson plan would continue to protect geographical minorities yet would weaken the current bias favoring number of square miles over number of people.[55] It would promote a two-party system but could mollify groups that feel marginalized under the current system as well as those who would feel marginalized without it. Nationwide, it would more accurately reflect each party's strength at the polls. It would not aid minor parties; however, no currently proposed reform plans are likely to produce miracles for minor parties. By weakening but not eliminating the small-state advantage, it would mean less of a shift in parties' campaign strategies than would direct popular elections with their greater emphasis on large population centers. Finally, it could decrease discord and promote compromise among the "red" and "blue" states.[56]

The neo-Wilson plan is as legitimate as any other and is attractive for what it would not do as well as what it would do. Other than the loss of the bonus votes for small states, it adds no negative outcomes to the present system. It could bring the country closer to majoritarian principles without the risks of direct popular vote. It does not embody a grandiose principle of democracy, but its appearance of pragmatism and compromise is very appealing. If public opinion and political circumstances should conspire to make it harder for small states to cling to their 1787 victory, the neo-Wilson plan could be their new bargaining chip. It continues to be excluded from the reform debate but belongs on the table for discussion by political scientists.

Conclusion

This chapter points to a need for further study and consideration by political scientists, elections administrators, and election reformers of four issues: (1) It is past time to abandon the notion of a meaningful large-state advantage in presidential elections beyond the simple fact that more people live in large states. Even the magnifier effect is, arguably, an illusion, since the voters who thereby deliver a large block of electors to a candidate do so on behalf of a large population. The fact is that small states are intentionally advantaged by the Electoral College. (2) To remain useful, voting power analysis needs more refinement. Further correction is needed in the incomplete causal modeling that confuses the separate effects of population with those of the Electoral College as an institution, and the modeling of coalition behavior needs to be enhanced to incorporate the effects of interjurisdictional coalitions (states). (3) Political scholars could offer more comparative perspective to the analysis of electoral reform to help assess the real risks and dangers in adopting institutional reforms. As other nations have demonstrated, democracy can operate quite successfully when the chief executive is chosen by a legislative assembly elected from single-member districts (as in England), or when an electoral system is designed to encourage multiple parties (as in proportional representation systems); and federal systems need not directly involve the regional units in the choice of the executive; (4) Study of sectional political culture and behavior is more important than ever. The thesis of a geosocial schism must be more rigorously studied. The election of 2000 highlights the importance of understanding links between regional cultures and state and federal policy.

The Electoral College played a direct role in raising doubts about the legitimacy of the 2000 election, and serious reform of the institution looms as a potentially thorny and intractable problem. Reform is not technically difficult, as the neo-Wilson plan demonstrates, but it is politically difficult. Even the deliberation over alternatives is likely to reenergize all the careless analysis and self-interested interpretation that has characterized the debate in the past, and the small states will oppose reforms that threaten their advantage. Yet, as we have noted before, deferral of confrontational issues through symbolic compromise does not necessarily ameliorate the harm that will ultimately result.[57] Failure to reform the Electoral College leaves in place a relentless reminder that the Constitution gave to a category of states a special advantage, which in the 2000 election appears to have brought them power and benefits at the expense of the others.

Notes

1. Cooke, *The Federalist*, 461.
2. See, for example, Gregg, "Electoral College," 24–25.
3. Madison, *Debates*, 267.
4. See, for example, Gregg, "Electoral College," 20–22.
5. Thach, *Presidency*, 81.
6. Quoted in Madison, *Debates*, 198–99.

7. See Sherman's views as recorded by Madison in *Debates*, 220, 267, 461, 515, 519.

8. Ibid., 220.

9. Ibid., 41–42; see also, Thach, *Presidency*, 85.

10. Thach, *Presidency*, 34, 88.

11. Madison, *Debates*, passim. See also, Thach, *Presidency*, 76–139, for a discussion of the process. The plan as adopted is found in Article II, Section 2, later altered slightly in Amendment XII. The phrase "constant two" is a descriptive term used in discussions of the Electoral College to refer to each state's two votes based on its Senate representation. The contingency plan, another part of the small-state victory, has been relegated to the accident-waiting-to-happen category by the development of political parties and the unit-vote system. Although an important issue in Electoral College reform, it is beyond the scope of this chapter.

12. For detailed studies of shifting alliances at the Constitutional Convention, see Thach, *Presidency*; Jillson, *Constitution Making*.

13. Peirce, *The People's President*, 82–86; MacBride, *The American Electoral College*, 29–34.

14. Slonim, "Designing the Electoral College," 34.

15. Longley and Peirce, *Primer 2000*, 24.

16. Ibid., 16; MacBride, *The American Electoral College*, 28–39.

17. Longley and Peirce, *Primer 2000*, 32–37; Best, *Choice of the People*, 10–15.

18. National Archives and Records Administration, Electoral College Homepage. In 1960, the counting of the popular vote in Alabama was made ambiguous by the partial use of uncommitted electors on the Democratic ballot. Robert Byrd received 638,822 votes and other candidates won 188,559. Kennedy has been officially credited with defeating Nixon in the popular vote by a margin of less than 120,000. Kennedy ultimately won 303 electoral votes. He could have given the electoral votes for hotly contested Illinois and divided Alabama to Nixon and still have won the election. See Peirce, *The People's President*, 100–109.

19. The nine states, in order of size, are California, New York, Texas, Florida, Pennsylvania, Illinois, Ohio, Michigan, and New Jersey.

20. See Longley and Peirce, *Primer 2000*, 150–53; also, Yunker and Longley, *The Electoral College*, 12–13.

21. All states use the winner-take-all or unit-vote system except Nebraska and Maine, which award electors according to the vote in congressional districts, with the "constant two" votes going to the statewide winner. However, all of Nebraska's votes went to Bush and all of Maine's went to Gore in 2000.

22. Mann and Shapely, "A Priori Voting Strength."

23. Ibid., 154.

24. Ibid., 157–58.

25. Longley and Peirce, *Primer 2000*, 153.

26. Ibid., 150.

27. Gelman and Katz, "How Much Does a Vote Count?"

28. Ibid., 14.

29. Longley and Peirce, *Primer 2000,* 164–65.

30. Rhodes, *Republicans in the South,* 25.

31. "Red Zone vs. Blue Zone"; Cook, "Stalemate." According to Cook, the map first appeared in *USA Today* on November 9, 2000.

32. "Red Zone vs. Blue Zone," 40.

33. Cook, "Stalemate," 223–27.

34. Sears and Valentino, "Race, Religion, and Sectional Conflict," 26–32.

35. Andersen and Heath, "Social Cleavage and Political Context."

36. Cook, "Stalemate," 220.

37. McConnell, Introduction, xvii–xviii; Uhlmann, "Creating Constitutional Majorities," 109–10.

38. See, for example, Krugman, "True Blue Americans."

39. Krugman, "True Blue Americans"; see also Ivins, "We're Too Numb, Dumb."

40. Andersen and Heath, "Social Cleavage and Political Context."

41. Hovey and Hovey, *CQ's State Fact Finder 1999,* 83; see also *CQ's State Fact Finder 2001,* 90, 92, 137, and *CQ's State Fact Finder 2002,* 87, 91, 206, 220.

42. Hovey and Hovey, *CQ's State Fact Finder 2002,* 39, 62, 131, 134, 140.

43. Cooke, *The Federalist,* 60–61.

44. See Amy, *Behind the Ballot Box,* 11–25.

45. See Longley and Peirce, *Primer 2000,* chap. 1.

46. Best, *Case Against Direct Election.*

47. See, for example, Bobbitt, "Parlor Games."

48. See gallup.com/poll/releases/pr010105.asp. The figure had dropped to 59 percent by December. Only 41 percent of Republicans preferred popular vote compared to 57 percent of independents and 75 percent of Democrats. In 1968 the overall level of support stood at 80 percent.

49. See Best, *Case Against Direct Election,* 142.

50. Ibid., 209.

51. See, for example, a discussion of the Lodge-Gossett plan in MacBride, *The American Electoral College,* 43–59.

52. Neale, "Electoral College: Reform Proposals."

53. Sayre and Parris, *Voting for President,* 119–20.

54. See Amy, *Behind the Ballot Box,* 12, 146, for discussions of the virtues of majority and mandate elections.

55. An argument may be made that this is desirable although undemocratic. See Amy, *Behind the Ballot Box,* 13.

56. "A good voting system should not intensify the discord between different political, religious, economic, and racial groups. Instead, it should promote dialogue, negotiation, and compromise among these groups." Amy, *Behind the Ballot Box,* 21.

57. Rainey and Rainey, "Distribution of Power," 28.

14 □

□

□

Electoral College Reform at the State Level

Choices and Trade-Offs

PAUL D. SCHUMAKER, UNIVERSITY OF KANSAS,
AND BRUCE I. OPPENHEIMER, VANDERBILT UNIVERSITY

Some of the concerns over the 2000 presidential election have focused on the crucial roles of federal principles and the American states. First, owing to the way electoral votes are allocated among the states and the way the electoral votes of the states are aggregated, Al Gore's 500,000 lead in the national popular vote failed to translate into an Electoral College victory.[1] Second, charges of bias, fraud, and miscounts in Florida highlighted the inadequacies and inconsistencies in how states administer presidential elections. The first concern has led to proposals for fundamental reform of the Electoral College, changes requiring amendment of the U.S. Constitution. The second concern has prompted more incremental reforms, generally involving the provision of technologies providing more accurate tabulation of the votes in each state. Intermediate to these fundamental and incremental reforms are possible changes in how states conduct their elections and allocate their electors in the Electoral College. This chapter considers such intermediate reform possibilities, and assesses the trade-offs involved in pursuing reform.

An Electoral College with State-Level Popular-Plurality Rules

The Founders adopted the Electoral College as a method for choosing the president employing federal principles that are interwoven throughout the Constitution. Federalism is evident in provisions giving each state a number of electors equal to its congressional delegation. Each state has representation in the House proportional to its population (a provision that reflects the interests of populous states) and two senators regardless of population (a provision that recognizes the equality of states and thus reflects the interests of small states). Federalism is also evident in provisions giving each state control over the process of selecting its electors. Initially, only some states determined electors by popular vote, but by 1840 most states had instituted a system using popular votes. During this early period in the nation's history, political parties emerged to nominate candidates, and most states adopted the unit rule (winner-take-all provision) that allocates all of the electors of a state to that party nominee receiving the most popular votes.

The Electoral College is a system for selecting a president that aggregates votes in two stages: (1) Elections are held within each state, and (2) are tallied to achieve a national total of the electors won in the various states. As the Constitution specifies, the candidate receiving more than half (270) of the 538 electors in the second stage wins the presidency. Even though more attention is devoted to the second stage, the first stage—the process to determine whether a state's electors will cast their ballots for the Republican or Democratic candidate—is more important in the sense that the results of state-level processes determine the results of the national tally.

Today each state holds a popular election, and in most states the candidate winning the most votes, or a "popular plurality," receives all of a state's electors. Maine and Nebraska are exceptions to this practice, as they aggregate popular votes within each congressional district as well as at the state level. In these states, the candidate with the most votes in a district gets an elector from that district, and the candidate with the most votes in the state as a whole gets two additional electors. The district plan illustrates the kind of intermediate reforms of the Electoral College that states might consider. However, other options are available to the states for reforming presidential elections within the Electoral College system.

State Options in Presidential Elections

Because democratic norms have become stronger since the Electoral College was adopted, states are unlikely to reduce popular influence in the selection and operation of electors. They could return the selection of electors to state legislators, but the threat by the Florida House to do so after the indecisive popular vote in Florida in 2000 was widely viewed as undemocratic and thus unacceptable. Continuing to have popular votes determine electors seems essential to any Electoral College reform at the state level. States could reduce any requirements binding electors to popular outcomes, but the occasional defections of "rogue voters" are usually seen as violations of democratic norms. Instituting reforms that create "automatic electors" and removal of any possibility that electors violate popular mandates are clearly consistent with democratic ideals.[2]

Almost all states thus employ rules and procedures in presidential elections having the following components: (1) there is a popular vote, (2) which is resolved by a statewide plurality rule (3) that results in the leading vote-getter attaining all of a state's electors, (4) who are often pledged to him through state legislation and are almost always committed to him because of party and personal loyalty and the norm of instructed delegation. When thinking about state-level reforms of the Electoral College, we assume that democratic norms require maintenance of the first component (popular elections) and may involve strengthening the fourth component (eliminating rogue electors). The second and third components provide the main possibilities for reform. States could adopt a majoritarian, rather than plurality, decision rule. States could also abandon their winner-take-all systems. Four major reforms at the state level might thus be considered.

1. *Adopt a Strict Majority Rule.* If one candidate receives a plurality (more votes than anyone else) but fails to get a majority (50 percent plus one) of the popular votes in a state, a state could require a runoff election within a few weeks. A strict majority rule would usually lead to a runoff election between the top two candidates whenever third-party or independent candidates received a large percentage of votes or when there was a very close margin of victory between the front-runners. For example, because of the votes received by Ralph Nader and others, neither Bush nor Gore approached a majority in Florida (and several other states); thus, if Florida had used a strict majority rule, a runoff between them would have been required. Such a process might have been preferable to the spectacle of recounting votes and looking for spoiled ballots and voting irregularities in every county of the state.

2. *Adopt an Instant Runoff.* A second version of majority rule would be to adopt the instant-runoff system used in Australian legislative elections, in choosing city council members in Cambridge, Massachusetts, and recently for choosing the mayor of San Francisco. This method—known as the "single-transferable vote" or "alternative vote" procedure in the comparative electoral

systems literature—would give voters the opportunity to rank their top choices for the presidency.[3] The top choice of each voter would initially be counted, and if one candidate won a majority, he or she would win in the state. But if no one received an initial majority, computer technology would "instantly" recalculate the results in the following manner: The candidate getting the fewest first-place votes would be eliminated, and his or her votes would be transferred to the second-ranked choice of each voter who chose the eliminated candidate. If this reassignment of votes did not result in one candidate receiving a majority, the candidate with the next lowest first-place votes would be eliminated, and the votes for that candidate would be transferred to the candidate ranked second (or third) on ballots cast for this newly eliminated candidate. This process would be repeated until one candidate achieved a majority. This method would ensure that the winner of a state's electoral votes had majority support from the state's voters, and it would avoid the time and cost of a subsequent runoff election.

3. *Adopt the District Plan.* States could abandon the unit rule and adopt the district plan. Under this reform, a candidate would win all of a state's electoral votes only if he or she won in each and every congressional district. In practice, neither Maine nor Nebraska has divided its electors since they adopted the district plan (in 1972 and 1992, respectively), because the statewide leader has also won in each congressional district. In principle, this plan would neverthe-less allow candidates having little or no chance to win at the state level to still pick up electors where they win in particular districts.[4] This plan could lead to a more equitable division of electors between candidates in closely contested states. Rather than having all twenty-five electors at stake in the recounts and challenges in Florida, both candidates would have captured electors in districts where they were strong, with only a few electors up for grabs in a few closely contested districts and in the state as a whole.

4. *Adopt Proportional Allocation.* Another alternative to the unit rule would be for the state to allocate its electors in proportion to the popular votes each candidate receives. For example, in a state with twenty electoral votes where three candidates split the state's popular vote 50–40–10, the candidate with 50 percent would get ten electoral votes, the candidate with 40 percent would get eight electoral votes, and the candidate with 10 percent would get two electoral votes. In practice, the proportions would not work out so neatly—if, in our example, the first candidate won 52 percent of the popular vote, he or she would be entitled to 10.4 electoral votes—and states would need to adopt some scheme for dealing with fractions. The Electoral College system assumes that electors

are real people who cast whole votes, rather than "automatic electors" who cast their votes to reflect strict proportionality. The procedure most often used to avoid fractions is the d'Hondt or highest-average system, used in proportional representation systems throughout the world. It rounds fractions upward, giving partially allocated electors to the candidates receiving the greater popular vote. While proportional allocation allows third parties and minority parties to win electors that would be denied them under the dominant unit rule, the d'Hondt system minimizes the number of electors awarded them. Again, states would have the option of d'Hondt or other rounding methods.[5]

Standards and Assessments of the Existing System

Each of these reforms has certain attractions. Any systematic evaluation of them, however, requires elaboration of broad standards or criteria regarding the effectiveness and fairness of elections. We here propose nine standards and illustrate their meaning and application by discussing how well they are (or are not) achieved by the Electoral College system as it operates on the national level and by the popular-plurality system as it operates on the state level to determine electors to the college. The standards and assessments offered here are intended to reflect the judgments of thirty-seven political scientists, including the authors, who participated in a broader project examining the Electoral College system and the leading alternatives to it.[6]

1. *Simplicity.* Simplicity is a virtue in electoral systems. Complex systems are poorly understood by voters, reducing their effective participation in elections. The Electoral College is clearly a complex system. Many citizens do not realize that they are in fact voting for electors rather than directly for a candidate. Most citizens have only the crudest understandings of the unit rule, the casting of electoral votes, the possibility of a House contingency election if no candidate gets a majority in the College, and so forth. In contrast, the popular-plurality system used in most states is unquestionably the simplest electoral system. We all participate in popular elections that apply the plurality ("first past the post") rule to determine winners. Most Americans probably regard this system as "democracy, pure and simple."

2. *Equality.* Voter equality, often expressed as "one man, one vote," is a fundamental feature of democracy.[7] The Electoral College is frequently criticized for violating this criterion, as the (formal) value of voting is not equal for all citizens. As was noted in the previous chapter, because all states are provided two electors regardless of population and because of other anomalies that arise

in the allocation of electors among states (such as the changes in population that occur between a census and an election), the value of voting is greater for citizens living in small states than for citizens of more populated states. There are, for example, 119,000 voters per elector in Wyoming compared to more than 450,000 voters per elector in Florida, Texas, and California.[8] The popular-plurality systems employed by the states in selecting electors to the College avoid such inequalities, as all votes in such systems count equally, absent any fraud or other irregularities. Such equality also seems to be achieved by the four reforms considered in this chapter, and so the application of the equality criterion does not help us differentiate the merit of these systems from the existing popular-plurality system. But this does not mean that all systems treat voters equally in broader senses of the term.

3. *Neutrality.* Voting systems are neutral if they lack bias or a built-in advantage favoring certain types of voters. However, voting systems that are formally equal can have characteristics that interact with other political and social conditions to create biases that challenge our conceptions of fairness. The Electoral College is alleged to have such biases. The most prominent example is the bias in favor of citizens in large and/or competitive states who are most courted by the candidates, as campaigns promise them policy benefits and expend more resources on them in pursuit of their crucial support. For instance, Florida was regarded as a toss-up between Gore and Bush in 2000, and its twenty-five electoral votes gave Floridians high "vote power"—the capacity to swing a key state in a close election.[9] Some conventional wisdom adds that minorities and the poor are disproportionately residents of such swing states, giving rise to the notion that the Electoral College contains a built-in advantage benefiting African Americans and the urban poor. While we are skeptical of the veracity of this claim, it illustrates a potential threat to neutrality in the system.[10]

The popular-plurality system also seems to have bias, as it benefits the major parties by disadvantaging third parties and independent candidates. Such candidates might be attractive to "sincere voters," but these voters have incentives under the popular-plurality system to instead be "sophisticated voters" who cast their ballots for their second choice, one of the major-party candidates, because they are wary of "wasting" votes on unelectable candidates. However, it is not clear that any electoral system avoids this sort of bias, and this matter can best be addressed by considering another standard for effective electoral systems, the criterion of sincerity.

4. *Sincerity.* Electoral systems promote sincere voting when they enable citizens to locate candidates who represent their principles and interests and when

these systems encourage citizens to vote for such candidates. Representation is increased and citizens gain opportunities for sincere voting when electoral systems enable a wide variety of parties and candidates to be credible contenders for office. Representation is reduced and citizens lose opportunities for sincere voting when electoral systems reduce their choices to two candidates, neither of whom represents the views of many voters. First-past-the-post electoral systems that give victory to only one candidate—the person getting the most votes—reduce representation, because candidates express middle-of-the-road positions intended to maximize their votes and because some voters abandon their preferred candidates who have little chance of winning.

The Electoral College is thought to reduce opportunities for representation and sincere voting because the unit rule used by the states puts a premium on coming in first in a state. It encourages potential supporters of third-party and independent candidates to be sophisticated voters who cast their votes for the lesser of two evils among the "electable" major-party candidates, to prevent their least preferred candidate from winning the state.

Overall, the popular-plurality elections used by states within the Electoral College system probably contribute to this reduced representation by narrowing contests to mainstream candidates and encouraging citizens to be sophisticated rather than sincere voters. But popular-plurality systems have a feature that can increase representation and sincere voting. Such systems can result in low thresholds for the percentage of votes needed to capture a state. If three candidates closely contest a state, one might win with only 35 percent of the vote. If four candidates closely contest an election, one might win with little more than a quarter of the vote, and so forth.

5. *Participation.* Voting systems promote participation when they reduce the costs and increase the benefits of voting. Because the chances are minuscule that one vote will decisively influence the outcome of a presidential election, voting under any electoral system will be a low-benefit activity.[11] But the Electoral College system makes it abundantly clear to voters in states where the outcome is preordained that their vote is meaningless, even if the national outcome is in doubt. In 2000, only a dozen states were regarded as "in play" when the election was held, giving voters in the rest of the states the sense that their votes could contribute nothing to the outcomes in their states and thus to the outcome of the close Bush-Gore contest. A national popular election could well have encouraged nonvoters in states that were safe for Bush or Gore to cast ballots, knowing that the outcome hinged on national popular totals to which their votes would contribute. Although a national popular voting scheme might

enhance the level of voter turnout, states face the question of whether any of the alternatives available to them would enhance turnout within their state.

6. *Legitimacy.* Electoral victory is the principle means by which American presidents acquire legitimacy, the constitutional right to exercise the powers of the office, and the moral obligation of others to obey the just commands of presidents. All fair and democratic electoral systems can confer legitimacy on victors, but for citizens to accept electoral outcomes, it helps for the winners to be clear, even in relatively close elections.

The Electoral College is thought to enhance presidential legitimacy because it frequently converts slim popular vote margins to decisive victory among electors in the College. For example, Richard Nixon's victory margin over Hubert Humphrey in 1968 was less than one percent, but he had a commanding 301 to 191 victory in the Electoral College. But the Electoral College is also thought to have features that can undermine legitimacy. If no candidate wins a majority in the College and the task of selecting the president falls to the House of Representatives, the public could feel deprived of its right to determine the president and thus question the legitimacy of the person so selected.[12] In the immediate aftermath of the 2000 election, many commentators and scholars predicted that Bush's legitimacy would be questioned because of the discrepancy between the outcome of the popular vote and the vote in the Electoral College.[13] However, both historical and contemporary events suggest that the Electoral College has effectively conferred legitimacy even when the House contingency has been invoked (as it was in 1824) and when the president has lost the popular vote (as in 1876, 1888, and 2000). With the possible exception of Abraham Lincoln in 1860, the victor in the Electoral College has been granted legitimacy even when elections have been close and controversial.

Elections decided by the plurality rule have conferred legitimacy on most governors and legislators in the states throughout our history, but such popular elections have a couple of features that worry analysts contemplating abolition of the Electoral College and replacing it with a national popular-plurality system. First, if citizens dispersed their votes broadly among many credible candidates, the winner could have far less than a majority of the votes, raising doubts that his mandate is sufficiently wide to confer legitimacy. Second, if the national popular vote were extremely close, the outcome could be in doubt as allegations of fraud and miscounts are made, investigated, and perhaps never completely resolved in various precincts and counties throughout the country. As illustrated in Florida in 2000, such problems can occur in the popular-plurality elections conducted in the states during the first phase of the Electoral College process. The question is whether these problems are significant enough to undermine the legitimacy of the outcome in the states and whether an alternative electoral system could avoid such problems.

7. *Governance.* While the Electoral College has successfully conferred legitimacy on presidents, not all presidents have been able to govern effectively. The capacity to govern in a pluralist society requires achieving considerable consensus on policy goals and limiting the capacity of opposing interests to cause stalemate. The American system of separation of powers is intended to make governance difficult, but historically our party system, dominated by two relatively centrist parties, has facilitated some effective governance. Governance is generally most effective when one party controls both the presidency and Congress and can claim widespread support for its policies. Governance is more difficult when different parties control the presidency and Congress, but if both parties are relatively pragmatic and centrist, they can still govern effectively. Especially in a large and diverse country like the United States, governance would be most difficult to attain if control over governmental institutions were fragmented among multiple parties, each representing narrow interests and/or uncompromising ideologies.

The Electoral College is thought to be an important ingredient in attaining effective governance in Washington because it helps maintain our two-party system with relatively centrist parties. The key to this result is the popular-plurality elections in the states that comprise the first stage of the Electoral College system. Because of the first-past-the-post feature of these elections, third-party and independent candidates are discouraged from competing and voters are discouraged from "wasting their votes" on such candidates. The question is whether alternative electoral systems available to the states would encourage a proliferation of parties, each representing distinct interests and having sufficient influence to contribute to stalemate and undermine effective governance.

8. *Inclusiveness.* Inclusiveness refers to the diversity of interests and ideals included within electoral and governing organizations. Inclusive parties and campaigns craft platforms that appeal to the interests of disparate groups and express principles that are broadly accepted. Sincere voters find within these platforms positive responses to their legitimate interests and the articulation of broad principles with which they agree. Inclusive governing coalitions adopt and implement policies that spread benefits broadly among the public and embody widely accepted notions of the common good.

Inclusiveness is related to centrism but is not identical with it. Centrist campaigns imagine that most citizens are grouped around a "median voter" having a preexisting set of preferences and ideals known through such indicators as public opinion polls. Inclusive campaigns imagine that citizens have fairly weak and diverse preexisting views that a median voter may not well represent. The goal of an inclusive campaign is to articulate policy goals that modify and strengthen the preferences of citizens, appealing to and activating as many members of as many groups as possible.

Supporters of the Electoral College claim that it is particularly effective at building inclusive campaign and governing organizations, because its rules make clear to presidential aspirants that they need support that is broadly distributed across the states to get the requisite majority of electors in the College.[14] Obviously, candidates whose appeal is limited to "the Southern vote" or "the urban vote" or "the farm vote" or other such "special interests" but ignore most aspects of America's diversity are unlikely to succeed. Less obviously, candidates whose appeal is to the median voter may fail to activate the support of broad segments of the public whose views are poorly expressed by the median voter. And even if appealing to the median voter were the best way of getting a popular plurality in a national election, a majority in the Electoral College may not be achieved unless that popular plurality is constructed in such a fashion as to get broad support across the states.

Nevertheless, it is questionable whether the Electoral College produces the kinds of supermajoritarian campaigns and governing coalitions that are attributed to it by its defenders. Certainly various ethnic and lifestyle groups feel ignored by both Democrat and Republican candidates. And other groups, like African Americans, report being taken for granted and not actively courted. Campaigns clearly have notions about where their votes do and do not lie, and they tend to ignore supporters in safe states and groups that they believe are unnecessary to building a winning electoral coalition in key swing states. Abolishing the Electoral College and adopting a national popular plurality system might remove such disincentives for inclusive politics, as all types of voters would be equally valuable in achieving electoral success, regardless of where they lived and how crucial their votes were to success in their states. However, a candidate could win a national popular vote with a relatively small plurality, and many citizens could well feel excluded from the governing coalition that emerged from such an electoral outcome.

Incentives for building inclusive campaigns seem mixed when popular-plurality methods are employed at the state level. In safe states, where one party is dominant or one candidate has an insurmountable lead, there is little incentive for campaigns to seek even larger majorities. However, in competitive states, the need to appeal to undecided and crucial blocs of voters can promote inclusive campaigning. The question is whether alternative systems can more consistently promote inclusive politics, even in states that are often uncompetitive.

9. *Feasibility.* National efforts to abolish the Electoral College and replace it with a national popular vote are not very feasible. There are huge institutional obstacles to amending the Constitution, including securing the approval of three-fourths of the states, many of which are advantaged by the present system. It is also unlikely that leaders of the major parties would seek to eliminate a system that has helped shield them from competition from new and third parties.[15] Because states have the constitutional authority to create their own rules for selecting electors to the College, reforms in the states do not have the same institutional barriers that exist at the national level.

Evaluating Alternatives to Popular-Plurality Systems at the State Level

Table 14.1 summarizes our judgments about the desirability and feasibility of moving away from the prevailing popular-plurality system that constitutes the first stage of the Electoral College system and employing each of the four alternatives at the state level. In this section, we compare these—the popular-majority system, the instant runoff, the district plan, and the proportional-allocation system—with the prevailing popular-plurality system.

Evaluating the Popular-Majority Alternative

As a method of determining electors at the state level, the popular-majority system has some attractions. Although the requirement of having a runoff election if no candidate gets a majority is more complex than having a single election determined by the plurality rule, the popular-majority system is relatively simple and familiar. Most states have both primary and general elections to determine their governors and other elected officials, so the possibility of a second (runoff) election between the top two vote-getters would not be foreign to voters.

This system could make a second-place finish in the initial balloting an important prize, propelling a candidate who would be eliminated as a "loser" in the popular-plurality system into a contender in a potentially vital runoff election. This possibility could encourage third-party and independent candidates as well as candidates who lost major-party nominations to compete aggressively in states adopting the popular-majority system. This situation could

Table 14.1 Evaluating Electoral Systems on Nine Criteria

Criteria	Electoral College (Nationally)	Popular Plurality	Popular Majority	Instant Runoff	District Plan	Proportional Allocation
Simplicity	most complex	most simple	relatively simple	relatively foreign and complex	relatively complex	relatively complex
Equality	unequal across states	equal within states	equal within states	equal within states	equal within states	equal within states
Neutrality	biases toward swing states	bias toward major parties	bias toward major parties reduced	bias toward Republicans likely	bias toward Republican evident	bias is not apparent
Sincerity	discouraged	discouraged	less discouraged	encouraged	discouraged	encouraged
Participation	discouraged in noncompetitive state	encouraged if adapted nationally	reduced in runoffs (voter fatigue)	encouraged	encouraged in certain districts	encouraged in all states
Legitimacy	conferred historically	threatened by weak pluralities, fraud, and recounts	enhanced (and threatened) by majority rule	enhanced by majoritarianism	enhanced by localizing recounts and irregularities	threatened if House contingency procedure is used
Governance	facilitated	facilitated	diminished	diminished	facilitated	diminished
Inclusiveness	unclear[a]	encouraged if states are competitive	unclear[a]	encouraged if districts are competitive	encouraged if districts are competitive	discouraged
Feasibility	status quo	status quo in most state	least likely	possible under very limited circumstances	most possible but still unlikely	possible under very limited circumstances

[a]Inclusiveness depends on a wide array of factors.

have both positive and negative effects for sincere voting. On the one hand, the greater number of candidates and parties would enhance the ability of sincere voters to find candidates who represented well their views. And the runoff provision might encourage voters to cast an initial ballot for their sincere choice, even if those candidates had little chance of success, on the assumption that they would have the opportunity to choose between the lesser of two evils in the second round. On the other hand, the runoff provision could encourage some insincere, strategic voting, as some voters might see the first round as an opportunity to cast protest ballots for candidates they little admire, simply to signal their unhappiness with the major-party candidates. In any event, the popular-majority system would reduce bias toward the nominees of the major parties.

Such a system could also make some contributions to enhancing legitimacy. As mentioned earlier, a runoff could erase doubts about who really won a close initial balloting accompanied by charges of miscounts and fraud. Additionally, the winner of the runoff could, of course, claim to be supported by a majority, thus giving greater legitimacy to his claim to a state's electors.

However, the popular-majority system also has some deficiencies. Voter participation might decline in the runoff, especially if supporters of defeated candidates are apathetic about the remaining candidates and alienated by a system that rejected their favorite candidates. And if the second-place finisher in the initial vote won in the runoff, the legitimacy of the outcome could be reduced, as citizens might wonder why the winner under a majority rule had any greater claim to victory than the winner under a plurality rule.[16] If third parties succeeded in either the initial or the runoff election, or even if they were simply spoilers who deprived the major parties of a first-round victory, they would gain a greater role in American politics, possibly acquiring sufficient power to thwart the governing capacity of the major parties. Suppose, for example, that Florida had had a popular-majority system in 2000. Because both Bush and Gore came up short of a majority in Florida, and yet needed that state to win in the College, both candidates would have had huge incentives to bargain with Ralph Nader, Pat Buchanan, and other eliminated candidates for the support of their voters in the runoff. Such bargains might include giving these candidates veto power over certain policy initiatives. Perhaps such bargains would involve providing the third-party candidates with important offices in the resulting administration, making it more inclusive in the sense that additional interests would be represented in the governing coalition. But the included third-party candidates could also be extremists who demanded noninclusive policy concessions that undermined the interests and principles of other groups within the governing coalition.

Finally, a delayed runoff has a number of disadvantages that might undermine the feasibility of a popular-majority system. For states conducting runoff elections, there are of course additional expenses. For the nation as a whole, there could well be unease and even resentment if the outcome remained undetermined until one state conducted its runoff election. And such a decisive runoff could generate tumultuous, intense, and perhaps vicious campaigning in order to put a candidate over the top. These possibilities might result in national opposition to states contemplating a popular-majority system involving delayed runoff elections.

Evaluating the Instant-Runoff Alternative

This innovative reform has attracted considerable national attention, but has a variety of possible difficulties that must be considered by any state contemplating employing it.[17] It normally permits voters to rank their top three candidates, a task that is certainly more complex than simply indicating one's most preferred candidate. It calls on voters to be fairly informed about an array of candidates and to be fairly analytical about assessing how the interests and ideals of these candidates relate to the voter's own views. Its complexity suggests that well-educated, upper-income voters could better understand and more effectively navigate the system than poorly educated and lower-income voters, and this suggests that voters for the Democratic Party may be less likely to vote in such a system (or more likely to cast spoiled ballots) than voters supporting the Republican Party. In short, the complexity of the instant runoff may interact with established patterns of partisan voting to create bias favoring Republicans. As the election in Florida in 2000 demonstrates, voters can be easily confused by even modest complexities in balloting.

Supporters of instant runoffs, however, doubt that such effects and biases would be significant. They correctly maintain that the existing popular-plurality elections within the Electoral College system already create biases in favor of both Republicans and Democrats, and that the instant runoff would provide more equal opportunities for third-party and independent candidates. They claim that many citizens do recognize the degree to which all candidates represent their interests and ideals, and that they can effectively rank their preferences based on such understandings. The instant runoff relieves the burden such citizens feel under the popular-plurality system of having to decide whether to be sincere, voting for a preferred candidate who has little chance of winning, or to be sophisticated, voting for a second-favorite candidate to avoid helping to elect the least-preferred candidate. In the instant-runoff system, the elimination of their preferred candidate would not result in their votes being wasted, as each such vote would be transferred to the second-most-preferred candidate if the election were sufficiently close to have their vote make any difference.[18]

Proponents suggest that the instant runoff may have other benefits as well. By encouraging third-party candidacies capable of turning out citizens who are apathetic about the major-party candidates and by enabling citizens to cast ballots representing both their sincere and their sophisticated preferences, the instant runoff might increase voter turnout. It could increase legitimacy, as the winning candidate would almost certainly be named as one of the preferred choices on a majority of ballots and thus be able to claim being supported by the majority of voters as well as being the most-supported candidate. It might also increase inclusiveness, as the major-party candidates would have added incentives to include proposals in their platforms that appealed to the interests and principles of supporters of third parties, in hopes that such voters would rank them second, and that the transferred votes they could receive under this system would ultimately lead to victory.

The instant runoff would almost certainly increase the role of third parties in the American political system, and this could complicate effective governance. Energized third-party and independent candidates could win in states having the instant runoff and perhaps deprive either major-party candidate of a majority in the Electoral College. To achieve that majority, the major-party candidates would again be prompted to negotiate agreements with third-party candidates for their electoral votes. The price for such votes could well be the capacity of third parties to obstruct many policy goals that the governing coalition would otherwise implement.

To reformers in some states, such a scenario might seem either remote or not entirely unattractive, and thus adopting the instant runoff might be feasible in some states having cultures conducive to third-party movements and independent candidates. The leaders of the Republican and Democratic Parties in the states would certainly be leery of any reforms that could undermine the dominance of their parties, but states having cultures conducive to innovations like the instant runoff might also be states having provisions for citizen initiatives. Through procedures of direct democracy, the resistance of the major parties could be circumvented and the instant runoff could be implemented.

Evaluating the District Plan

Unlike the instant-runoff and popular-majority systems, the district plan would, from the point of view of voters, involve almost no changes from the popular-plurality method used now in most states. The actual ballots need have no changes from those currently employed, and there would still be only one casting of ballots. Election administrators would face the additional complexity of counting the ballots for each district, as well as in the state as a whole, but this change would be fairly invisible to most voters.[19] The district plan could, however, simplify one task facing election administrators. If there are allegations of fraudulent and miscounted ballots, they could focus their energies on those districts where suspicions of voting irregularities are most compelling and where reexamination of the ballots could influence the election outcome.

The district plan has several other attractions beyond its relative simplicity. Perhaps most important, it could increase voter turnout.[20] Competitive districts within safe states could be transformed from places ignored by candidates into battlegrounds for swing electoral votes. Local parties that previously felt they had no significant role to play could become energized in competitive districts, enhancing their get-out-the-vote efforts. Citizens in such districts would see that their votes actually mattered. Of course, many congressional districts are not very competitive, but voters could believe that their votes would still matter in the determination of the two state-level electors, if the state as a whole was competitive. In short, more districts would be in play under the district plan than under the statewide popular-plurality system, stimulating the greater involvement of local parties and the greater participation of citizens.

It is unlikely, however, that the district plan would affect the basic structure of our two-party system. Congressional elections now waged in the districts are mostly two-party affairs, because their first-past-the-post feature encourages citizens to be sophisticated voters who do not waste their votes on third-party and independent candidates. Elections for presidential electors in the districts would have the same features.[21] By maintaining the two-party system, the district plan would also facilitate and perhaps enhance effective governance. Under the district plan, presidential candidates could be more closely tied to the congressional candidates of their party, and stronger presidential coattails might reduce divided government and strengthen cooperation between the president and members of the House. The district plan might also result in a bit more inclusiveness. To attract supporters in newly competitive districts, presidential aspirants and first-term presidents would have incentives to devise proposals and policies that serve the interests or appeal to the principles of voters who could previously be ignored.

The biggest problem with the district plan would appear to be its Republican bias. Analysts have found that the nationwide implementation of the district plan would result in more electoral votes going to Republicans than has been the case under the more neutral popular-plurality system. For example, under the district plan, Nixon would have defeated Kennedy in 1960, and Ford would have tied Carter in 1976.[22] It is estimated that Bush would have achieved an additional seventeen votes under the district plan in 2000, defeating Gore 288 to 250.[23] The best explanation for this phenomenon is that the boundaries of congressional districts are often drawn by Republican-dominated state legislatures who understand the advantages of packing Democratic voters, especially minorities and the urban poor, into a few specific districts. In any event, Democrats seem to be more highly concentrated in some congressional districts, while Republicans have thinner majorities in a larger number of districts. This enables Republicans to do better under the district plan than under the popular-plurality system. This points to the related problem of how the boundaries of congressional districts are drawn, already a highly partisan process. Enhancing the stakes that are involved in it would only enhance the contentiousness of the redistricting process.

The district plan may be relatively feasible, because it is consistent with—and even represents an extension of—the federal principles in the Constitution and because it would not compromise the dominance of the major parties in the states. However, two strategic considerations limit the circumstances under which the district plan is likely to be adopted. If one party is dominant in a state and can normally deliver the entire bloc of electors to its candidate, it would probably resist adoption of a system that enabled the minority party in the state to claim electors in a few competitive districts. And if a state is large, dropping the unit rule could diminish its influence in the presidential campaign. One of the major reasons that states adopted the unit rule in the first place was the perception that having electors vote as a bloc enhanced a state's importance to candidates, who would thus pay more attention to their concerns. Populous states that are most viewed as having decisive blocs of electors thus would have the greatest disincentives for adopting the district plan. Florida, for example, considered the district plan, but dropped the idea, fearing the reform would dilute its influence. Small states, like Maine and Nebraska, have less to lose from trying this reform. These considerations about losing influence by abandoning the unit rule also apply, of course, to the proportional-allocation plan.

Evaluating Proportional Allocation

Like the district plan, proportional allocation would be relatively simple to implement, at least from the point of view of voters. Under this scheme, citizens would vote using customary ballots, procedures, and schedules. The major formal change would be in the way that electors in the College were allocated as a result of how citizens cast their ballots, as the winner-take-all feature would be replaced by allocating electors pledged to candidates in proportion to the outcome of the popular vote.[24]

Proportional allocation would have several advantages. If the district plan would encourage more participation than the popular-plurality system, proportional allocation would encourage more participation than the district plan. Under the district plan, only competitive districts would be in play. With proportional allocation, the entire state including every district in the state would be in play. Parties that are dominant in the state and in particular districts could not assume electors were safely in their column, as some electors could and would be peeled off by minority, third-party, and independent candidates. All parties would thus gain fresh incentives to compete aggressively for each and every elector to be allocated. Citizens in noncompetitive states (or districts) would no longer see their votes as irrelevant to the outcome. Voting would be encouraged, as voters would no longer need to worry about wasting their votes on their unelectable first choices, as independent and third-party candidates could win some electors even if they trailed other candidates and won fairly small percentages of the popular vote.

Proportional allocation would eliminate the bias in favor of the major parties that exists under first-past-the-post systems like the popular-plurality system. Though this would make the electoral system more neutral, it would complicate governance. Proportional allocation would produce party fragmentation, making effective governance difficult. To reduce such fragmentation and to limit the role of narrow or special-interest candidates and fringe parties, proportional-allocation plans might require candidates to attain some minimal percentage of popular votes—typically 5–10 percent—to qualify for any electors. Of course, such requirements would be important only in larger states, as a candidate winning about 10 percent of the popular vote would not qualify for any electors unless the state had ten electors to allocate. One allocation formula, the d'Hondt system, allocates seats in a manner that reduces representation of minor parties and favors major parties, and thus appears to be the preferred method of proportional allocation if the goal is to obtain a better balance between governance and representation.

A related problem with proportional allocation is that inclusiveness may also be discouraged. While popular-plurality systems encourage competition between two broad and fairly inclusive parties, proportional allocation can reward with electors those candidates and parties that represent narrow interests and clear ideological commitments that appeal to sizable minorities in the state but offer little and may be offensive to broader segments of the public.

Another drawback of proportional allocation is that the electors won by such third parties and independent candidates could become spoilers, whose main role would be to deprive candidates of the major parties of an Electoral College victory. If states that adopted proportional allocation also made electors legally bound to represent those citizens who voted for specific candidates, bargaining between third-party candidates and major parties within the Electoral College would be foreclosed. In such circumstances, the House contingency procedure, required by the Constitution when there is no majority among electors in the College, would be invoked. Under this procedure, the results of the popular votes in all states would be discarded, and the state delegations in the House of Representatives, each having a single vote, would determine which of the top three vote-getters in the College should be president. Perhaps John Quincy Adams had sufficient legitimacy to be a reasonably effective president when selected by such a procedure in 1824, but democratic norms have evolved greatly since then, and it is questionable that a person selected by such a process today would be accorded much legitimacy.

The obstacles to adoption of proportional allocation are thus fairly great. The leaders of the Democratic and Republican Parties would certainly oppose a reform that strengthened third parties and independent candidates. Perhaps this reform could be adopted by a citizen initiative in states whose cultures are receptive to innovation.

Conclusions

Reformers who reach the judgment that two or more of these systems are superior to their current system will want to compare such highly regarded reforms with one another. Our own judgment is that each alternative has limitations as well as strengths. Because we doubt that any alternative is clearly superior to the prevailing system, we leave to others who are more enthusiastic about state-level reform than ourselves the task of determining the best alternative. This is not to say that we would oppose states adopting any of these reforms. We believe that states are important laboratories of democracy and think it entirely appropriate for states seeking to improve democratic performance to ex- periment with any of these reforms. We recognize that state experimentation with these alternatives could yield important information about the consequences of employing these alternatives, and that such information could be valuable in future debates about how to structure presidential elections nationally.

Notes

1. The "plus two" allocation of two electors to states regardless of population gives small states disproportionate influence in the Electoral College and is one reason for George W. Bush's victory over Gore in the College. See Rainey and Rainey, "Distribution of Power." Aggregating electoral votes on the basis of the winner-take-all rule employed by most states advantages candidates who lose decisively in some states while achieving narrow popular victories in other states. Had Florida used a proportional allocation rule, Gore would have captured twelve electoral votes there, enough to ensure his victory in the Electoral College. Had all states employed the d'Hondt proportional allocation method discussed below, Gore would have led Bush in the Electoral College, but neither would have achieved a majority, and the House would have decided the outcome—in favor of Bush. See Herron, Francisco, and Yap, "Election Rules and Social Stability," 154.

2. Caraley, "Constitutional Right."

3. For a further discussion of the alternative vote, see Reynolds and Reilly, *Handbook of Electoral Systems Design*.

4. While the district plan normally assumes the winner would be determined by plurality rule, winners could also be determined by majority rule with runoffs.

5. For discussion of the d'Hondt and other rounding systems, see Reynolds and Reilly, *Handbook of Electoral Systems Design*.

6. This project is discussed in detail in Schumaker and Loomis, *Choosing a President*.

7. Dahl, *On Democracy*, 37.

8. See Frey, "Regional Shifts." Two considerations prompt some analysts to discount criticisms of the Electoral College based on such inequality. First, the "constant two" factor in the distribution of electors provides an element of equal treatment for the states as important units in our federal system, independent of the number of citizens within them. The fact that the value of the vote is greater for citizens in small states is simply a by-product of providing some equality among states. Second, it is argued that voters in small states like Wyoming can influence the selection of only three electors, while the voters in large states like California can influence the selection of as many as fifty-four electors. Thus voters in large states may have greater "voting power" or the capacity to decide the election in important swing states.

9. Longley and Peirce, *Primer 2000*, 147-61.

10. Lineberry et al., "Social Cleavages."

11. See Shactar and Nalebuff, "Follow the Leader."

12. Schumaker and Loomis, *Choosing a President*, 201–2.

13. In *Primer 2000*, Longley and Peirce foresaw precisely this problem. Had it not been for the Florida controversy, perhaps the public would have focused more on the fact that Bush was not the popular-vote winner and questioned his legitimacy.

14. Judith Best testifying on Proposals for Electoral College Reform to the House Committee on the Judiciary, Subcommittee on the Constitution, H.J. Res. 28 and H.J. Res. 43, September 4, 1997.

15. Schumaker and Loomis, *Choosing a President*, 1–6.

16. Democratic theory does not insist on either majority rule or plurality rule, but instead claims that the winner under the agreed-upon rules has the legitimate claim to office. But feelings that an outcome is illegitimate can be enhanced when people believe that the outcome is due to flaws and limitations of procedure rather than to some clear and reliable expression of the popular will.

17. The Center for Voting and Democracy is perhaps its strongest supporter. See their Web site at www.fairvote.org.

18. However, it can be argued that such a system could also make irresponsible voting rather costless, as voters could list detested fringe candidates as their first choice as a means of expressing their distaste for the front runners. This could undermine both the legitimacy and the governing capacity of the eventual winner.

19. Currently there is no need to determine the votes for each candidate in each congressional district, and thus states do not report such data. Indeed, some precincts and counties span district lines, requiring voting analysts to estimate, rather than precisely count, the outcomes at the district level. The district plan would, of course, require election administrators to redraw the boundaries of some voting precincts to coincide with congressional districts.

20. There is evidence that adoption of the district plan has enhanced voter participation in Maine. See Stein et al., "Citizen Participation," 132.

21. Third-party candidates might nevertheless win in specific districts. For example, Ross Perot almost claimed one district in Maine in 1992.

22. Polsby and Wildavsky, *Presidential Elections*, 251.

23. Bensen, "Presidential Election 2000 Study," at www.polidata.org.

24. There are different allocation formulas for handing "rounding issues" and these are relatively complex. Reformers who propose proportional allocation would have to deal with the complexity of alternatives and be able to defend such possibilities as the d'Hondt system. Administrators would also have to make the allocations according to somewhat complex rules. But such complexity would not cause much confusion among voters, who merely would have to mark their ballots in traditional ways.

 ELECTION REFORM

15 ☐

☐

☐

The Elusive Promise of Democratic Elections?

VICTORIA A. FARRAR-MYERS, UNIVERSITY OF TEXAS—ARLINGTON

> As Thomas Paine once said: "The right to vote is the primary right upon which all other rights are based." Therefore, there is no greater challenge facing [Congress] than restoring Americans' faith in our electoral process. . . . What we are engaged in today . . . is not any discussion or debate about the past. . . . This bill is about the future, what we can do to try to make our election systems more fair, to bring them up to date, to make it possible for people to cast votes more easily, and to see to it that those who may want to corrupt the system somehow will find their job far more difficult. . . . While the problems that took place in Florida [in 2000] brought the flaws in our election system to the Nation's attention, these are systematic problems that have existed in many states for many years.

—Senator Christopher Dodd (D-CT)

At the Founding, the idea that our representative democracy would have popular sovereignty as its cornerstone seemed to make the new national government structure seem less remote and more democratic. The Framers also ensured that the citizenry would have opportunities to express this popular sovereignty through regular and recurrent elections of our governmental officials. In addition, the constitutional provision to have the states dictate the time, place, and manner of elections was a way to mollify those at the Founding who thought national government would become too distant for individuals to remain engaged.

Even at the Founding, though, the electoral process was ripe for influence-wielding, persuasion, and corruption. The delicate balance between popular sovereignty and democracy was difficult in the early years, since those that voted were limited to white, male, landed gentry. With the passage of time, the debate over political equality, and thus democracy itself, has been a driving force behind much of the reforms in the electoral process. Whether it was the expansion of suffrage with the passage of the Fifteenth and Nineteenth Amendments, the Voting Rights Act of 1965, or the one-person-one-vote statement articulated in the Supreme Court decision *Baker v. Carr,* political equality and reforms designed to achieve such have remained at the forefront of our political lexicon.

The ongoing debate regarding such issues as political equality always remains just below the surface, ready to erupt when events highlight the existing barriers to achieving the goals of democracy and popular sovereignty. Therefore, it is not surprising the events surrounding recent elections—in particular the presidential election of 2000—shed light on several key issues that bring to the forefront ideas of how current electoral structures can function to meet our desired ends of representation, participation, political equality, and, ultimately, the expression of popular sovereignty. Such ends serve as a goal to which voters and citizens strive through the electoral process. The nation's ability to obtain each of them, however, has been called into question as the very structures designed to help achieve them seem to be producing unanticipated and, in some instances, undesirable consequences.

Representation

The conceptions of representation in the American system range from the view that representatives should filter public opinion (a view generally held by the Federalists at the Founding) to the idea (more akin to the Anti-Federalists' view) that elected officials should mirror the public. Regardless of which conception one favors, however, elections in a representative democracy call forth the notion that those who run for and are elected to office are to some extent reflective of the whole body—that they share the general interests and opinions of the public at large and will work for the public's benefit. Although this image is the ideal, it often becomes confronted with the limitations of the structures, rules, and processes that define the current electoral system.

For example, campaigns and elections today are candidate-centered, meaning that an individual can choose to run and campaign individually, and the electorate focuses on personal characteristics of that individual. More traditional mechanisms such as party organizations have been pushed aside, and their resources no longer play as important a role in electing officials. Candidate recruitment now has become about who has the money, connections, and ambition to step forward. In addition, traditional grassroots campaigns are sometimes difficult to organize around party, and are oftentimes driven by issues. Although these developments have, to some extent, freed candidates from having to be part of a "party machine" to be nominated and elected, they also have placed a greater burden on those running for office to obtain for themselves the resources necessary to campaign effectively.

With the barriers to campaigning fairly high, quality challengers are often unwilling to enter races in which they are underfunded and have little or no infrastructure, such as the party used to provide, to draw upon. As a result, the pool of potential candidates willing to run for office shrinks, with the fear that those candidates who remain may be beholden to special interests that are prepared to help fund their campaigns, or that those candidates who are wealthy enough to fund their own campaigns independently (the so-called millionaire candidates) are simply buying their way into office. The implications for representation are that the choices available to voters are reduced and that those candidates in the pool may not adequately reflect the citizenry. Although voters are always required to select from among a small, finite number of candidates in any given election, the barriers to campaigning may limit the number and quality of viewpoints that candidates express in that election.

These issues regarding access to the campaign and electoral processes become heightened for women and minority candidates. Historically, women and minorities have not had the same access to campaign resources as white male candidates. Time has narrowed this gap to some degree—for example, women elected to Congress have proven to be as successful as their average male counterparts in fund-raising.[1] Further, as the ranks of women and minorities grow among elected officials, these questions will subside further. Given the barriers that have existed, both in the original Constitutional design and in modern practice, many will remain vigilant of the status of women and minority candidates to ensure that there is no "backslide." But as long as the percentages of women and minority elected officials continue to be smaller than their percentages generally in the population, the question of representation for these groups will remain.

Another important component of successfully running for an office today is the need for name recognition and exposure. Building such recognition takes a long time, and as a result, candidates for office at any level need to start planning and running earlier than in years past. This is best exemplified by the presidential election system, which over the last several election cycles has seen candidates start running years in advance, thus creating an "invisible primary."

Candidates and potential candidates are evaluated by the public, the media, and donors who judge how viable that person's candidacy *may* be. Those that do not stimulate enough early reaction or do not raise enough funds often will withdraw from the presidential race before the first official voting primary takes place.

Elizabeth Dole represents the best example of this invisible primary phenomenon during the 2000 presidential election cycle. When she first entered the race, many pundits viewed her as a potentially strong challenger for the Republican presidential nomination. When she was unable to raise enough money, however, she withdrew, leaving Republican primary voters without the opportunity to express their support for her and her views.

In addition to the difficulties that candidates face in accumulating sufficient resources to permit them to present their views, the advent and growth of interest groups has made the marketplace of ideas even more crowded. These interest groups have spent millions on issue ads and in some cases "express advocacy" ads that, critics say, only serve to drown out candidates in the process. The increased involvement of interest groups acting on their own behalf in campaigns creates a "catch-22" for the goals of representation and democratic elections. On the one hand, by expressing their views, interest groups add to the political discourse, particularly on issues that candidates seeking office might not otherwise address. From a pluralist perspective, out of this proliferation of voices will emerge a sense of the public's will, providing a basis on which the elected officials can act to represent their constituents. On the other hand, given the disparity in resources between many organized interests and the ordinary, unaffiliated voter, and among interest groups themselves, the amount, intensity, and duration of certain groups' messages can be considerably stronger than others. As a result, some contend, voters may focus on the singular message of a particular interest group instead of the views of the candidates themselves. This calls into question whether elections can truly be "representative" of anything other than special interests.

Although many scholars, when questioning how representative current elections are, bemoan the breakdown of parties, one should not forget that political parties too were once seen as "factions" and sources of vice in the political system. Therefore, it seems quite ironic to blame the decay of representation on their predicament. What these scholars are missing is that the waning of parties in the electorate and as organizations has led other components of the electoral system—interest groups and candidate-centered strategies—to adapt and to be adapted to compensate and fill the vacuum.

One common set of reforms that might help alleviate some of the problems outlined above includes such proposals as public financing of congressional elections and free media airtime for candidates. The underlying premise of these proposals is that the cost of modern campaigning for any office deters quality candidates from running; if the financial burdens of campaigning are eased and all candidates are afforded a more equal share of available resources, more and better candidates will emerge. This in turn will improve the nature and quality of representation by our elected officials. Whether these proposals, if enacted, would actually improve the representative nature of our electoral system remains an open question. However, they do raise key issues to keep in mind. What truly is of concern is whether and to what extent the modern adaptations noted above have helped elections fully serve their key purpose in the American democratic system, or whether we need to acknowledge that the emerging trends in modern elections may facilitate the goals of democracy only to a point. The answer to that question directs how rigorously electoral and campaign finance reforms like those mentioned need to be pursued.

Participation and Political Equality

The common lesson that voters drew from the 2000 election controversy in Florida was severalfold. For one thing, the Electoral College did not seem to make sense. For the first time in more than a century, the popular-vote winner did not win the presidential election. Further, registration and voting mechanisms seemed arcane and in some instances unfair, as the outcome of the presidential election turned, in part, not on the policy positions of the candidates but on their positions on "butterfly" and other ballots. In addition, despite efforts by such organizations as MTV and the World Wrestling Federation to stimulate participation among young voters, this group of the electorate was generally considered to be tuned out. Indeed, a great deal of discussion focused on the lack of civic engagement and turnout among all voters.

The concept of the citizenry's participation in the electoral process is fundamental to the American form of democracy. It is not enough that the political system ensure the right to vote; voters need to exercise that right. The right to vote is one of the primary bases of equality. In theory, every voter is the same in the voting booth; every lever that is flipped, every hole that is punched, and every mark that is made counts the same. The electoral process, however, offers numerous deterrents that force us to assess continually how closely our practice conforms to that theory.

Although these deterrents are not new, the 2000 presidential election shed light on subjects that have largely been hidden in the shadows. As noted above, the Electoral College came under sharp criticism (at least on the surface) from both Democrats and Republicans, liberals and conservatives, for imposing an added, perhaps unnecessary, layer to the process of electing the president. Although arguing the pros and cons of the Electoral College is beyond the scope of this chapter, critics do present a compelling argument that the Electoral College framework distorts political equality. In a straight popularity-style election, all citizens' votes would count the same, regardless of where they lived, but with the Electoral College, certain votes may be seen as not counting. For example, a voter in Texas—George W. Bush's home state, where he served as a very popular governor—could have voted for Bush, Gore, Nader, or not voted at all, and that person knew going into Election Day that it did not matter. His or her vote was not going to affect whether Bush received Texas's electoral votes.

Another deterrent to voting that received prominent attention in 2000 involves absentee ballots. A small, but significant, number of voters will cast absentee ballots in any given election; this includes military personnel who are serving away from their homes and who are sworn to protect and defend such important constitutional rights as the right to vote. Absentee voters undertake the added burdens of obtaining and casting an absentee ballot in a timely fashion in the belief that their one vote matters. In 2000, because of the importance of counting every vote in states with close outcomes, local election boards had to make sure they included these absentee ballots in their final counts. Reports came out, however, that such diligence was not always the case—that, sometimes, local election boards would not count some or all absentee ballots unless the result might turn on that count. Such practices may leave some voters who would otherwise make the effort to cast an absentee ballot to ask, "Why should I even bother if my vote is not going to be counted?"

The form of ballot used was another component of the electoral process receiving scrutiny in the wake of the 2000 election. The choice of the form and technology used for ballots is left to individual counties. For a multitude of reasons, ranging from cost of equipment to historical factors, a variety of ballots and voting mechanisms are used throughout the nation. The 2000 election, though, made phrases like "butterfly ballot," "hanging chad," and "dimpled chad" part of the political vernacular. It further demonstrated that simply going to the voting booth is not enough—that a person's vote still may not count, or not count as intended, because of some error attributable to the form of the ballot or the manner in which the vote is cast and counted.

Reforms

As we have seen, certain procedural mechanisms in the electoral process impede our attaining the goal of "one person, one vote." There are deterrents in the system that discourage people from voting in the first place; if voters do turn out, there are additional common reasons why their vote may not have the same effect as someone else's. In the wake of the 2000 election, numerous reform proposals started to be bandied about in an attempt to ease some of the procedural and administrative burdens of attaining the goals of greater participation and political equality.

One such reform proposal was to move toward a national ballot style and voting mechanism—that is, requiring each county to use the same form of ballot and use the same mechanism for counting votes. One of the problems with such a proposal, however, is that it flies in the face of the structure of federalism, in which states are constitutionally provided with the authority to determine the time, place, and manner of elections. A national ballot requirement would take this authority away from the localities and centralize it in Washington.

If federalism leads to a diversity in standards for conducting elections, with all the implications that holds for political equality, it also affords certain benefits that might present more promise of reform. For instance, a national standard for a ballot is a somewhat unrealistic effort in moving toward the elusive goal of democratic elections. In the present system, each state and locality can serve as a laboratory of democracy, in which different methods to resolve problems like those discussed herein can be tried. Some states, among them Oregon, are exploring such emerging technologies as the Internet to address some of the traditional problems associated with conducting elections. Suppose a voter is traveling on Election Day or otherwise unable to make it to the polls—no problem, just point and click, and your vote is cast. If states and localities are allowed to try different methods of conducting voting and elections, they may hit upon solutions that enhance participation and political equality.

Political participation takes forms other than voting. For example, people can contribute money to a campaign as an additional way to support their favored candidates. Unlike voting, where everyone has the same resource (one vote), the world of campaign finance presents an uneven playing field. Some individuals have far greater resources than others to contribute to political campaigns. In addition, although entities such as interest groups and political action committees (PACs) do not have the right to vote, they do have the right to raise and distribute funds to candidates.

The elections of 2000 set all sorts of campaign financing records. George W.

Bush opted not to collect federal matching funds during the Republican prima-ries. Freed from the fund-raising constraints connected with receiving match-ing funds, Bush raised more than $91 million for his primary campaign. During the primaries, Al Gore, Bill Bradley, and John McCain each raised more than $42 million, and Steve Forbes contributed that much to his own campaign. On the congressional level, candidates collectively spent more than $1 billion seek-ing seats in the House and Senate—the first time that barrier had been broken. Contributions to political parties also were up during the 1999–2000 election cycle when compared to the previous presidential election cycle of 1995–96. A significant portion of this increase was attributable to "soft money"—that is, unregulated funds that are supposed to be used for party-building activities such as voter registration and get-out-the-vote drives. Both the Democratic and Republican national party committees raised more than $245 million in soft money during the 1999–2000 election cycle, representing a 98 percent and an 81 percent increase over 1995–96, respectively.[2] With so much money flowing around the political system, many voters were left to conclude that, without money, they had no chance of participating in this component of the electoral system or of influencing candidates. Taken further, many voters were left with the feeling that their one vote could not possibly make a difference against the sea of contributions flowing into candidates' "war chests."

In 2002, Congress passed the Bipartisan Campaign Reform Act, the first major change in the nation's federal campaign finance laws since the 1970s. Representative Christopher Shays, the lead sponsor of the bill in the House of Representatives, characterized the legislation as "aim[ing] to end the current system in which corporate treasury and union dues money drowns out the voice of individual Americans by banning soft money and closing the sham 'issue ad' loophole."[3] In addition, the act increased the maximum amount an individual could give to a presidential, House, or Senate candidate from $1,000 to $2,000 (to be increased with inflation). One problem with the act, however, is that it will not necessarily stimulate greater participation, especially in the form of turnout, by average voters.[4] Furthermore, the skewed level of finan-cial resources among the various actors in the electoral process will remain, serving as a continuing deterrent to achieving political equality. These are simply factors inherent in the system to which the nation must respond.

Popular Sovereignty

The Framers of the Constitution were deeply influenced by the writings of Montesquieu and Rousseau and by the concept of the social contract—that is, the idea that the body politic is a "public person . . . formed by the union of all persons."[5] For Rousseau, sovereignty was "nothing less than the exercise of the general will."[6] James Madison expressed his understanding of these issues in *Federalist 39:*

> What, then, are the distinctive characters of the republican form [of government]? . . . If we resort for a criterion to the different principles on which different forms of government are established, we may define a republic to be, or at least may bestow that name on, *a government which derives all its powers directly or indirectly from the great body of the people,* and is administered by persons holding their offices during pleasure, for a limited period, or during good behavior.

The emphasized portion of the above quotation captures the essence of popular sovereignty in the American form of government—that the authority of the government flows from its citizens. Although the individual goals of representation, popular participation, and political equality are important in their own right, they all serve to facilitate the expression of popular sovereignty, which, as Madison noted, is one of the principle criteria for distinguishing a republican form of government from others.

Such was the perception more than two hundred years ago, but in so many ways the political world today is vastly different. Not only has the electorate expanded, but the principles that Madison and the rest of the Framers focused on—the principles that they were trying to ensure would be reflected in the new national government—have since then been given definite expression in the minutest forms through legislation, court cases, and practice. That practice, as we have seen throughout this chapter, oftentimes falls far short of the principles underlying our political system.

For example, the Framers sought as a compromise to incorporate the principle of dual sovereignty—that is, protecting the states' rights while still providing sufficient authority to the national government. The need to placate the states by reserving to them the time, place, and manner of elections empowered them to decide how to administer elections, even those for national offices. The wisdom of this decision has been called into question many times, but no more so than in the wake of the 2000 elections when the lack of standardization, the diversity of systems, and issues as detailed as what time polls are open all raised questions regarding the validity of our electoral systems, and, therefore, whether our mechanisms for expressing popular sovereignty really work.

Given this, one may ask: does popular sovereignty remain the grand principle that its ideal poses, or is it today just a limited notion and justification for those elected to claim legitimacy as representatives of the whole? If the latter, then the problems and issues raised by the 2000 election, while perhaps of concern, are inevitable. After all, from a political perspective, an elected official can accomplish more when he or she can claim to have some form of mandate from the people.

Such a view, however, is perhaps dangerously cynical. The expression of popular sovereignty in the American political system, while somewhat flawed in its execution, remains the cornerstone principle of a republican form of government. It is *one* principle, however—one that must interact with other fundamental values. As a result, the system is one where divergent rules of election administration can still dictate the substantive outcomes of elections. Although it may seem disconcerting, this is nevertheless the way things will likely remain.

That does not mean that the system is not open to improvement. What the nation's political leaders and citizenry must keep in mind, however, are the consequences their decisions will bring. The quotation of Senator Dodd at the start of this chapter, taken from the recent Senate debates regarding campaign reforms emerging from Election 2000,[7] calls to mind that changes made today not only affect the present and future functioning of elections but also have ramifications for each of the ends of representation, participation, political equality, and the expression of our popular sovereignty.

Conclusion

One could easily criticize the current state of the electoral process in the United States and be skeptical about the promise of any so-called reforms. After all, many of the problems discussed above stem from developments that at one time or another appeared to be reforms. Furthermore, the lessons that can be drawn from the 2000 elections—from turnout to campaign finance to election administration—all lead to a pessimistic view of the state of democratic elections in America.

Turn these lessons upside-down, however, and perhaps the system is generally working the way it is supposed to do. One needs to remember that elections in the American political system are a means to achieving the ends of representation, participation, political equality, and the expression of popular sovereignty, but they are not substitutes for these ends—or, in Rousseau's words, "the election of rulers is a function of government, and not of Sovereignty."[8] Elections are the method by which we select our leaders to govern ourselves. Although the electoral system may be flawed, the system still works, as the nation has continuously selected its leaders and experienced peaceful transitions of power through elections.

Certainly the electoral system can be improved to achieve the goals that Senator Dodd enunciated in the opening quotation: making the system fairer, more modern, easier to use, and more steadfast against corruption. Perhaps most important, the system needs to be improved to restore the lost faith of voters in the electoral processes. Furthermore, any present reforms, like those that preceded them, will come with unintended consequences that will need to be continuously monitored and, when necessary, addressed through additional reforms.

Despite the flaws in the electoral system, though, the primacy of popular sovereignty in the U.S. political system remains. The general will is still expressed through the participation of the citizenry and through the actions of elected officials. The fact that the electoral system has continued on, even after the heavy criticisms levied against it recently, is perhaps the greatest lesson that can be taken from the election of 2000.

Notes

1. Farrar-Myers, "Susan B. Anthony Dollars."
2. "FEC Reports Increase in Party Fundraising for 2000," Federal Election Commission press release, May 15, 2001, at http://www.fec.gov/2001news.html.
3. Statement of Rep. Christopher Shays, at http://www.house.gov/shays/hot/CFR/index.htm (emphasis added).
4. See Farrar-Myers, "Reforming the Reforms."
5. Jean-Jacques Rousseau, The Social Contract, bk. 1, chap. 6.
6. Ibid., bk. 2, chap. 1.
7. Congressional Record, February 13, 2002, S710.
8. Rousseau, The Social Contract, bk. 4, chap. 3.

16

□
□
□

The Fiasco in Florida

Fertile Ground for Electoral Reform

BLAIR BOBIER, PACIFIC GREEN PARTY OF OREGON

Throw the word *democracy* into a discussion of U.S. history and politics and it will likely produce one of three reactions. One unsentimental response is "The United States is not a democracy, it is a constitutional republic." Another, offered in the context of a socioeconomic analysis, is "The United States is not a democracy, it is a plutocracy." The third response, rarely heard in the days following the 2000 presidential election, is "The United States is the greatest democracy in the history of the world."

The unsentimental view, favored by certain academic types, conservative commentators, and America's aristocrats, is that the United States is not, was never intended to be, and (hopefully, according to them) never will be a democracy. This view notes that the Framers were the white, wealthy elites, who viewed "democracy" as something unsavory—government by the people, the merchants, tenants, and peddlers, as opposed to a government that left governing to the rich and educated. According to this view, the working-class and uneducated masses were incapable and undeserving of governing.

Consider that of all the governing institutions created by the Framers—the federal courts, the presidency, the Senate, and the House of Representatives—only the members of the House were elected directly by "the people." And "the people" who were eligible to vote were wealthy, white landowners. Various laws throughout history have prevented women, African Americans, Native Americans, Chinese, Japanese, Catholics, Jews, and poor whites from voting. Strange as it may seem from today's perspective, women were not granted the right to vote until the Nineteenth Amendment was adopted in 1920 and African Americans were routinely denied voting rights until the civil rights legislation of 1965, less than four decades ago. More recently, charges of discrimination against African American voters played a prominent role in the 2000 presidential election controversy in Florida.

To put it succinctly, only the members of the House of Representatives were elected directly by the people they were intended to represent: white men who owned real property. Federal judges and Supreme Court justices were, as they are today, all appointed. The president was, and is, elected *not* by the people but by the Electoral College. U.S. senators were chosen by their respective state legislatures until 1913, when the Seventeenth Amendment provided for their direct election.

Although the United States has embraced democratic ideals and is evolving into a more diverse and pluralistic society, it still has a long way to go before it can truly claim to be a democracy. Following the election in 2000, women, who made up more than 50 percent of the population, constituted only 13 percent of the Senate, and no African Americans were serving in the Senate, yet it is estimated that millionaires, who comprise considerably less than 1 percent of the country's population, held 28 percent of the Senate seats. In some ways the United States has evolved little in its 225-plus years of existence, and the controversies that stemmed from the 2000 election in Florida, although troubling, are in retrospect not that surprising.

The Electoral System

The Mother's Milk of Politics

"Money," according to a time-honored political axiom, "is the mother's milk of politics." The combined spending total for all elections in the United States in the year 2000 was $3 billion. To put that amount in perspective, it is greater than the entire federal budget of any country in Central America that year, and more than Switzerland spent on defense. Needless to say, the influential role of money in politics needs to be carefully examined, especially since some analysts claim that money does *not* buy elections. The question to pose then is: What does it buy? One answer: access and influence. People and industries that give big money to elected officials receive access in return. Meetings are set up. Phone calls are returned. Favors are granted. Legislation is drafted. Since relatively few people contribute to political campaigns—let alone contribute substantial sums—the money coming from relatively few people is a major determinant of government policy.

Whether or not money buys elections, it is surely poured into them. One of the major expenditures of any political campaign is advertising, primarily television commercials. The interesting thing about this medium is that we, the people, own the television airwaves. Government leases the broadcast rights to large corporations, who pay a pittance for these rights. The corporations, in turn, charge an arm and a leg for commercial time. Candidates pay the exorbitant fees and raise more money from wealthy contributors to pay for the commercials. But it does not have to be this way.

Barriers to Participation

The American electoral process is rife with barriers to participation—unless one has, or has access to, a lot of money and chooses to run as a Republican or a Democrat. Although there recently have been some prominent assaults on the two-party system, most notably Ross Perot's and Ralph Nader's presidential campaigns and the success of independent governor Jesse Ventura in Minnesota, many states make running as a third-party or independent candidate especially difficult. It was not always like this. So-called third parties have a long and rich history in this country and were rather successful in the early part of the twentieth century.

It was this success in particular that prompted Democrats and Republicans in state legislatures across the nation to enact ballot access laws making it more difficult—and in some cases impossible—for third parties to place candidates on the ballot. Typically these laws called for new or smaller parties to obtain thousands of signatures on petitions in order to run candidates. Some states required that candidates or parties pay huge filing fees. Third parties were forced to meet these stringent requirements in each election unless their candidates received a certain percentage of the vote. In some states, these percentages were set so high they were rarely, if ever, met.

Winner Take All

Unlike most Western European and South American democracies, which use forms of proportional representation, the United States uses the winner-take-all method to elect its Congress and legislatures. With proportional-representation elections, the emphasis shifts from individual candidates to party platforms, from personalities to issues. Political parties win seats in the legislature based on the percentage of votes they receive. For example, if a party wins 10 percent of the vote, it gets approximately 10 percent of the seats in the legislature. Although the threshold or minimum percentage varies from country to country, a party can win representation with as little as 0.67 percent of the vote in the Netherlands, whereas the threshold is 5 percent in Germany, New Zealand, and Russia.

Proportional representation much more accurately reflects the will of the voters. Hypothetically, if it was used in a U.S. legislative election in which 45 percent of voters voted for Democrats, 35 percent for Republicans, 10 percent for Greens, and 5 percent for Libertarians, the seats in the legislature would be allocated to all parties accordingly. By contrast, in order to win such a seat in the United States at present, a candidate needs to win either a plurality (more votes than anyone else receives) or, in some places, a majority (50 percent plus one) in that district. If a candidate wins an election with, say, 55 percent of the vote, 45 percent of voters have cast ballots for a losing candidate and wind up with no representation. In a three-way race with plurality voting, a candidate could win with 34 percent of the vote. In this case, the *vast majority* of voters would have voted for losing candidates.

Because of the high threshold needed to win election in the United States (usually 34–51 percent) compared to countries that use proportional representation (0.67–5 percent), it is difficult for smaller parties to win any representation at all. Winner-take-all elections tend to produce a "two-party system," which really is not a system at all but rather a result: two major parties that gravitate toward the philosophical middle of the electorate. Proportional representation, on the other hand, produces multiparty democracies where a wider spectrum of political views are represented.

Countries using proportional representation also tend to have higher voter turnout and better electoral representation of women and minority ethnic groups.

Lack of Real Competition

In many election years, the reelection rate of incumbents in the U.S. Congress has been higher than it was for the members of the former Soviet Union's Politburo, which was widely ridiculed for sham elections. In the 2000 elections, a whopping 98.5 percent of incumbents were reelected, most by landslides. This is not because Congress is doing such a wonderful job, or even because its members use their office and its perks (free mailings to boast of their accomplishments, for example) to their advantage. It's because congressional districts are generally drawn to favor one of the two major parties over the other. The Democrats and Republicans, in other words, divide up the political map between themselves.

Some districts, therefore, are safe for Republicans—it is almost impossible for a Democrat to get elected there—while other districts are safe for Democrats. Rare are the "swing" districts, where neither party has the advantage and the seat can change hands from party to party from one election to another.

Apathy or Informed Abstentions?

Voter turnout in the United States is among the lowest in western democracies. Moreover, nonvoters tend to be less affluent and less educated than voters. Are nonvoters apathetic? Are voter registration requirements or voting procedures too difficult or too stringent? Some nonvoters say voting does not make any difference at all. Are they failing to perform their civic duty or are they effectively voting for "none of the above," rejecting all the candidates and the government en masse?

One unusual and fascinating election that may shed some light on this subject was Jesse Ventura's 1996 victory in Minnesota as a third-party gubernatorial candidate. Ventura's brash and unorthodox campaign challenged not only the two major parties but conventional campaign wisdom as well. By actively courting *nonvoters* in a state that allows voter registration right up until Election Day, Ventura shocked the pollsters, pundits, and political establishment when thousands of people turned out to register and vote for him.

Ventura's election suggests that many nonvoters are not as apathetic as they are unmotivated by politics, viewing it as business as usual. It also suggests that laws requiring people to register to vote weeks before an election are unnecessary barriers that prevent them from participating in the democratic process just when it starts to get really exciting.

Burnout and Boredom?

There are many and frequent elections in the United States. There are elections for local, state, and federal offices. There are primary, runoff, and general elections. U.S. representatives and many state legislators are elected every two years, the president every four. Many other countries have longer legislative terms and do not hold primaries, which means that they have fewer elections less often than the United States.

While some may see so many elections as a sign of a robust participatory democracy, it should also be considered whether they overwhelm and bore the average citizen.

The Fiasco in Florida and Its Aftermath

The controversial 2000 presidential election—and the fiasco at its epicenter in Florida—introduced millions of Americans to the intricacies of the electoral process. Everything from the design of ballots to the role of the Electoral College became topics of heated debate and a source of material for late-night comedians on television. In one fell swoop, a controversy raged that incorporated the election of a president who lost the popular vote, charges that African American and Jewish voters had suffered discrimination, and accusations of impropriety and even treason on the part of elections officials and the U.S. Supreme Court, respectively.

Since the outcome of the election of the world's most powerful individual, the president of the United States of America, appeared to hinge on some five hundred votes in Florida, it would seem that the election proved how important it is to vote and that voting really does matter. On the other hand, the election proved to many people that voting does not matter at all: the loser of the popular vote won, and the only vote that mattered was the 5–4 vote of the Republican-dominated U.S. Supreme Court that effectively installed George W. Bush as the forty-third president.

Yet, despite the idiosyncrasies and made-for-TV controversies of the 2000 election, in many ways it was totally unremarkable. As usual, barely half of the eligible voters bothered to vote. Distinguished and credible third-party candidates were ignored. And for the third presidential election in a row, the winner received less than a majority of the popular vote: Bill Clinton's 1992 and 1996 presidential campaigns were won by 43 percent and 49 percent of the popular vote, respectively.

Flunking the Electoral College

Much like the design of most of the American government, the Electoral College is an inherently antidemocratic institution. Created as yet another device to buffer the federal government from the American people, the Electoral College—and *not* the American people—elects the president. Each state has a number of votes in the Electoral College equal to its representatives in the U.S. House and Senate. Because each state has two senators, regardless of population, states with fewer people receive greater representation in the Electoral College. If you live in Montana, Alaska, Hawaii, or Idaho, your vote counts more than someone's in Florida, New York, Texas, or California.

Some scholars have suggested that the Electoral College's origins were not only elitist but racially discriminatory as well. At the outset of the nation's history, blacks were not allowed to vote, yet each was included in the population census as an insulting three-fifths of a person. Therefore, states with large slave populations received greater representation in both Congress and the Electoral College, increasing the power of slaveholders at the expense of the enslaved.

Like slavery and powdered wigs, the Electoral College is an historical anachronism that has no place in modern America. If not abolished, it should at least be reformed. Currently, every state except Nebraska and Maine allocates its electors by a winner-take-all process: if a candidate wins a plurality of the vote in one of those forty-eight other states, that candidate wins all its electors. Electors should either be allocated in proportion to the popular vote earned or, better yet, the Electoral College should be abolished and replaced by a direct vote of the people. To ensure that the winning candidate has the support of a majority of voters, the election should be conducted using instant runoff voting, or IRV.

"Money Doesn't Talk, It Swears"—Bob Dylan

After years of inaction or downright hostility to stemming the massive flow of private money into the public political process, Congress finally passed a campaign finance reform bill in 2002, although its passage owes more to the Enron scandal than to the fiasco in Florida. The Shays-Meehan bill bans "soft money" contributions to the national political party committees but it also raises the allowable amount of "hard money" contributions to congressional and presidential candidates. Those who equate money and property with a First Amendment free-speech right have challenged the Act in court. Although it is seen by some as a step in the right direction, others are skeptical. It remains to be seen if it will survive judicial scrutiny and, if so, how effective it will be and the extent to which its loopholes will be exploited.

There is no question, however, that money is a corrupting influence in politics and that the American system of campaign "contributions" has, in effect, condoned legalized bribery. Who do you think has a better chance of getting an audience with the president or a member of Congress—the guy who fixes your car or a wealthy contributor to political campaigns? A look at the guest list of the Lincoln Bedroom in Bill Clinton's White House or the composition of Vice President Dick Cheney's Energy Policy Task Force shows that Democrats and Republicans are equally corrupted.

Perhaps even more disturbing is the amount of money raised by congressional incumbents in "safe" districts when most of them are virtually guaranteed reelection anyway. If a member of Congress is raising money that is not really needed to win an election, than what does that money buy? Fortunately, states such as Maine and Massachusetts are taking the lead in innovative "clean elections" laws, and these are models that can be used by other states and perhaps even at the federal level.

Make Your Vote Count

The *majority* of voters cast their ballots for losing candidates in the 2000 presidential election—as they did in 1996 and 1992. A direct popular vote using instant runoff voting (IRV) would change this and ensure that the winner has earned the support of a majority of voters. With IRV, voters rank the candidates in order of preference, marking a "1" next to their favorite candidate, a "2" for their second choice, "3" for their third choice, and so on. If any one candidate receives a majority of first-choice votes, that candidate wins and the election is over. If, however, no candidate gets a majority, then a "runoff" is held—instantly. Just as in a traditional two-round, go-back-to-the-polls-a-second-time runoff, the candidate with the fewest votes is eliminated. With IRV, though, voters have already marked their second choice on their ballots, so there is no need to go back to polls: a computer can instantly retabulate the votes. The process of eliminating candidates and retabulating the vote is done until one candidate receives an outright majority.

IRV allows people to vote their conscience and feel like they do not have to support the lesser of two evils in order to make their vote count. In jurisdictions where IRV replaces two-round runoffs, it can save time and money and increase voter turnout. In 2002, San Francisco became the first major U.S. city to adopt IRV elections for local offices, although Cambridge, Massachusetts, has successfully used another, similar "preference voting" method for many years. London uses IRV to elect its mayor, Ireland uses it to elect its president, and it is used at various levels of government in Australia.

With Liberty, Justice, and Representation for All

Although IRV would be a vast improvement in the way mayors, governors, presidents, and other executive officers are elected in the United States, it still does not solve the issue of fair representation in Congress and state legislatures. A "democracy" using winner-take-all elections provides representation for electoral winners only, while democracies using proportional representation strive to provide representation to all voters. There is a big difference between a right to vote and a right to representation.

The United States, in addition to its winner-take-all representation and notoriously low voter turnout, is also one of the least representative democracies in another way. Although the population of the United States has more than tripled in the past ninety years, the size of the House of Representatives has stayed constant at 435 members since the 1920s. The British House of Commons has one member for every 90,188 people; the South African National Assembly has one member for every 108,553 people, while the U.S. House of Representatives has one member for every 645,632 citizens. Many activists and scholars champion proportional representation, but the idea of increasing the size of the House is a relatively novel one, perhaps most notably supported by Representative Alcee Hastings of Florida. Nonetheless, both ideas—especially in tandem—would provide much more representation of people in government.

Reform: Fixing a Broken System

The mechanics of voting machines may not exactly excite people, but folks might get a lot more interested when they learn that outdated and malfunctioning voting machines deprived as many as *six million* Americans of their right to vote in the 2000 elections. Although separate studies conducted by Caltech/MIT and the Institute of Government Studies at U.C.–Berkeley in 2001 differed on what is the best voting technology, they agreed on the worst: punch cards. In February of 2002, a federal judge in Los Angeles agreed and ruled, in response to a lawsuit brought by the ACLU, that California had to replace punch-card voting machines by the 2004 elections.

Around the nation, nearly two thousand election-reform bills were introduced in state legislatures, but only a fraction of them passed, most likely because they required funding not seen as a priority given the recession of 2001–2003, the terror attacks of September 11, 2001, and wars in Afghanistan and Iraq. The situation could now change dramatically because a federal elections bill passed that provides funding to states for modernizing voting equipment.

Florida was the exception to the rule and enacted an omnibus election-reform bill that decertified punch cards, set standards for recounts, funded voter and poll-worker education, and centralized voter databases. Much more quietly, the state of Florida changed procedures that were said to have blocked tens of thousands of eligible Florida voters, mostly Democrats and a disproportionate number of them African Americans, from casting their ballots. A lawsuit by the NAACP is pending with regard to these allegations.

Opening Up the Process

Americans love choices—fifty-seven channels on cable, thirty-one flavors of ice cream, and enough varieties of breakfast cereal to eat something different every day of the month—yet its citizens accept a force-fed diet of only two political parties. Yes, three or four or five major parties might be more cumbersome than two, but it would certainly be more interesting—and more democratic. Besides, efficiency should not be the overriding consideration of governance. Too many regimes have made efficiency and expediency their priorities. China's one-party system is a model of efficiency. And the United States is just one party away from that.

Ralph Nader, who arguably has accomplished more in his lengthy public service career than Al Gore and George W. Bush combined, was not invited to participate in the 2000 presidential debates, and was even barred from attending one debate despite holding a ticket for admission. There is something seriously wrong with this picture. Presidential debates need to be sponsored by an independent nonpartisan (or *multi*partisan) commission and open to candidates beyond the two major parties.

Restrictive ballot access laws, enacted to create and perpetuate a two-party stranglehold on elections, need to be changed. And we the people need to reclaim our public airwaves and demand free television and radio time for all ballot-qualified candidates.

Voting and voter registration also need to be easier. Allowing same-day (Election Day) voter registration greatly increases voter turnout and should be implemented nationwide. Why is Election Day in the middle of the week when most people have to work, anyway? Making Election Day a holiday or moving it to the weekend is a sensible, and easily accomplished, democratic improvement.

Increased Awareness and Activism

Although the 2000 election plunged our nation into a crisis and produced a topsy-turvy result, it has increased both awareness of the electoral process and prodemocracy activism. The Pro-Democracy Convention in Philadelphia in 2001 brought together hundreds of citizens from across the country, an annual Democracy Summer training institute was created in Florida to teach students and activists about electoral reforms, and a coalition of activists and organizations created a Voters' Bill of Rights as a rallying point for democratic improvements.

Conclusion

The United States is an evolving democracy, and the fiasco in Florida not only highlighted the electoral system's shortcomings but also acted as a catalyst for election and campaign-finance reform. Fortunately, voting machines are being modernized, as a result either of legislation or of lawsuits. But there is still a long way to go in fulfilling the promise of American democracy. Many years of struggle produced voting rights for women, African Americans, and others historically denied the right to vote. Today's challenges are no less important. Big money, winner-take-all elections, and archaic institutions like the Electoral College deny Americans the right to representation. To modernize a rallying cry from the first American Revolution, "Voting without representation is tyranny."

The Declaration of Independence tells the American people that "it is their Right, it is their Duty" to change the nature of their government when it is no longer providing for their peace and happiness. We stand on the shoulders of giants. We owe it to them and to ourselves to create an electoral system befitting the diverse and modern nation that is twenty-first-century America.

17 ☐
☐
☐

Is Election Reform Necessary? Yes!

JOAN KARP, PRESIDENT, LEAGUE OF WOMEN VOTERS
OF SOUTH PALM BEACH COUNTY

In the wake of the controversial 2000 election in Florida, the question of the need for sweeping reforms in the way elections are administered has been raised. According to Carolyn Jefferson-Jenkins, then national president of the League of Women Voters, arguing for election reforms in the September/October 2001 issue of *The National Voter*:

A study of U.S. election systems by the League of Women Voters Education Fund finds that huge numbers of citizens are being disenfranchised because the systems don't work. State officials often pass the buck to local officials; local officials are often apathetic and uninformed.

Among the problems: Fear of fraud is often used to keep certain people away from the polls. The poor, the elderly, the uneducated, and racial and ethnic minorities are particularly burdened. Registration procedures are too complex. So are the methods for absentee voting, as well as the procedures for actually casting a ballot.

Registration lists are often incomplete. Staff at the polling places are poorly trained. Bilingual staff isn't available when needed. Officials too often act as if voting were a privilege, rather than a right.

Sounds like a good description of today's problems, right? Except that this study was done in 1972—almost three decades before the current furor over Election 2000. The similarities with today's election crisis show just how intractable some of the problems are, and how long the league has been fighting to over-come them.

Not much has changed since this 1972 survey. However, the population in Palm Beach County has grown tremendously in size and diversity in the last three decades. Additionally, the advent of around-the-clock media coverage did not occur until after 1972. These two new factors contributed greatly to the nature, extent, and visibility of the problems experienced by Florida in November 2000.

Reactions to the 2000 Election

In Palm Beach County, Florida, the voters were angered and appalled by many facets of the election in 2000. The biggest issue was the infamous butterfly ballot, followed closely by the fact that some ballots did not line up properly when inserted into the old punch-card voting machines. Contrary to the portrayal in the media and by late-night comedians, the difficulties with aligning the ballots occurred irrespective of whether a voter was experienced or inexperienced. Another problem was that some voters were told they were not on the registered-voter rolls the day of the election, and poll workers were unable to phone in to the elections office for confirmation because of overloaded phone lines.

The League of Women Voters of South Palm Beach County (LWVSPBC) held a new-member orientation coffee the Saturday after Election Day. Even though it was scheduled as the main item of business, we were unable to get to our orientation program because the women who attended were so focused on the election, which still remained in limbo at this point. Several people at this meeting had been poll workers and had firsthand knowledge of all the problems. One of the positive consequences of the election was that our league chapter gained more than sixty members. These new members were motivated directly by the election debacle and had the desire to do something to ensure that the problems would not happen again.

The anger continued throughout 2001. A public hearing in October 2001 to solicit reactions to Florida's proposed rules for standardizing vote counting saw angry voters recapping what happened to them at the polls. While this was not very constructive for the hearing, it was indicative of the dire need for reform and reflected both the sentiment of much of the county and the mood found at other similar public meetings.

The Governor Reacts

Immediately after the final vote counts in December of 2000, Florida governor Jeb Bush appointed a bipartisan task force to recommend voting reforms. This task force comprised twenty-one members—ten each of Democrats and Republicans, and one unaffiliated member chosen by the other twenty. With a deadline of March 1, 2001, to bring their recommendations to the Florida legislature, the task force planned hearings all around the state to obtain citizen input.

League Positions

The League of Women Voters is a national organization in existence since 1920, with a presence in all fifty states. Membership is open to all citizens, male and female. It is a grassroots organization. Each state has a state league, and within each state are local leagues. Dues paid to local leagues support the state and national organizations as well.

Our mission statement: The League of Women Voters is a nonpartisan organization that promotes political responsibility through informed and active participation of citizens in government and acts on selected governmental issues.

The League of Women Voters of the United States and the League of Women Voters of Florida have long-standing positions on reforming elections. Positions are the result of local league study and combined consensus. These positions allow leagues at all levels to lobby for reforms in all possible venues.

It was obvious to the directors of our league chapter that the members needed to act regarding an array of issues pertaining to the problems experienced in the 2000 election. We immediately formed a committee to get ideas from the members. Eighteen members came forward to participate. We decided our goal would be to present our opinion at the February 1, 2001, task force hearing.

The LWVSPBC started with the Florida league's established positions and decided which ones to concentrate on for lobbying. For organizational purposes, we broke into groups to allow different discussions. When league members reconvened, we had a prioritized list that became a three-minute testimony, and a more detailed written version to submit to the task force. Other local leagues around the state as well as the league's state board testified at various hearings. The hearings were televised on C-SPAN. My testimony to the governor's task force follows:

I am Joan Karp, president, League of Women Voters of South Palm Beach County, speaking also for the West Palm Beach Area League of Women Voters. The League of Women Voters of Palm Beach County thanks you and all the other groups and committees around the state for all the effort toward election reform. I thank you for the opportunity to present the league's views.

The League of Women Voters of Florida believes that democratic government depends on the informed and active participation of its citizens, and that fundamental to this participation is the right to vote and equal access to the ballot.

The league has long-standing positions on election reform. Over the years, some of our positions have been incorporated into the laws, but there are still many that we feel need to be enacted. We are in agreement with many of the points put forward in the last several weeks since this task force has been in place. I will touch on a few points that we feel require special emphasis and may not yet have been addressed. Additionally, I am submitting in writing a longer list of positions and suggestions in five categories that address our priorities.

We feel the following are of major importance:

1. *Equipment and Ballots.* Statewide standardized equipment and ballot design are essential. Further, market testing by a large group of people of the process from the time a voter walks into the polling place through ballot counting and possible recounting is crucial. That, of course, includes the ballot itself.

2. *Equal Access.* Use every means possible to guarantee accurate up-to-date voter lists. Borrow techniques from the U.S. Post Office, telemarketers, IRS, who are able to find most of us. Also, enlist assistance of the federal government to develop standards and procedures for overseas and military ballots.

3. *Registration Forms.* New application forms should be developed that are more easily read, especially the required fields.

4. *Crossover Primaries.* The legislature should eliminate the loophole in the current law that allows a write-in candidate to preclude opposing party members from voting in a primary when only candidates from one party are running for a particular office. This loophole disenfranchised some people in one district in Palm Beach County this year.

5. *Conflict of Interest.* All election officials (supervisors, canvassing board members, Secretary of State, etc.) should be prohibited from active participation in candidates' campaigns.

6. *Nonpartisan Elections.* Supervisors of Elections should be elected on a nonpartisan basis.

7. *Poll Workers.* Consider job-sharing to decrease hours of poll workers, and drawing from a larger pool for poll workers (e.g., college students).

8. *Felons.* Voting rights should be automatically restored when a felon has paid his debt to society. Florida is among only thirteen states that deny this. This change would resolve one of the issues that created problems at the polling place.

The LWVSPBC also endorsed the recommendation by the supervisors of elections that provisional ballots be provided when a voter's eligibility cannot be determined at the polls. Additionally, two letters-to-the-editor sent to our three local papers were published. The first in November of 2000 urged the officials to "make every vote count"—that is, to count all the ballots that officials were discarding because of various "chad" problems, and vowed that the LWVSPBC would increase our voter education in the future. The second letter, at the end of February of 2001, chastised the legislature for giving election reform a low priority even before the task force's report was due and the legislative session started.

Results

In general, the league was pleased with the reforms the legislature passed in the 2001 session. Here is a short summary:

· Punch cards, paper ballots, mechanical lever machines, and central-count voting systems were prohibited. Two methods now approved are touch-screen and scanned ballots. (Palm Beach County decided on touch-screen, and the county commissioners agreed to pay for these.)

· Money was earmarked for voter education and poll worker training. Poll workers must complete a specified number of hours of training. A manual of procedures must be at each polling place.

· Absentee ballots became "convenience ballots." That is, you do not need a reason to vote absentee. The military and overseas ballot process was simplified.

· Provisional ballots will be available for voters whose eligibility cannot be determined at the polls. Those ballots will be counted only if/when eligibility is determined.

· Statewide uniform procedures for recounts, certifications, and the like are required and were established later by the Department of Elections.

· The second primary, or runoff primary, has been eliminated for 2002 only. (This was not a task force recommendation but came from the legislature, which subsequently also eliminated the 2003 primary. The legislature will determine whether this should continue in future elections.)

In spite of this positive result, some elements of the task force's recommendations as well as of the league's list of reforms were omitted. These include:

· Limiting political activity of members of local and state canvassing boards

· Nonpartisan election of the supervisors of elections (something the supervisors wanted as well, which became a reality through a ballot question in the 2002 election)

· Allowing government workers to serve as poll workers

· Restoring the voting rights of ex-felons by easing Florida's onerous process of application for rights restoration (Governor Jeb Bush promised to do so, but this is not yet in the statutes at the time of this writing)

· Public campaign financing, which was weakened by stating that campaign contributions from out of state would not count toward qualifying for matching public financing.

Where Are We Now?

The LWVSPBC is actively involved in voter registration and education initiatives and in getting-out-the-vote programs. Since Palm Beach County has all new voting machines, we have joined in a coalition of several groups whose sole purpose is to assist the county supervisor of elections in voter registration and demonstrating the new touch-screen voting to the citizenry.

The members of our Speakers Bureau have been out in the community explaining the voting reforms to various organizations, homeowners associations, churches, corporations, and so forth. In 2000 we spoke to thirty-eight different groups in South Palm Beach County. With the additional wrinkle of new voting districts for the November 2002 elections, and eleven proposed constitutional amendments on the ballot, we had thirty-six speaking engagements. For 2004, we prepared a voter's manual in three languages that describes the registration and voting processes, along with descriptions of the elective offices.

Members of our Voters Service Committee devised a program that we present to each senior class in the five public high schools in our area. We talk to the students about the various elections held in the county, and why one vote counts, and we register students to vote who are at least seventeen years of age.

We also participate in the Democracy Network (DNet), the league's online voters' guide. Citizens can go online for information on all candidates on the ballot in one place (www.dnet.org). DNet is also a helpful service for the candidates—it allows them to respond to their opponents and provides a forum for their positions, at no cost to them. The league's position is to invite all candidates to participate in the service. Many do.

On the local (municipal and county) level, we hold candidate forums where there are at least two candidates for an office. As a nonpartisan organization, the league never endorses any candidates, and does not allow campaigning at any of our public meetings.

Even though much remains to be done to ensure that elections are fair, inclusive, open, and accurate, progress has been made. Voters and citizens as well as organizations such as the League of Women Voters and community groups can play a role—and must play a role—in both administering and improving elections. This is one of the important lessons learned from the 2000 election controversy in Florida. Election reform is necessary, and it is possible.

CONCLUSION

18 □
　　□
　　□

"This Is Guatemala"

MICHAEL A. GENOVESE, LOYOLA MARYMOUNT UNIVERSITY

The ballots made no results. The counters made the result.

—Boss Tweed

The 2000 presidential election in the United States was a cynic's paradise, and a democrat's nightmare. With a plot seemingly taken from a baroque Graham Greene novel of colonial corruption and imperial arrogance, Election 2000 challenged many of the sacred assumptions Americans once held about the integrity of the electoral process and the legitimacy of their governmental system. Called into question were the core democratic values Americans long took for granted.

As this book amply demonstrates, Election 2000 was anything but ordinary. Indeed, it was an international embarrassment for the United States. After decades of monitoring elections in other countries to ensure democratic standards, the United States found itself trying to explain to others why the leader of the free world could not even get a vote count right! One e-mail widely circulated in the aftermath of the November 2000 election highlighted the hypocrisies of America's patronizing celebration of its premier status as an advanced, sophisticated democracy. Entitled simply "Imagine," it quoted a Zimbabwean politician as saying children should study the U.S. election event closely because it shows that election fraud is not only a Third World phenomenon. To make his case, the character in the e-mail invited his audience to

· Imagine that we read of an election occurring anywhere in the Third World in which the self-declared winner was the son of the former prime minister and that former prime minister was himself the former head of the nation's secret police/intelligence agency.

· Imagine that the self-declared winner lost the popular vote but won based on some old colonial holdover from the nation's predemocratic past (the Electoral College).

· Imagine that the self-declared winner's "victory" turned on disputed votes cast in a province governed by his brother!

· Imagine that the poorly drafted ballots of one district, a district heavily favouring the self-declared winner's opponent, led thousands of voters to vote for the wrong candidate.

· Imagine that hundreds of members of that most-despised caste were intercepted on their way to the polls by state police operating under the authority of the self-declared winner's brother.

· Imagine that six million people voted in the disputed province and that the self-declared winner's "lead" was only 327 votes. Fewer, certainly, than the vote-counting machines' margin of error.

· Imagine that the self-declared winner and his political party opposed a more careful by-hand inspection and recounting of the ballots in the disputed province or in its most hotly disputed district.

· Imagine that the self-declared winner was himself the governor of a major province, which had the worst human rights record of any province in his nation and actually led the nation in executions.

· Imagine that a major campaign promise of the self-declared winner was to appoint like-minded human rights violators to lifetime positions on the high court of that nation.

None of us would deem such an election to be representative of anything other than the self-declared winner's will to power. All of us, I imagine, would wearily turn the page thinking that it was another sad tale of a Third World country.

There exists, in the "world's most powerful democracy," the distinct possibility that the loser won the election—that, in effect, a democratic election may have been stolen. After 105 million citizens voted, it was a handful of justices by a 5–4 vote who finally selected a president, their vote largely along party lines. Along the peculiar path from election to selection were a series of macabre, bizarre, and unbelievable twists and turns that do indeed call into question the honesty, integrity, and viability of the American system of elections.

Table 18.1 Close Presidential Elections

Closest Races by Electoral Vote

Year	Losing Candidate	# Earned	Short of Victory	Winning Candidate
1876	Samuel J. Tilden	184	1	Rutherford B. Hayes
1916	Charles E. Hughes	254	12	Woodrow Wilson
1884	James G. Blaine	182	19	Grover Cleveland
1976	Gerald R. Ford	240	29	Jimmy Carter
1880	Winfield S. Hancock	155	30	James A. Garfield
1888	Grover Cleveland	168	33	Benjamin Harrison

Closest Races by Popular Vote

Year	Winning Candidate	Losing Candidate	Vote Margin	% of Total
1876	Rutherford B. Hayes	Samuel J. Tilden	-254,235	-3.02
1888	Benjamin Harrison	Grover Cleveland	-90,596	-0.80
1880	James A. Garfield	Winfield S. Hancock	1,898	0.02
1884	Grover Cleveland	James G. Blaine	25,685	0.25
1960	John F. Kennedy	Richard M. Nixon	118,574	0.17

Adapted from Ceaser and Busch, *The Perfect Tie,* 134; and Larry J. Sabato, *Overtime!: The Election 2000 Thriller,* New York: Longman, 2002, 120–21.

Political Parity and Shifting Winds

Arguably the closest, certainly the longest, demonstrably the costliest presidential campaign in history, this contest will be remembered for the strange thirty-six-day election aftermath, in which five Supreme Court justices finally selected the candidate, from their own party, who lost the popular vote and may have actually lost the Electoral College vote. It was not supposed to be this way—not in America.

How is one to understand and put into proper perspective the peculiarities of Campaign 2000 and Election 2000? The postelection swirl of events perplexed rather than enlightened us. So many ups and downs, so many possible outcomes hanging on a single judge's decision or the interpretation of what to do about a dangling, dimpled, or pregnant chad. It was, Louis Menand wrote, "the civics course from hell."[1]

Americans had been accustomed to waking up on the day after the election and knowing who would be their president. But on November 8, 2000, the campaign may have officially ended but a new contest was just beginning. It would last five weeks. As James Ceaser and Andrew Busch note, "There were two major questions at that moment that no one could answer: who would win, and who would decide who would win."[2] We now know that George W. Bush won; we also know that it was the U.S. Supreme Court that ultimately handed him the presidency. In the end, Bush became president in one of the closest elections in presidential history. Not only was the presidential contest close—too close to call—but the Senate ended with a 50–50 split between the two major parties (only to be broken a few months later when Vermont Republican James Jeffords left his party to become an Independent and vote with the Democrats). In the House of Representatives, the Republicans had a razor-thin majority. At the state level, there was also a near-even split in party control. In state legislatures, the Democrats controlled 25 lower houses, the Republicans 24; the Republicans controlled 24 state senates, the Democrats 21. Only among governors, where Republicans held a 29–19 advantage after the election, was there any measurable gap between the power of the parties. In major-city mayoral contests, the Democrats came out slightly ahead of the Republicans.

George W. Bush was elected president without a majority. Governing in the best of times is difficult enough. But governing without a majority when your legitimacy is in question is especially difficult. There was a rough parity between the parties, and with no governing majority and no electoral mandate, along with political equilibrium and voter volatility, George W. Bush was handed the presidency, but with little power. Surprisingly, Bush was able to assume office with few challenges to his legitimacy.

With no consensus or majority, American politics has flip-flopped dramatically in the past quarter century. From the Democratic center-left (Carter), the nation lurched to the Republican hard right (Reagan), then back to the Republican center-right (Bush). Then, as a reaction to the impact of Reagan, who had shifted the center of political gravity to the right, Democrat Bill Clinton took his party from left to center and captured the White House. But two years later, with fears he was moving too far to the left, the voters again lurched hard right in 1994 with Newt Gingrich's Republican Revolution. That was to fizzle out, and a centrist Clinton easily won reelection in 1996. Then the Republicans launched a new frontal assault on Clinton with impeachment, only to be beaten by a president whose popularity remained above 60 percent. The impeachment polarized the public, but many appear to have been frustrated with the Republicans for attempting to remove a president with high approval ratings. Comedian Dennis Miller even "ranted" that the Republicans were "more out of step with the rest of America than Joe Cocker in a line dance." This event was followed by a close, indecisive election in 2000 in which George W. Bush became president. The country had been on a political and ideological roller coaster and was now coming off a real ride in the weeks after the 2000 election. Observers of the American political scene were more likely to emerge from their inquiries with whiplash than insights. In this context of parity, no majorities, and shifting political winds, coupled with an age of cynicism, the election of 2000 makes "some" sense.

The Gory Details—or, Gore Happens

> Life is terribly deficient in form. Its catastrophes happen in the wrong way and to the wrong people. There is a grotesque horror about its comedies, and its tragedies seem to culminate in farce.
>
> —Oscar Wilde, *The Critic as Artist*

How in the world could Al Gore have lost the 2000 election? Conditions pointed to an easy Gore victory: peace and prosperity. An overwhelming majority of Americans believed that the country was "going in the right direction." All electoral voting models concluded that good times benefited the incumbent president and his party. So, how did Gore lose? Of course, he may not have lost. But that is beside the point at this late date. The election should never have been close enough to allow the fiasco in Florida to determine the outcome. Did Gore lose? Did Bush win? Did Clinton cost Gore the election?

The Gore team had an important early strategic decision to make: Do we embrace Clinton and his successes, or do we avoid Clinton and the scandal baggage? Their polls suggested and their inclination was to avoid Clinton. It was a huge risk and, as it turns out, probably a fatal mistake.

With Clinton, one had to accept the good with the bad, but by avoiding Clinton and his strong record of accomplishments, Gore relinquished the opportunity to run on the record and propose "more of the same." True, that "same" meant different things to different people. But all the anti-Clinton voters were already in the Bush camp. All the pro-Clinton voters were already behind Gore. It was the independent voters who Gore feared might be turned away by the Clinton problems. This meant running away from the Clinton strengths as well. "I'm my own man," Gore announced to a national audience at the Los Angeles Democratic Convention. Al Gore ran a campaign abandoning the strong record of the Clinton presidency.

During the postelection recount battle, the Gore strategy—textbook strategy for the candidate trailing in the vote count—was to hold off any final state certification decisions while attempting, by whatever means available, to establish as broad and inclusive a vote-counting regime as possible. Given the peculiarities of Florida's voting procedures, there was reason to believe that, if all the votes were properly and accurately counted, Gore had a good chance to win. The chief enemy of this strategy was time: the calendar conspired against the Gore team's strategy. And in the end, the clock ran out for the Gore campaign.

Son of a Bush—or, Bush Happens

> The ordinary American voter does not object to mediocrity. He has a lower conception of the qualities requisite to make a statesman than those who direct public opinion in Europe have. He likes his candidate to be sensible, vigorous, and, above all, what he calls "magnetic," and does not value, because he sees no need for, originality or profundity, a fine culture or a wide knowledge.
>
> —James Bryce, *The American Commonwealth*

So we have said: It should never have been a contest. Economic and world conditions favored the incumbent party, and the Bush challenge should have been a faint threat to Gore during times of peace and prosperity. Bush took an early lead in the race for the Republican Party nomination; he had raised more money than had ever been raised in any campaign, was able to fend off a primary-season challenge from maverick John McCain, and won his party's nomination rather easily . His general election campaign theme of "compassionate conservativism" reflected the impact of Bill Clinton as much as it reflected Bush's own goals and ideology. Clinton did to the Republicans what Reagan a decade earlier had done to the Democrats: forced them to either move to the political center or face electoral defeat. Clinton moved the Democrats to a left-center position, delivered on peace and prosperity, and took the nation to a centrist posture. Reagan moved the nation from center-left to center-right; Clinton moved the nation back to center. Bush had no choice but to go where the votes were, the center, and take his party with him. He ran a centrist campaign, and Republicans, desperate after eight years of Democratic control of the White House, held their noses and moved along with him toward the center. At least for the campaign. Governing would be another story.

During the postelection contest, Bush's strategy was clear and simple: delay, delay, delay. When one is ahead in a potential recount battle, the calendar becomes a chief ally. The longer Bush drew out the process—the Bush team referred to this as "mudballing"—the more likely it was that time would run out for Al Gore. Any stalling tactic, any roadblock, any way to stifle a recount would help Bush protect his slim lead. His campaign sat on the ball and let the clock run out, so to speak.

Kathleen Harris, Florida's secretary of state and Bush's campaign cochair for Florida, barely bothered to conceal her partisan intentions, making decision after decision that favored the Bush cause. In the end, there just was not enough time for a fair and accurate recount. The Bush team saw to that. Justice takes time, and time was on Bush's side. Bush held nearly all the strong cards: a lead after Election Day, the ability to delay when time was of the essence, a brother who was governor of the contested state, his state cochair serving as the state's chief elections officer, and a politicized and friendly U.S. Supreme Court if he needed it.

Who Really Won—or, Chad Happens

> I am not naive enough to think that the candidate with the most votes should win an election. That's the kind of uninformed, romantic, antediluvian belief that I clung to until about thirteen days ago. We now know that it is the candidate with the best lawyers who should win an election.
>
> —Joel Achenbach, *It Looks Like a President Only Smaller*

Who would have won Florida, and thus the presidency, had not the U.S. Supreme Court halted the recount? Had time not been an issue, had the state officials in Florida been able to accurately count the vote, would Bush or Gore have emerged as the victor? Alas, we may never know the answer. So few votes separated the two candidates that—depending on how the votes were counted, and which votes—each candidate could reasonably claim that he was the "real winner." If nothing else, the Florida fiasco revealed the fragile, complex, and dark underside of the electoral machinery. Most of the failures of Florida's vote counting system were errors of carelessness, confusion, and stupidity, not crimes or fraud. Confusing butterfly ballots may have been a mistake, but they were not the result of malice. Dangling, dimpled, pregnant, and other chads were not an attempt to manipulate the vote outcome unfairly. They were the flawed outcome of a flawed process.

The one truly disturbing charge to emerge from the Florida vote aftermath was found in the report of the U.S. Civil Rights Commission, which concluded that Florida's election was marred by "significant and distressing" barriers put in the way of African Americans who were attempting to vote. These likely Gore voters were, it seems, prevented from voting in alarming numbers. The Commission charged that the Florida election was marked by "injustice, ineptitude and inefficiency," and it urged the Justice Department to investigate whether laws were violated, maintaining that this disenfranchisement was not "isolated or episodic" but that, rather, African American voters were nearly ten times more likely than white voters to have their ballots rejected in Florida.

Bush v. Gore v. the Supreme Court—or, Scalia Happens

> If I should need to name, O Western World, your powerfulest scene and show,
> 'Twould not be you, Niagara—nor you, ye limitless prairies—nor your huge rifts of canyons, Colorado,
> Nor you, Yosemite . . .
>   I'd name—the still small voice vibrating—America's choosing day . . .
> Texas to Maine—the Prairie States—Vermont, Virginia, California,
> The final ballot-shower from East to West.
>
> —Walt Whitman, "Election Day, November, 1884"

As events in Florida unfolded at a bewildering pace; as each day seemed to bring a decision that favored one candidate, only to be reversed the next day; as the outcome remained as uncertain as the process was confusing, both camps began to believe that the issue would ultimately be decided in the courts— either Florida's or the U.S. Supreme Court. With shortness of time dictating events, the Supreme Court felt it had to cast the final deciding vote in the 2000 election. Politically, no one should have been surprised that this very partisan court sided with Bush, yet constitutional scholars had reason to feel surprise at the questionable grounds on which the Court made its decision. The majority, appointed by Republican presidents, had fairly actively embraced and promoted the Republican Party agenda. But in *Bush v. Gore* the Court had to violate its "constitutional principles" to satisfy its partisan goal. In order for the Court to side with Bush, it had to abandon its firm commitment to federalism and overturn the decision of the Supreme Court of Florida. The Court had to swallow its previous logic on the sanctity of states' rights and undermine the very foundation on which its adherence to federalism was based. Ironically, the action that gave Bush the victory went against the principles that Bush and the Republican Party held up as their fundamental beliefs. This very court had time and again sided with states against the federal government, citing infringement of state prerogative as the grounds for striking down federal laws ranging from a ban on guns near schools to a statute allowing rape victims and battered spouses to sue their assailants in federal court. But in *Bush v. Gore* the Court that had consistently exalted state sovereignty put politics over principle.

The decision of the majority in the case was both confused and confusing.

It is difficult to find a respectable constitutional scholar who will defend it. The effect of the muddled decision was to effectively force Gore to concede defeat.[3] Are we to take the logic of the Court seriously, or must we merely consign their case to the laws of power politics? If the legal positions of Bush and Gore were reversed, could anyone imagine the Court making the decision it made? In *Bush v. Gore* partisanship trumped law; politics trumped justice. The exit wound left by this case was eloquently noted in a dissent by Justice John Paul Stevens, who considered the damage done to the Court's respect and to the law:

> The endorsement of that [Bush's] position by the majority of this Court can only lend credence to the most cynical appraisal of the work of judges throughout the land. It is confidence in the men and women who administer the judicial system that is the true backbone of the rule of law. Time will one day heal the wound to that confidence that will be inflicted by today's decision. One thing, however, is certain. Although we may never know with complete certainty the identify of the winner of this year's Presidential election, the identity of the loser is perfectly clear. It is the Nation's confidence in the judge as an impartial guardian of the rule of law.

Lessons of the 2000 Election—or, Breakdown Happens

> The health of any democracy . . . depends on a small detail: the conduct of elections. Everything else is secondary.
>
> —José Ortega y Gasset

What are we to make of Election 2000 and its bizarre aftermath? What lessons can we draw from this most unusual of presidential contests? One strand of thought suggests that, precisely because the 2000 election was so unusual, we should be wary of drawing broad conclusions. The events in Florida were, so the argument goes, unique and thus unlikely to be repeated. True, the events of Florida are not likely to be soon repeated, but apart from the peculiarities of the Florida controversy, there is much we can learn from what happened in the aftermath of November 2000 in particular and from the election more generally.

The Gore campaign reminds us that during times of peace and prosperity, the incumbent should blanket himself or herself in a cloak of achievements, regardless of the potential downside of defending a president or a record that is less than perfect. Gore's decision to run apart from or away from Clinton's— and his own—record seems in hindsight to have been a huge mistake.

Table 18.2. The 2000 Vote Breakdown

	Vote share	Gore	Bush
Gender			
Men	48%	42%	53%
Women	52%	54%	43%
Race			
White	81%	42%	54%
Black	10%	90%	9%
Hispanic	7%	62%	35%
Asian	2%	55%	41%
Other	1%	55%	39%
Age			
18–29	17%	48%	46%
30–44	33%	48%	49%
45–59	28%	48%	49%
60+	22%	51%	47%
Education			
No high school	5%	59%	39%
High school grad	21%	48%	49%
Some college	32%	45%	51%
College grad	24%	45%	51%
Postgrad	18%	52%	44%
Income			
< $15,000	7%	57%	37%
$15–$30,000	16%	54%	41%
$30–$50,000	24%	49%	48%
$50–$75,000	25%	46%	51%
$75–$100,000	13%	45%	52%
> $100,000	15%	43%	54%

Source: Voter News Service.

During the postelection phase, it is unfair to be too harsh on any of the participants. Should Gore have moved sooner? Should he have called for an immediate statewide recount? Done this? Done that? It was all too confusing at the moment to expect perfection from any campaign. Fighting three wars at once—legal, political, and public relations battles—created inherent tensions that could never be fully reconciled. As a staff writer of the *Washington Post* wrote, "Every day the participants were forced to make potentially huge decisions, with little time to think."[4] Under such circumstances it is best to be a bit forgiving. Both campaigns pursued their own self-interest. We could and should expect nothing else. The Bush and Gore campaigns had one and only one goal in mind: winning. To that end, Bush behaved no better or worse than Gore.

Without question, respect for the nation's electoral system was damaged. Events in Florida exposed the fragility of democracy generally, and more specifically how vulnerable the system was to technical breakdown. The dark secret of election vulnerability—that inaccuracies infect the system and that there is a very real margin-of-error problem—has now been exposed. If the Florida fiasco compels systematic improvements, it will be a benefit to democracy.

Elections are not self-executing mechanisms. They require laws, regulations, funding, and honorable people to fulfill the democratic requirements of fairness. Those who control the machinery of government can, to a degree, shape both the rules of engagement (preelection) and the outcomes (postelection). In the case of Florida, the postelection opportunity either to remain neutral and fair or to engage in partisanship presented itself from day one. Nearly all the important levers of power in Florida were in the hands of the Republican Party. From the governor (the brother of one candidate) to the secretary of state (said candidate's state cochair), Republicans had the opportunity to shape, if not wholly determine, the outcome of the race. In almost every case, the decisions made by those in power demonstrably aided the cause of George W. Bush. It may be that the Bush campaign was in the right in each instance. But it hardly seems statistically probable. Self-interest drove the Bush team to oppose a full and fair counting of the votes in Florida. Florida officials cooperated in this opposition at almost every turn. Elections, as we have learned, are vulnerable to partisan power plays.

In the aftermath of the Florida fiasco, calls to "reform" the Electoral College sprang up from across the country. This anachronistic institution is at fault, the critics charged; it undermines democracy and lets the loser win. Indeed, the loser of the popular vote did win, which must strike one as decidedly undemocratic. But is abolishing the Electoral College the answer? I confess sympathy with the many who wish to have the president directly elected by popular vote. It satisfies my democratic prejudices. But I also fear the possibility that—as so often has happened in the past—reform may deform. What, one must ask, are the unintended consequences of reform? Would smaller states suffer? Would the party system be undermined? It would appear that this debate is purely academic, because the country has tried many times historically to right past wrongs by abolishing the Electoral College. It has not been done; I suspect it will not be done.

The media received a big black eye as a result of its coverage on election night. Calling Florida for Gore prematurely, then withdrawing the state from the Gore column, then prematurely awarding the state to Bush, all proved to be an embarrassment born of the pressures of competition and the propensity to rush to judgment ahead of the facts. By early December, Gallup polls reported record levels of public distrust of the media, with 65 percent saying that the major news organizations could not be trusted to "get the facts straight."

And what of the American public? What can be said of their response to Election 2000? Did the public demonstrate concern that an election may have been stolen? No, not in the way and to the extent that they should have. If anything, the public expressed mild interest and little emotional attachment. During the 1996 campaign, Republican presidential candidate Bob Dole crossed the country attacking Clinton's character flaws while asking, "Where's the outrage?" He was met with yawns. Two years later, when the Republicans made their case for the impeachment of President Clinton, the public failed to embrace the cause. Then in 2000, when a presidential election may have been stolen, the public looked on with confusion and amusement. Where, indeed, was and is the outrage?

Part of the answer may be that the presidency itself has changed. In the post–Cold War pre-terrorism era, the presidency seemed less necessary and less important than it used to be. Is the presidency getting smaller, and do we care less about its health and stature? The public plays the role of uninterested observer. Politics becomes merely a spectator sport and the presidency part of the spectacle of a political circus. The president is now the nation's celebrity-in-chief, supplying entertainment that may be interesting but seems only somewhat important. This is a sad loss. A diminished presidency may have seemed a good idea amid peace and prosperity, but will it be capable of governing when needed to act and lead the nation?

If the presidency seems diminished, did the events in Florida damage the legitimacy of the institution and George W. Bush as president? How could it not? Amazingly—and probably befitting the previous statements—Bush assumed office with all the legitimacy necessary to govern. There were few who questioned his right to occupy the office, and while his may have been a tainted victory, it was recognized as legitimate. The "legal coup d'état" did not undermine Bush's ability to govern. Whether this is good or bad is debatable. Today, in an age of terrorism, the president's legitimacy goes unquestioned.

Most damaged by the Florida case is the U.S. Supreme Court. By its blatantly biased decision, the Court opened the curtain exposing itself as political and partisan. Twice did the Court—devoted though it is to the principle of federalism—overrule the Florida Supreme Court on their interpretation of state election law, and did so on questionable grounds. The Court diminished itself by its willingness to abandon principle. If there is a real loser in this bizarre event full of losers, it is, as Justice Stevens noted, the high court.

Conclusion: Theft Happens?

> And the loser now will be later to win,
> For the times, they are a changin.'
>
> —Bob Dylan

Did George W. Bush "steal" the election in Florida? Lamentably, we may never be able to say for certain who actually won Florida in 2000. The closeness of the vote in Florida reflected a closeness of political perspectives and practices in the country. There is today no effective governing majority. America has become a largely centrist nation. The pendulum swung left in the 1960s, back right in the 1980s, and the 2000 election was fought on the moderate low ground, with neither candidate inspiring much affection or respect.

That is not to say that all is lumped in the middle. Election 2000 confirmed the realignment of the South squarely into the Republican fold. It also extended the urban/rural divide. Gore won 71 percent of the urban vote; Bush won 59 percent of the rural and small-town vote—or what columnist Mike Barnicle calls the "Wal-Mart versus Martha Stewart vote." The nation is also divided by race and, to a lesser degree, by gender. Ninety percent of African Americans, 62 percent of Hispanics, and 55 percent of Asian Americans voted for Gore. Fifty-four percent of whites voted for Bush and 53 percent of men (the figure was much higher for white males), while 54 percent of women voted for Gore. The wealthy voted for Bush, the poor for Gore.

In the end, America endured and the presidency survives. But one is left with a haunting question: Is there any other mature democracy in which George W. Bush would have assumed office? We might hope the nation would learn from the experience of the 2000 election, but it seems precious little has been learned.

Perhaps H. L. Mencken's words on democracy provide some comfort, and perhaps not:

> I confess, for my part, that it greatly delights me. I enjoy democracy immensely. It is incomparably idiotic, and hence incomparably amusing. Does it exalt dunderheads, cowards, trimmers, frauds, cads? Then the pain of seeing them go up is balanced and obliterated by the joy of seeing them come down.
>
> Is it inordinately wasteful, extravagant, dishonest? Then so is every other form of government: All alike are enemies to laborious and virtuous men. Is rascality at the very heart of it? Well, we have borne that rascality since 1776, and continue to survive. In the long run, it may turn out that rascality is necessary to human government, and even to civilization itself—that civilization, at bottom, is nothing but a colossal swindle.
>
> I do not know: I report only that when the suckers are running well, the spectacle is infinitely exhilarating. But I am, it may be, a somewhat malicious man: My sympathies, when it comes to suckers, tend to be coy. What I can't make out is how any man can believe in democracy who feels for and with them, and is pained when they are debauched and made a show of. How can any man be a democrat who is sincerely a democrat?

Notes

With apologies to Guatemala, this essay's title is attributed to Ron Klair, Al Gore's Florida campaign advisor; see Nakashima, Von Drehle, et al., *Deadlock,* 71. The remark by Boss Tweed is quoted in Remnick, "Talk of the Town."

1. Menand, "Talk of the Town."

2. Ceaser and Busch, *The Perfect Tie,* 171.

3. See Bugliosi, *The Betrayal of America*; Dershowitz, *Supreme Injustice*; Dionne and Kristol, *Bush v. Gore*; Gillman, *The Votes That Counted*; Issacharoff, Karlan, and Pildes, *When Elections Go Bad*; Posner, *Breaking the Deadlock.*

4. Nakashima, Von Drehle, et al., *Deadlock,* 247.

Appendix A. Chronology of the Events of Election 2000

Nov. 7   Election Day; TV networks mistakenly announce Gore winner in Flor-
         ida, then retract announcement, only to later announce Bush winner
         in Florida, then retract second mistake; day ends with no clear winner
         in presidential election

Nov. 8   Gore leads in national popular vote; no apparent winner in Florida
         (also Oregon and New Mexico), with 37 electoral votes remaining at
         stake, including Florida's "make-or-break" 25 votes

Nov. 9   Gore asks for *hand* recounts in four contested counties in Florida
         (Broward, Miami-Dade, Palm Beach, Volusia); machine recount nar-
         rows Bush's already thin lead in Florida (327 votes after *machine* re-
         count); Florida secretary of state Katherine Harris rejects effort to
         extend deadline for submitting vote count

Nov. 11 Bush petitions U.S. District Court to stop Florida recount

Nov. 13 Court denies Bush's request

Nov. 14 Due date for Florida counties to submit vote totals

Nov. 15 Bush appeals to U.S. Court of Appeals the U.S. District Court ruling
         allowing Florida recount to continue; Florida secretary of state asks
         for recount to be stopped, but Florida Supreme Court denies petition

Nov. 16 Florida Supreme Court allows (by unanimous decision) Broward and
         Palm Beach Counties to continue their recount; Democrats sue Semi-
         nole County for fraudulently allowing Republican Party officials to
         correct incomplete Republican ballots cast in the race (suit will be
         dismissed)

Nov. 18 Due date for ballots mailed in from overseas to be counted; absentee ballots increase Bush lead to 930 votes

Nov. 21 Florida Supreme Court moves November 14 due date for submitting vote count back to November 26 to allow adequate time for recount; Florida Supreme Court orders secretary of state to accept manual recounts submitted before November 26

Nov. 22 Bush asks U.S. Supreme Court to consider actions of Florida Supreme Court

Nov. 24 U.S. Supreme Court agrees to hear Bush appeal

Nov. 26 Florida secretary of state declares Bush winner in state

Nov. 27 Gore files suit to challenge vote certification

Dec. 1 Florida Supreme Court denies Gore's request for immediate recount in Palm Beach County; oral arguments before U.S. Supreme Court begin

Dec. 4 Leon County Circuit Court judge denies Gore's request to extend the recount and ruling; U.S. Supreme Court declines to review election questions and remands case back to state

Dec. 5 Democrats in Florida sue, alleging ballot irregularities in two counties (Martin and Seminole)

Dec. 6 U.S. Court of Appeals, Eleventh Circuit, rejects Bush's bid to stop manual recounts

Dec. 8 Florida Supreme Court overturns lower court decision, orders statewide hand recount of undervotes; Florida Supreme Court supports Gore's appeal (by 4-3 vote) and orders hand count of questionable ballots in Miami-Dade and certification of previously discarded Gore votes in Miami-Dade and Palm Beach Counties; Bush appeals this ruling to U.S. Supreme Court

Dec. 12 Due date for Florida to submit vote of presidential electors; U.S. Supreme Court reverses (by 5-4 vote) Florida Supreme Court and stops recount

Dec. 13 Gore concedes election to Bush

Dec. 18 Electoral College meets in state capitols to cast votes; Bush 271, Gore 266

Jan. 6 Joint session of Congress meets to count Electoral College votes, declares Bush president

Jan. 20 Bush assumes office

Appendix B. Glossary of Terms

Chads

Chad Perforated part of a ballot; area appearing next to candidate's name in punch-card ballot designed to be punched out by voter

Dangling chad Either a hanging or a swinging chad

Dimpled chad chad still attached to ballot but bulged, apparently in unsuccessful or inadvertent attempt to perforate chad while voting

Hanging chad chad still attached to ballot by only one corner

Pierced chad chad still attached to ballot but pierced by voting instrument in apparent attempt to vote

Pregnant chad chad still attached to ballot but pierced and dimpled/bulged

Swinging chad chad still attached to ballot by two corners

Types of Voting Equipment

Datavote In this variation of punch-card ballots, a staplerlike tool creates holes on the card with sufficient force that prescoring of ballot cards is unnecessary. Unlike standard punch-card systems, information on candidates and ballot questions is printed directly on the Datavote card.

Electronic systems With electronic voting, using Direct Register Electronic machines (DRE), voter choices directly enter electronic storage, using touch screens, push buttons, or keyboards.

Machines are typically programmed to prevent overvoting. The most common models are "full faced," showing all contests at once, like lever machines, and a flashing red light alerts voters to the contests in which they have not voted.

Lever machines Each candidate's name is assigned to a lever on a rectangular array of levers on the face of the machines. The voter pulls down selected levers to indicate choices. Interlocks in the machines prevent overvoting.

Optical scanning Large ballots similar to those of paper ballot systems are used, allowing information about candidates to be printed directly on the ballot. Voters mark their choices using a pen or pencil. Ballots are counted by a machine that uses light or infrared as a sensor to discern which oval or rectangle the voter marked from a set of choices. Some precinct-based scanning machines are programmed to allow voters to check their ballots for overvotes.

Paper ballots Candidates' names are printed next to boxes that voters mark, on large ballot forms that are counted manually. Because counting by hand is time intensive, these remain in use mostly in small counties with few contested offices.

Punch cards Information about the ballot choices is provided in a booklet attached to a mechanical holder and centered over a punch card, which is inserted by the voter. To cast a vote, a stylus or other punching device provided is used to punch holes at the appropriate locations on the card, forcing out the inside of a prescored area in the shape of a rectangle.

Election Terminology

Absentee voting a way people can vote when they are unable to get to the polls; voting occurs on a special form and is mailed in to the elections office

Apportionment process of reallocating voters within a legislative district to reflect changes in population, usually done after a new census; also called redistricting

At-large election	election in which candidates for office must compete throughout the jurisdiction as a whole
Baker v. Carr	Supreme Court decision (1962) giving voters right to use courts to rectify malapportionment of legislative districts
Bandwagon effect	tendency of voters to vote for perceived winners, following lead of media, which declare some candidates winners and others losers
Black codes	laws passed by southern states after the Civil War that denied legal rights to newly freed slaves; related to Jim Crow laws
Boll Weevils	conservative Democrats, mainly from the South, who often vote with the Republican Party
Closed primary	primary election restricted to registered members of one political party; *see* **Open primary**
Convention	gathering of political party delegates to select candidates and set policy
Dixiecrat	one of a group of southern segregationist Democrats who formed the States' Rights Party in 1948
Electoral College	delegates from the individual states who cast the final ballots for president and vice president
Exit poll	election-day survey of voters leaving the polling places
FEC	Federal Election Commission, created in 1975 as a result of legislation in 1971 and 1974 regulating campaigns; enforces federal laws on campaign financing
15th Amendment	Constitutional amendment (ratified 1870) prohibiting infringement of right to vote on the basis of race
Frontloading	selecting an earlier date in the presidential primaries to increase the state's visibility and influence in the election
Frontrunner	candidate whom political pros/media portray as **likely winner**
General Election	election among party nominees held on the first Tuesday after the first Monday in November
Gerrymandering	Designing legislative districts for political purposes, to aid one candidate or a group in gaining office.
GOP	Grand Old Party; Republican Party, formed in 1856
Incumbent	current holder of an office
IRV	Instant runoff voting is an election reform that asks voters

	to rank candidates in order of voter preference in the event no candidate wins a majority (in elections requiring a majority). IRV takes the place of actually administering a runoff election.
Lame duck	incumbent holding office only until inauguration of elected successor; also, incumbent in last permitted term
19th Amendment	Constitutional amendment (ratified 1920) giving women the right to vote
Open primary	primary election in which party members, independents, and members of other parties may vote
Platform	statement of a candidate's or political party's positions on issues
Plebiscite	direct vote by all the people on a public measure
Precinct	boundaries established based on population and convenience of voters and used by registered voters living in the area to cast votes
Primary election	election within a party to decide, for a given office, which candidate will represent the party in the general election
Referendum	procedure whereby the state legislature submits proposed legislation to the voters for approval
Roll-off	drop off in voting on the ballot when the voter fails to cast a vote for such items as referenda or initiatives
Straw poll	unscientific poll used to gauge public opinion
Tracking poll	continuous survey that enables a campaign or the public to chart rises or falls in support

Appendix C. Chronology of Election History

1789 George Washington elected first president

1800 In outcome unforeseen by Founders, Thomas Jefferson and Aaron Burr tie for presidency; Electoral College hung, so House of Representatives selects Jefferson after many ballots; first major electoral realignment as Jefferson's Democratic Republicans replace Federalists as ruling party (1800–28)

1804 First "reform" of Electoral College (Amendment XII) requires "distinct" ballots for president and vice president

1824 John Quincy Adams defeats Andrew Jackson for presidency but without majority of Electoral College; election tainted by allegations that Adams made deal to gain support of electors

1828 Second major electoral realignment as Jackson wins presidency, Jacksonian Democrats rule government (1828–60)

1830s Presidential nominating conventions replace old caucuses

1840 William Henry Harrison elected as first Whig Party president

1860 Abraham Lincoln elected as first Republican Party president; Civil War party realignment (1860–96)

1865 Slavery ends; Reconstruction begins to enfranchise blacks in South

1870 Amendment XV extends voting rights to black males

1876 Rutherford B. Hayes defeats Samuel J. Tilden in Electoral College by 185-184 margin but fails to win popular vote

1877 Reconstruction ends; southern states deny blacks full political enfranchisement and voting rights through use of grandfather clauses, literacy tests, poll taxes, and more

1888	Benjamin Harrison defeats Grover Cleveland in Electoral College but does not carry popular vote
1890s	Progressive Era (until 1920) ushers in reforms such as voter registration requirements, direct primaries, secret ballots
1896	Electoral realignment favors Republican Party (1896–1932)
1913	Amendment XVII provides for direct election of U.S. senators
1920	Amendment XIX extends voting rights to women
1930s	Electoral realignment favors Democratic Party (1932–68)
1933	Amendment XX establishes noon on January 20 after election as start of presidential term; discusses vice presidential succession after death of president
1951	Amendment XXII limits president to two terms in office
1961	Amendment XXIII grants electoral votes to District of Columbia
1962	*Baker v. Carr* Supreme Court ruling affirms "one man, one vote" principle
1964	Amendment XXIV eliminates poll taxes
1965	Voting Rights Act passed
1967	Amendment XXV clarifies chain of succession upon death or removal of president
1971	Amendment XXVI reduces voting age from 21 to 18
1993	"Motor-voter" law makes it easier to register to vote
2000	Controversial presidential election between George W. Bush and Al Gore

Appendix D. Election Reform Resources

Resources

Ballot Access News (www.ballot-access.org). A monthly newsletter covering ballot laws, lawsuits, and minor party efforts.

Center for Voting and Democracy (www.fairvote.org). The nation's leading organization focusing on proportional representation and instant runoff voting.

Democracy Summer (www.democracysummer.org). A new initiative promoting electoral reform issues.

Books

Amy, Douglas J. *Behind the Ballot Box: A Citizen's Guide to Voting Systems.* Westport, Conn.: Praeger, 2001.

Ceaser, James W., and Andrew E. Busch. *The Perfect Tie: The True Story of the 2000 Presidential Election.* Lanham, Md.: Rowman & Littlefield, 2001.

Dionne, E. J., Jr., and William Kristol, eds. *Bush v. Gore: The Court Cases and the Commentary.* Washington, D.C.: Brookings Institution Press, 2001.

Dudley, Robert L., and Alan R. Gitelson. *American Elections: The Rules Matter.* New York: Longman, 2002.

Greene, Abner. *Understanding the 2000 Election: A Guide to the Legal Battles That Decided the Presidency.* New York: New York University Press, 2001.

Jamieson, Kathleen Hall, and Paul Waldman, eds. *Electing the President 2000:*

The Insiders' View: Election Strategy from Those Who Made It. Philadelphia: University of Pennsylvania Press, 2001.

Keyssar, Alexander. *The Right to Vote: The Contested History of Democracy in the United States.* New York: Basic Books, 2000.

Longley, Lawrence D., and Neal R. Peirce, *The Electoral College Primer 2000.* New Haven: Yale University Press, 1999.

Magleby, David B., ed. *Financing the 2000 Election.* Washington, D.C.: Brookings Institution Press, 2002.

Pomper, Gerald M., ed. *The Election of 2000: Reports and Interpretations.* New York: Chatham House, 2001.

Posner, Richard A. *Breaking the Deadlock: The 2000 Election, the Constitution, and the Courts.* Princeton, N.J.: Princeton University Press, 2001.

Sabato, Larry J., ed. *Overtime! The Election 2000 Thriller.* New York: Longman, 2002.

Watson, Robert P., and Colton C. Campbell, eds. *Campaigns and Elections: Issues, Concepts, Cases.* Boulder, Colo: Lynne Rienner, 2002.

Wayne, Stephen J. *The Road to the White House 2000: The Politics of Presidential Elections.* New York: St. Martin's Press, 2000.

Recent Election Reform Reports

Advancement Project, "America's Modern Poll Tax: How Structural Disenfranchisement Erodes Democracy," 2001 (www.advancementproject.org/reports/master.pdf).

Brady, Henry E., Justin Buchler, Matt Jarvis, and John McNulty. "Counting All The Votes: The Performance of Voting Technology in the United States," Survey Research Center and Institute of Governmental Studies, University of California, Berkeley, 2001 (ucdata.berkeley.edu/new_web/countingall thevotes.pdf).

Caltech/MIT Voting Technology Project, "Residual Votes Attributable to Technology: An Assessment of the Reliability of Existing Voting Equipment," 2001 (vote.caltech.edu or www.hss.caltech.edu/~voting/CalTech_MIT_Report_version2.pdf).

Caltech/MIT Voting Technology Project, "Voting: What Is, What Could Be," 2001 (www.vote.caltech.edu/Reports/index/html).

Center for Governmental Studies, University of Virginia, "The Report of the

National Symposium on Presidential Selection," 2001 (www.goodpolitics. org/reform/nssreport_entire.pdf).

Constitution Project, Forum on Election Reform, "Building Consensus on Election Reform," 2001 (www.constitutionproject.org/eri/index.htm).

Election Center's National Task Force on Election Reform, "Election 2000: Review and Recommendations by the Nation's Elections Administrators," 2001 (www.voternet.org/electionreformreport/).

Election Reform Information Project, "What's Changed, What Hasn't, and Why: Election Reform Since November 2000," 2001 (www.electionline.org/ site/docs/pdf/electionline.report.10.22.2001.pdf).

Eric A. Fischer, "Voting Technologies in the United States," CRS Report for Congress, 2001 (cnie.org/nle/crsreports/risk/rsk-55.cfm).

Thomas E. Mann, "An Agenda for Election Reform," Brookings Institution, 2001 (www.secstate.wa.gov/elections/pdf/brookings_report.pdf).

National Association of Secretaries of State, "NASS Election Reform Resolution," February 2001 (www.nass.org/pubs/pubs_electionres.html); July 2001 (www.nass.org/issues/electionres_7.17.01.html); July 2002 (www.nass.org/ issues/electionres_7.28.02.html).

National Association of State Election Directors, "Federal Election Recommendations," 2001 (www.nased.org/nased801.pdf).

National Commission on Election Standards and Reform, "Report and Recommendations to Improve America's Election System," 2001 (www.secstate. wa.gov/elections/pdf/nacoreport.pdf).

National Commission on Federal Election Reform, "To Assure Pride and Confidence in the Electoral Process," 2001 (reformelections.org).

National Conference of State Legislatures, "Voting in America: Final Report of the NCSL Elections Reform Task Force," 2001 (www.ncsl.org/programs/ press/2001/electref0801.htm).

U.S. Commission on Civil Rights, "Voting Irregularities in Florida During the 2000 General Election," 2001 (www.usccr.gov).

U.S. General Accounting Office, "Elections: Perspectives on Activities and Challenges Across the Nation," 2001 (www.gao.gov/new.items/d023.pdf).

U.S. General Accounting Office, "Elections: Statistical Analysis of Factors That Affected Uncounted Votes in the 2000 Presidential Election," 2001 (www.gao.gov).

U.S. House of Representatives, Committee on Government Reform, Special

Investigations Division, Minority Staff, "Income and Racial Disparities in the Undercount in the 2000 Presidential Election," 2001 (www.house.gov/reform/min/pdfs/pdf_inves/pdf_elec_nat_study.pdf).

U.S. House of Representatives, Committee on the Judiciary, Democratic Investigative Staff, "How to Make Over One Million Votes Disappear," 2001 (www.house.gov/judiciary_democrats/electionreport.pdf).

Appendix E. The League of Women Voters, "Election Reform Survey Summary Findings"

Findings from a survey fielded by the League of Women Voters of the United States through its local leagues indicate that election administration processes work well only "sometimes" or "usually." Rarely do they "always" work as they should. Given that elections can be won or lost by extremely narrow margins, these levels of performance are not acceptable. "'Good enough' is not good enough."

Findings also indicate that the treatment of voters is seriously deficient. To ensure that voters' voices are heard, it is imperative that election administration practices be improved to make voters the central concern of the voting system.

The survey was fielded by the league between June and August 2001 and gathers benchmark information against which election administration reforms at the federal, state, and local levels can be evaluated. Of the nearly 1,000 state and local leagues, 460 reported, representing a broad cross-section of the country, including local leagues in major metropolitan, suburban, and rural areas in forty-seven states and representing jurisdictions that account for almost half of all registered voters. Findings from these local leagues provide a window on election administration procedures across the country.

Highlights from the survey findings that indicate a need for better treatment of voters include:

· Voters' names are not regularly getting onto voter registration lists, resulting in voters being turned away.

· Voting machines do not consistently function properly.

· There are not sufficient numbers of voting machines in many locations.

· Voters frequently have to stand in long lines when waiting to vote.

· Visually impaired voters do not consistently have access to private and independent voting.

· There are insufficient numbers of poll workers, and those who do work the polls usually do not receive adequate training and are required to work long hours—as much as twelve to sixteen hours at a stretch. These conditions can contribute to poll workers becoming discourteous or unhelpful toward voters.

· There is inadequate communication by elections officials, especially regarding changes in the location of polling places.

The league's findings echo those made by other commissions, task forces, and the General Accounting Office (GAO) and point to several areas that need attention: voter access, vote counting, the election workforce, and voter education. The league's findings are based on quantitative information gathered through interviews by league members with state and/or local elections officials. Qualitative assessments are based on local leagues' experience with and participation in election administration in their communities.

Based on years of work around voting and civic engagement, the league has reinvigorated its efforts, especially in light of the irregularities seen in the November 2000 elections. The league's work plays out at the national, state, and local levels and draws on the strengths of the league's unique structure. With a presence in all fifty states, the District of Columbia, Puerto Rico, the Virgin Islands, and Hong Kong, and in hundreds of communities across the country, the league is uniquely positioned to carry forward election reform at all levels and continues to be engaged at all levels to see that reforms, when needed, are implemented.

The league's election reform work includes a variety of legislative and educational approaches. The league's national staff continues to press for bipartisan federal legislation that provides funds for and federal guidance on election reforms at the state and local levels, as well as ongoing support for and implementation of existing voter rights laws.

State and local leagues have advocated for election reform for years with elected and appointed officials at all levels. While these legislators and officials may be waiting for federal funding and guidelines, state and local leagues are already in the process of advising them on reforms that need to be legislated and implemented at the state and local levels.

Beyond legislative reforms, the league at all levels is engaged in educating voters and the public about public policy issues. The league also works to facilitate voter interaction with officials and to facilitate civic engagement, broadly defined. One of its educational efforts is its nationwide online voter education service, DemocracyNet (DNet), which tracked more than nine thousand state and local candidates and hundreds of initiatives during the 2001 elections. DNet showed a preelection spike in viewership with more than three million "hits" in the two weeks before Election Day.

As election reform moves forward at all levels, the league continues to see a pressing need to address the concerns and challenges confirmed by its survey findings. Elected officials at all levels are faced with unprecedented public policy issues and it is perhaps now more important than ever that the public have venues for input regarding domestic, foreign, public, and fiscal policy—and that elected officials hear from constituents. Given this heightened need for exchange and with important elections coming up in 2004, it is imperative that reforms are made that ensure that *every* vote *always* counts.

Key Findings and Policy Recommendations

The survey examined processes in four key categories: Voter Access, Vote Counting, the Election Workforce, and Voter Education. Following are highlights of findings together with the league's public policy recommendations to remedy identified problems.

Voter Access

Voters do not have consistent and reliable access to voting.

· Local voter registration systems are not always compatible with the voter registration systems of the department of motor vehicles. Just over a third of reporting leagues indicate that computerized lists are compatible, while another third report that they are not. When they are not, the names of citizens who register to vote through their local departments of motor vehicles are not consistently getting onto the formal voter registration lists maintained by the county.

· Poll workers do not always have a fast and accurate way to confirm voter registration on election day. While 65 percent of reporting leagues report that there is a way to verify names that do not appear on lists, about one-fourth report that there is no quick and accurate way to do so. This frequently results in voters being turned away and votes being lost.

· Voters sometimes have to wait in long lines to vote. More than 50 percent of reporting leagues indicate that voters have to wait longer than half an hour to cast their votes, and 40 percent of reporting leagues indicate that only "usually" are there sufficient numbers of machines.

· Voters with disabilities do not have consistent access to voting. More than half of reporting leagues indicate that their jurisdictions do not have a voting option that allows blind and visually impaired voters to vote privately and independently. One-quarter of reporting leagues indicate that technology and polling places are "never" accessible for the visually impaired.

· While findings show that elections officials in 88 percent of reporting jurisdictions say there is access for voters in wheelchairs, 30 percent of reporting leagues indicate that polling places are only "usually" accessible for those with physical disabilities.

Policy Recommendations

· The league urges that state governments be required to establish and maintain a statewide, computerized, interactive database as a mechanism for linking all relevant voter registration agencies (such as the department of motor vehicles and elections offices) and as a means of assuring that each polling place has quick and reliable access to the official list.

· Leagues are working to ensure that their state governments create statewide, uniform, nondiscriminatory standards to ensure that no eligible voter is removed erroneously from the voter registration list and to provide procedural safeguards that ensure notice and opportunity to correct errors for all voters who may be erroneously purged from lists.

· The league also is lobbying to ensure that provisional ballots are provided to voters so that no registered voter is sent away from the polls without being able to cast a vote and to ensure that the vote is counted if the person is eligible to vote.

· At the federal level, the league is lobbying for legislation that protects and ensures compliance with the Voting Rights Act (including its bilingual ballot provisions), the National Voter Registration Act, the Voting Accessibility for the Elderly and Handicapped Act, and other voter protection laws.

· At the federal and state levels, the league is lobbying for legislation that ensures that citizens with disabilities can vote privately and independently at each polling place.

· At the local and county levels, leagues are urging officials to work with local disability organizations prior to election day to ascertain their needs and to ensure that disabled voters have full, nondiscriminatory access to the ballot and to polling places.

Vote Counting

Tabulation of results is not consistent and reliable.

· Less than 37 percent of reporting leagues indicate that machines "always" work properly. This means that voters cannot be assured that their votes will count.

· More than 48 percent of reporting leagues indicate that machines only "usually" work properly. This is an unacceptably high error rate for the constitutionally protected right to vote.

· Less than half indicate that their jurisdictions have machines with error correction technology, although 83 percent of reporting leagues indicate that their jurisdictions do have procedures that allow voters to correct ballot mistakes—if voters know to ask. Voters thus are too often unable to correct those mistakes of which they are aware.

· Half of reporting leagues indicate that absentee ballots are always received by those who apply for them, while 40 percent report that absentee ballots are only "usually" received.

Policy Recommendations

· Leagues are working with state officials to adopt the voluntary voting equipment standards established by the Federal Election Commission.

· The league is lobbying for federal and state funding for new machines that meet federal technology standards for error rates, undervote/ overvote, access, and an audit trail.

· Local leagues are working with local officials to evaluate and upgrade, if necessary, maintenance and storage procedures for all types of voting equipment as well as procedures for providing techni- cal expertise and needed repairs on election day.

· State leagues are lobbying for improvements in the administration and counting of absentee ballots with the recommendation that absentee ballots be required to arrive at the election office by election day.

Election Workforce

Election workers are not given the support they need to do their jobs success- fully. Too often, the result is less than optimum treatment of voters.

· Only 34 percent of reporting leagues indicate that there are "always" enough polling place workers; half indicate that there are only "usually" enough polling place workers. This is the crucial interface for the voter with the election system—and it is not working.

· Most leagues report that poll worker training is a one-time session and lasts for only 1–3 hours.

· Only 72 percent of reporting leagues feel that training is always or usually sufficient.

· Only 52 percent of reporting leagues indicate that jurisdictions train poll workers before every election.

· Less than 30 percent of reporting leagues indicate that jurisdictions offer split shifts for their election workers; more than 60 percent of reporting leagues indicate that poll workers do not have the option of working split shifts. This means that many poll workers end up working as much as twelve to sixteen hours straight on election day.

· Given these conditions, it is no surprise that almost half of reporting leagues say that there are complaints of rude, unhelpful, or uncoop- erative poll workers.

Policy Recommendations

· State and local leagues are working to promote innovative and effective methods of poll worker recruitment and training and are working to secure adequate compensation for poll workers.

There is a great need for serious attention to the election workforce, with an emphasis on training and improving the conditions under which these people work on election day.

Voter Education

Communication between elections officials and voters is insufficient.
· Reporting leagues indicate that 42 percent of jurisdictions do not send out sample ballots before the election. This makes it difficult for many voters to participate meaningfully in the process.
· While 45 percent of reporting leagues indicate that voters are notified about the availability of provisional ballots, almost 25 percent of reporting leagues indicate that voters are not notified about provisional ballots.
· More than 71 percent of reporting leagues indicate that voters only "usually" know how to work the voting machines on election day. This is a prime area for voter education by schools, civic organizations, and election officials.
· Almost half report that ballots are only "usually" clear and easy to understand.
· While half of reporting leagues indicate that voters are given sufficient notice when polling locations have changed, almost one-third report that voters are only "usually" given sufficient notice.

Policy Recommendations
· Leagues are lobbying state governments to create statewide, uniform, nondiscriminatory standards that include public and voter notification of polling place locations.
· Leagues are working with government officials to expand voter information activities, including:
· providing all registered voters with sample ballots before election day;
· providing all voters with information regarding their appropriate polling place locations;
· providing public and voter notification of voters' rights at the polling place.

Conclusion

A great deal of work remains to be done to ensure that going to the polls and voting works well for all citizens all the time, and to ensure that every vote is always counted. Given that elections can be won or lost by very narrow margins, and given the role elected officials play in determining important public policy issues, it is imperative that fair and accessible elections are assured.

The League of Women Voters has served for all of its eighty-four years as a champion of democracy. The league will continue its work and has rededicated itself to making democracy work for all citizens. With members in hundreds of communities across the country, the League of Women Voters is uniquely positioned to carry forward this important work.

The League of Women Voters Survey of Local Election Administration

IA. Voter Access Objective Data

	Yes	No	Unsure	No response
1. Is the local computerized list of registered voters compatible with the Department of Motor Vehicles system?	36.17%	33.77%	23.53%	6.54%
2. Do poll workers in your county have laptop computers with the list of registered voters available to check the status of voters?	2.83%	93.03%	0.65%	3.49%
3. If your county polling places do not have laptop technology, is there a quick and efficient means to check the status of voters?	64.27%	24.62%	3.27%	7.84%

	Yes	Y/all	Y/some	No	Unsure	No response
4. Are blind and visually impaired citizens able to vote privately and independently at all or some of the polling places?	0.65%	18.52%	13.29%	56.21%	6.54%	4.79%

	Yes	No	Unsure
5. Is the voting technology at the polling places accessible to voters in wheelchairs?	88.24%	4.36%	1.74%
6. Is assistance provided for voters who are not fluent in English?	35.95%	44.01%	11.98%

IB. League Assessment of Voter Access

	Always	Usually	Sometimes	Never	Don't know	No response
7. Are voters who registered at Department of Motor Vehicles or other agencies on the registration list on Election Day?	21.13%	52.94%	13.51%	1.53%	6.10%	4.14%
8. Are technology and polling places accessible for the visually impaired?	25.27%	16.34%	12.42%	24.62%	12.20%	8.50%
9. Are technology and polling places accessible for those with physical disabilities?	54.68%	30.94%	7.84%	1.09%	0.65%	4.14%
10. Do voters wait in lines longer than half an hour to vote?	1.31%	0.87%	53.59%	35.73%	3.49%	4.36%
11. Is language assistance provided for non-English-speaking voters?	4.14%	12.20%	18.52%	37.40%	18.74%	6.54%

IIA. Vote Counting Objective Data

	Election day	Absentee voting	Early voting	Provisional voting
12. What type(s) of voting machines are used in your county? (check all that apply)				
Datavote	3.92%	4.36%	1.74%	1.74%
Direct Recording	12.85%	3.05%	9.15%	1.09%
Mechanical	14.60%	0.65%	0.22%	0.22%
Optical Scan	44.66%	25.49%	21.57%	19.61%
Votomatic	17.86%	19.83%	11.11%	13.29%
Paper	10.46%	32.24%	9.80%	15.25%

	Yes	No	Unsure	No response
13. Do the voting machines in your jurisdiction have error correction technology?	39.65%	42.92%	16.99%	13.51%
14. Do machines or procedures in your jurisdiction allow voters to correct mistakes?	83.22%	9.37%	2.40%	5.01%

IIB. League Assessment of Vote Counting

	Always	Usually	Sometimes	Never	Don't know	No response
15. Are absentee ballots received by voters who apply for them?	49.02%	40.09%	0.44%	0.22%	5.88%	1.96%
16. Is there a sufficient number of voting machines at each polling place?	48.15%	39.65%	2.18%	0.22%	0.44%	6.97%
17. Do machines work properly for voters?	36.60%	48.15%	0.44%	0.22%	0.44%	11.76%

IIIA. Election Workforce Objective Data

	Manual	Video	One-time	Series
18. How are poll workers trained?	49.46%	26.80%	55.34%	33.99%

	0 hrs.	1–3 hrs.	3–6 hrs.	6–9 hrs.	10+ hrs.	No response
19. How many hours are involved in training for the general election?	2.40%	80.17%	8.28%	2.18%	1.53%	5.01%

	Yes	No	Unsure	No response
20. Is training compulsory for first-time workers?	80.16%	15.25%	1.74%	1.96%
21. All workers before every election?	52.15%	42.05%	2.40%	2.61%
22. Do workers have the option of working split shifts?	29.41%	63.40%	2.83%	3.92%

IIIB. League Assessment of Election Workforce

	Always	Usually	Sometimes	Never	Don't know	No response
23. Is there a sufficient number of polling place workers?	34.42%	49.89%	8.28%	2.18%	0.44%	0.65%
24. Is there sufficient training for volunteers working at polling places?	32.03%	39.87%	13.07%	1.96%	4.14%	4.79%

	Always	Usually	Sometimes	Never	Don't know	No response
25. Are poll workers representative of the community?	27.02%	44.88%	14.60%	3.49%	4.79%	1.09%
26. Are there complaints of rude, unhelpful, or uncooperative election/ polling place workers?	0.65%	1.53%	45.75%	32.90%	12.64%	2.40%
27. Are poll workers or election officials familiar with federal laws that protect against racial discrimination at the polling place?	41.18%	23.75%	4.79%	1.53%	21.79%	2.83%

IVA. Voter Education Objective Data

	Yes (To reg'd voters)	Yes (To all households)	Yes (To houses with reg'd voters)	No	Unsure
28. Do elections officials send out sample ballots?	19.83%	2.83%	4.36%	42.48%	2.18%

	PSA	Newspaper	Mailing	Other
29. How are voters notified if there is a change in polling place locations?	17.86%	55.77%	73.64%	15.69%

	Yes	No	Unsure	No response
30. Do officials offer voters training classes on how to use voting equipment?	40.31%	48.15%	4.36%	7.19%
31. Are voters notified about the option to vote by provisional ballots?	45.32%	23.97%	15.90%	14.81%

IVB. League Assessment of Voter Education

	Always	Usually	Sometimes	Never	Don't know	No response
32. Do voters know how to work the voting machines?	12.42%	71.4%	3.27%	0.00%	0.87%	9.80%
33. Is the ballot layout clear and easy to understand?	42.70%	48.37%	5.45%	0.00%	0.22%	0.87%

	Always	Usually	Sometimes	Never	Don't know	No response
34. Can voters easily contact the elections office to verify registration or locate poll?	59.26%	27.23%	8.28%	1.53%	0.87%	0.65%
35. Are voters given sufficient notice when polling place locations are changed?	49.89%	29.41%	7.84%	0.65%	5.66%	4.36%

Bibliography

Amy, Douglas J. *Behind the Ballot Box: A Citizen's Guide to Voting Systems.* Westport, Conn.: Praeger, 2001.

Andersen, Robert, and Anthony Heath. "Social Cleavage and Political Context: A Comparative Analysis of the United States, Britain, and Canada." Paper presented at the American Political Science Association annual meeting, San Francisco, August 2001.

Asher, Herbert, Russell Schussler, and Margaret Rosenfield. "The Effect of Voting Systems on Voter Participation." Paper presented at the Midwest Political Science Association annual meeting, Milwaukee, April 1982.

Bartels, Larry M., and Lynn Vavreck, eds. *Campaign Reform: Insights and Evidence.* Ann Arbor: University of Michigan Press, 2000.

Bensen, Clark H. "Electoral College Warfare," March 18, 2001 (www.polidata.org/prcd/wpr1c20z.pdf); "Presidential Results by Congressional District 2000," March 2001 (www.polidata.org/prcd/prcdoo.htm).

Best, Judith. *The Case Against Direct Election of the President: A Defense of the Electoral College.* Ithaca, N.Y.: Cornell University Press, 1975.

————. *The Choice of the People? Debating the Electoral College.* Lanham, Md.: Rowman & Littlefield, 1996.

Bobbitt, Philip. "Parlor Games." In *Constitutional Stupidities, Constitutional Tragedies,* edited by William N. Eskridge and Sanford Levinson, 18–21. New York: New York University Press, 1998.

Brady, Henry E., Justin Buchler, Matt Jarvis, and John McNulty. "Counting All the Votes: The Performance of Voting Technology in the United States." University of California, Berkeley, 2001. University document/unpublished manuscript.

Brady, Henry E., Sidney Verba, and Kay Lehman Schlozman. "Beyond SES: A Resource Model of Political Participation." *American Political Science Review* 89 (1995): 271–94.

Bugliosi, Vincent. *The Betrayal of America: How the Supreme Court Undermined the Constitution and Chose Our President.* New York: Thunder's Mouth Press, 2001.

Bullock, Charles S., III, and Richard E. Dunn. "Election Roll-Off: A Test of Three Explanations." *Urban Affairs Review* 32, no. 1 (1996):71–86.

Burnham, Walter Dean. "The Changing Shape of the American Political Universe." *American Political Science Review* 59, no. 1 (1965):7–28.

CalTech/MIT Voting Technology Project. "Residual Votes Attributable to Technology: A Preliminary Assessment of the Reliability of Existing Voting Equipment." 2001 (www.hss.caltech.edu/~voting/CalTech_MIT_Report_Version2.pdf).

———. "Voting: What Is, What Could Be." 2001 (www.vote.caltech.edu/Reports/index/html).

Campaign Reform: Insights and Evidence: Report of the Task Force on Campaign Reform. Princeton, N.J.: Pew Charitable Trusts and Woodrow Wilson School of Public and International Affairs, Princeton University, 1998.

Caraley, Demetrios. "Why Americans Deserve a Constitutional Right to Vote for Presidential Electors." *Political Science Quarterly* 116, no. 1 (2001):1–3.

Carter, Jimmy, Gerald R. Ford, Lloyd N. Cutler, and Robert H. Michel. *To Assure Pride and Confidence in the Electoral Process: Report of the National Commission on Federal Election Reform.* Washington, D.C.: Brookings Institution Press, 2002.

Cauchon, Dennis. "Errors Mostly Tied to Ballots, Not Machines." *USA Today,* November 7, 2001, A6.

Ceaser, James W., and Andrew E. Busch. *The Perfect Tie: The True Story of the 2000 Presidential Election.* Lanham, Md.: Rowman & Littlefield, 2001.

Cigler, Allan, Joel Paddock, Gary Reich, and Eric Uslaner. "Changing the Electoral College: The Impact on Parties and Organized Interests." In *Choosing a President,* edited by Paul D. Schumaker and Burdett A. Loomis, 87–101. New York: Chatham House, 2002.

Citrin, Jack. "Comment: The Political Relevance of Trust in Government." *American Political Science Review* 68 (1974):973–88.

Citrin, Jack, and Donald Phillip Green. "Political Leadership and the Resurgence of Trust in Government." *British Journal of Political Science* 16 (1986):431–53.

Clarke, Harold D., and Alan C. Acock. "National Elections and Political Attitudes: The Case of Political Efficacy." *British Journal of Political Science* 19 (1989):551–62.

Cook, Rhodes. "Stalemate: The 'Great' Election of 2000." In *Overtime! The Election 2000 Thriller,* edited by Larry J. Sabato, 219–27. New York: Longman, 2002.

Cooke, Jacob E., ed., *The Federalist.* Middletown, Conn.: Wesleyan University Press, 1961.

Cooper, Mary H. "Is America's Democracy in Trouble?" *Congressional Quarterly Researcher* 10, no. 36 (2000):1–28.

Cronin, Thomas E. Foreword to *The Choice of the People? Debating the Electoral College,* by Judith Best. Lanham, Md.: Rowman & Littlefield, 1996.

Dahl, Robert A. *On Democracy.* New Haven: Yale University Press, 1998.

Darcy, R., and Anne Schneider. "Confusing Ballots, Roll-off, and the Black Vote." *Western Political Quarterly* 42, no. 3 (1989):347–64.

Degler, Carl N. *In Search of Human Nature: The Decline and Revival of Darwinism in American Social Thought.* New York: Oxford University Press, 1991.

Delli Carpini, Michael X., and Scott Keeter. *What Americans Know About Politics and Why It Matters.* New Haven: Yale University Press, 1996.

Dershowitz, Alan M. *Supreme Injustice: How the High Court Hijacked Election 2000.* New York: Oxford University Press, 2001.

Dionne, E. J., Jr., and William Kristol, eds. *Bush v. Gore: The Court Cases and the Commentary.* Washington, D.C.: Brookings Institution Press, 2001.

Dugger, Ronnie. "Annals of Democracy." *New Yorker,* November 7, 1988, 40–58.

Easton, David. *A Systems Analysis of Political Life.* New York: Wiley, 1965.

Engstrom, Richard L., and Victoria M. Caridas. "Voting for Judges: Race and Roll-off in Judicial Elections." In *Political Participation and American Democracy,* edited by William Crotty, 171–91. Westport, Conn.: Greenwood Press, 1991.

Epstein, Richard A. *Forbidden Grounds: The Case Against Employment Discrimination Laws.* Cambridge: Harvard University Press, 1992.

Farrar-Myers, Victoria A. "Reforming the Reforms: Recent Campaign Finance Reform Proposals." In *Campaigns and Elections: Issues, Concepts, Cases,* edited by Robert P. Watson and Colton C. Campbell. Boulder, Colo.: Lynne Rienner, 2003, 99–118.

———. "A War Chest Full of Susan B. Anthony Dollars: Fundraising Issues for Female Presidential Candidates." In *Anticipating Madam President,* edited by Robert P. Watson and Ann Gordon. Boulder, Colo.: Lynne Rienner, 2002, 81–94.

Fellner, Jamie, and Marc Mauer. "Losing the Vote: The Impact of Felony Disenfranchisement Laws in the United States." Report prepared for Human Rights Watch and The Sentencing Project, March 2001 (http://www.hrw.org/reports98/vote).

Fields, Barbara Jeanne. "Slavery, Race, and Ideology in the United States of America." *New Left Review* 181 (1990):95–118.

Fischer, Eric A. "Voting Technology in the United States." Congressional Research Service report, 2001 (March 21 update). cnie.org/nle/crsreports/risk/rsk-55.cfm.

Frey, William H. "Regional Shifts in America's Voting Age Population." Population Studies Center, University of Michigan, report 1–459, 2000.

Gans, Curtis. "Electoral College Reform." *Congressional Digest,* January 2001, 12.

Gelman, Andrew, and Jonathan N. Katz. "How Much Does a Vote Count? Voting Power, Coalitions, and the Electoral College." Social Science Working Paper 1121, California Institute of Technology, 2001.

Gillman, Howard. *The Votes That Counted: How the Court Decided the 2000 Presidential Election.* Chicago: University of Chicago Press, 2002.

Ginsberg, Benjamin, and Robert Weissberg. "Elections and the Mobilization of Popular Support." *American Journal of Political Science* 22 (1978):31–55.

Greenhouse, Linda. "Collision With Politics Risks Court's Legal Credibility." *New York Times,* December 11, 2000.

Gregg, Gary L., II. "The Origins and Meaning of the Electoral College." In *Securing Democracy: Why We Have an Electoral College.* Wilmington, Del.: ISI, 2001, 13–26.

Haider-Markel, Donald, Melvin Dubnick, Richard Elling, David Niven, and Paul Schumaker. "The Role of Federalism in Presidential Elections." In *Choosing a President,* edited by Paul D. Schumaker and Burdett A. Loomis, 53–73. New York: Chatham House, 2002.

Hamilton, James T., and Helen F. Ladd. "Biased Ballots? The Impact of Ballot Structure on North Carolina Elections in 1992." *Public Choice* 87 (1996):259–80.

Hansen, Bruce E. "A Precinct-Level Demographic Analysis of Double-Punching in the Palm Beach Presidential Vote." University of Wisconsin, 2000. Manuscript.

Herron, Erik S., Ronald A. Francisco, and O. Fiona Yap. "Election Rules and Social Stability." In *Choosing a President,* edited by Paul D. Schumaker and Burdett A. Loomis, 143–60. New York: Chatham House, 2002.

Herron, Michael C., and Jasjeet S. Sekhon. "Overvoting and Representation: An Examination of Overvoted Presidential Ballots in Broward and Miami-Dade Counties." *Electoral Studies* (forthcoming).

Hetherington, Marc J. "The Political Relevance of Political Trust." *American Political Science Review* 92 (1998):791–808.

House Committee on Government Reform, Special Investigations Division, Minority Staff. "Income and Racial Disparities in the Undercount in the 2000 Presidential Election." 2001 (www.house.gov/reform/min/pdfs/pdf_inves/pdf_elec_nat_study.pdf).

Hovey, Kendra A., and Harold A. Hovey. *CQ's State Fact Finder.* Washington, D.C.: CQ Press, annually 1999–2002.

Issacharoff, Samuel, Pamela S. Karlan, and Richard H. Pildes. *When Elections Go Bad: The Law of Democracy and the Presidential Election of 2000.* New York: Foundation Press, 2001).

Ivins, Molly. "We're Too Numb, Dumb to be Outraged by Financial Scandals." *Lexington Herald-Examiner,* May 22, 2002, A17.

Jefferson-Jenkins, Carolyn. "League of Women Voters." *Congressional Digest,* January 2001, 29.

Jillson, Calvin C. *Constitution Making: Conflict and Consensus in the Federal Convention of 1787.* New York: Agathon Press, 1988.

Joyce, Amy. "A High Speed Disconnection." *Washington Post,* October 5, 2000.

Kimball, David C., and Chris T. Owens. "Where's the Party? Eliminating One-Punch Voting." Paper presented at the Midwest Political Science Association annual meeting, Chicago, April 28–30, 2000.

Kimball, David C., Chris T. Owens, and Katherine McAndrew. "Who's Afraid of an Undervote?" Paper presented at the Southern Political Science Association annual meeting, Atlanta, November 9, 2001.

Knack, Stephen. "Who Uses Inferior Voting Technology?" Paper presented at the Public Choice Society annual meeting, San Antonio, March 2001.

Knack, Stephen, and Martha Kropf. "For Shame! The Effect of the Community Cooperation Context on the Probability and Voting." *Political Psychology* 19 (1998):585–99.

———. "Invalidated Ballots in the 1996 Presidential Election: A County-Level Analysis." *Journal of Politics* 65, no. 3 (2001):891–97 (w.vote.caltech.edu/Reports/knack-kropf32.pdf)

———. "Roll-off at the Top of the Ballot: Intentional Undervoting in American Presidential Elections." National Commission on Federal Election Reform, 2001. Manuscript.

———. "Voided Ballots in the 1996 Presidential Election: A County-Level Analysis." *Journal of Politics* 65, no. 3 (2003):881–97.

———. "Who Uses Inferior Voting Technology?" *PS: Political Science & Politics,* September 2002, 1–8.

Koch, Kathy. "The Digital Divide." *Congressional Quarterly Researcher* 10, no. 3 (2000): 43–50.

Kousser, J. Morgan. *The Shaping of Southern Politics: Suffrage Restriction and the Establishment of the One-Party South, 1880–1910*. New Haven: Yale University Press, 1974.

Krugman, Paul. "True Blue Americans." *New York Times,* May 7, 2002, A31.

Lichtman, Allan J. "Report on the Racial Impact of the Rejection of Ballots Cast in the 2000 Presidential Election in the State of Florida." U.S. Commission on Civil Rights, 2001.

Lineberry, Robert L., Darren Davis, Robert Erikson, Richard Herrera, and Priscilla Southwell. "The Electoral College and Social Cleavages." In *Choosing a President,* edited by Paul D. Schumaker and Burdett A. Loomis, 161–75. New York: Chatham House, 2002.

Longley, Lawrence D., and Alan G. Braun. *The Politics of Electoral College Reform.* New Haven: Yale University Press, 1972.

Longley, Lawrence D., and Neal R. Peirce. *The Electoral College Primer 2000.* New Haven: Yale University Press, 1999.

Lott, John R., Jr. "Non-Voted Ballots and Discrimination in Florida." Yale University, 2001. Manuscript.

Lowi, Theodore J., and Benjamin Ginsberg. *American Government: Freedom and Power.* 5th ed. New York: W. W. Norton, 1999.

Lupia, Arthur, and Matthew D. McCubbins. *The Democratic Dilemma: Can Citizens Learn What They Need to Know?* New York: Cambridge University Press, 1998.

Lutz, Donald, Philip Abbott, Barbara Allen, and Russell Hansen. "The Electoral College in Historical and Philosophical Perspective." In *Choosing a President,* edited by Paul D. Schumaker and Burdett A. Loomis, 31–52. New York: Chatham House, 2002.

MacBride, Roger Lea. *The American Electoral College.* Caldwell, Idaho: Caxton, 1963.

Madison, James. *The Debates in the Federal Convention of 1787.* Edited by Gaillard Hunt and James Brown Scott. New York: Oxford University Press, 1920 (www.constitution.org/dfc/dfc-002.htm).

Mann, Irwin, and L. S. Shapely. "The A Priori Voting Strength of the Electoral College." In *Game Theory and Related Approaches to Social Behavior,* edited by Martin Shubik. New York: Wiley, 1964.

Máther, George B. *Effects of the Use of Voting Machines on Total Votes Cast: Iowa, 1920–1960.* Iowa City: Institute of Public Affairs, University of Iowa, 1964.

McConnell, Mitch. Introduction to *Securing Democracy: Why We Have an Electoral College,* edited by Gary L. Gregg II. Wilmington, Del.: ISI, 2001.

McWilliams, Wilson Carey. "The Meaning of the Election." In *The Election of 2000,* edited by Gerald M. Pomper. New York: Chatham House, 2001):177–201.

Menand, Louis. "The Talk of the Town." *New Yorker,* November 27, 2000, 67.

Miller, Arthur H. "Political Issues and Trust in Government, 1964–1970." *American Political Science Review* 68 (1974):951–72.

Nakashima, Ellen, David Von Drehle, et al. *Deadlock: The Inside Story of America's Closest Election.* New York: Public Affairs, 2001.

Neale, Thomas H. "The Electoral College: Reform Proposals in the 107th Congress." Washington, D.C.: Congressional Research Service, Library of Congress report RL30844, CRS-9, 2001.

Nichols, Stephen M. "State Referendum Voting, Ballot Roll-off, and the Effect of New Electoral Technology." *State and Local Government Review* 30 (Spring 1998):106–17.

Nichols, Stephen M., and Gregory A. Strizek. "Electronic Voting Machines and Ballot Roll-Off." *American Politics Quarterly* 23, no. 3 (1995):300–318.

Oliver, Eric J. "The Effects of Eligibility Restrictions and Party Activity on Absentee Voting and Overall Voter Turnout." *American Journal of Political Science* 40, no. 2 (1996):498–513.

Peirce, Neal R. *The People's President: The Electoral College in American History and the Direct-Vote Alternative.* New York: Simon & Schuster, 1968.

Piven, Frances Fox, and Richard A. Cloward. *Why Americans Still Don't Vote: And Why Politicians Want It That Way.* Rev. ed. Boston: Beacon Press, 2000.

Polsby, Nelson W., and Aaron Wildavsky. *Presidential Elections.* 10th ed. New York: Chatham House, 2000.

Popkin, Samuel L. *The Reasoning Voter: Communication and Persuasion in Presidential Campaigns.* Chicago: University of Chicago Press, 1991.

Posner, Richard A. *Breaking the Deadlock: The 2000 Election, the Constitution, and the Courts.* Princeton, N.J.: Princeton University Press, 2001.

Rainey, Glenn W., Jr., and Jane Gurganus Rainey. "Reexamining the Distribution of Power in the Electoral College: The 'Constant Two,' the 2000 Election, and Emergent Geosocial Cleavage in America." Paper presented at the Southern Political Science Association annual meeting, Atlanta, November 2001.

"Red Zone vs. Blue Zone." *Newsweek,* January 22, 2001, 38–41.

Remnick, David. "The Talk of the Town." *New Yorker,* December 4, 2000, 35.

Reynolds, Andrew, and Ben Reilly. *The International IDEA Handbook of Electoral Systems Design.* Stockholm: International Institute for Democracy and Electoral Assistance, 1997.

Rhodes, Terrel L. *Republicans in the South: Voting for the State House, Voting for the White House.* Westport, Conn.: Praeger, 2000.

Rusk, Jerrold G. "The Effect of the Australian Ballot Reform on Split Ticket Voting, 1876–1908." *American Political Science Review* 64, no. 4 (1970):1220–38.

Russett, Cynthia Eagle. *Sexual Science: The Victorian Construction of Womanhood.* Cambridge: Harvard University Press, 1989.

Saltman, Roy G. *Accuracy, Integrity, and Security in Computerized Vote-Tallying.* Gaithersburg, Md.: National Bureau of Standards, 1988.

Sayre, Wallace S., and Judith H. Parris. *Voting for President: The Electoral College and the American Political System.* Washington, D.C.: Brookings Institution, 1970.

Schmidt, Benno C., Jr. "Black Disenfranchisement from the KKK to the Grandfather Clause." *Columbia Law Review* 82 (1982):835–905.

Schudson, Michael. *The Good Citizen: A History of American Civic Life.* New York: Martin Kessler, 1998.

Schumaker, Paul. "Analyzing the Electoral College and Its Alternatives." In *Choosing a President,* edited by Paul D. Schumaker and Burdett A. Loomis, 10–30. New York: Chatham House, 2002.

Schumaker, Paul D., and Burdett A. Loomis, eds. *Choosing a President: The Electoral College and Beyond.* New York: Chatham House, 2002.

Sears, David O., and Nicholas A. Valentino. "Race, Religion, and Sectional Conflict in Contemporary Partisanship." Paper presented at the American Political Science Association annual meeting, San Francisco, August 2001.

Shactar, Ron, and Barry Nalebuff. "Follow the Leader: Theory and Evidence on Political Participation." *American Economic Review* 89, no. 2 (1999).

Shocket, Peter A., Neil R. Heighberger, and Clyde Brown. "The Effect of Voting Technology on Voting Behavior in a Simulated Multi-Candidate City Council Election." *Western Political Quarterly* 45, no. 2 (1992):521–37.

Slomin, Shlomo. "Designing the Electoral College." In *Inventing the American Presidency*, edited by Thomas E. Cronin. Lawrence: University Press of Kansas, 1989.

Smith, Rogers M. "Beyond Tocqueville, Myrdal, and Hartz: The Multiple Traditions in America." *American Political Science Review* 87, no. 3 (1993):549–66.

Stein, Robert M., Paul Johnson, Daron Shaw, and Robert Weissberg. "Citizen Participation and Electoral College Reform." In *Choosing a President*, edited by Paul D. Schumaker and Burdett A. Loomis, 125–42. New York: Chatham House, 2002.

Stiefbold, Rodney P. "The Significance of Void Ballots in West German Elections." *American Political Science Review* 59, no. 2 (1965):391–407.

Tate, Katherine. *From Protest to Politics: The New Black Voters in American Elections.* Enl. ed. New York: Russell Sage Foundation; Cambridge, Harvard University Press, 1994.

Teixeira, Ruy, and Joel Rogers. *America's Forgotten Majority: Why the White Working Class Still Matters.* New York: Basic Books, 2000.

Thach, Charles C., Jr. *The Creation of the Presidency, 1775–1789: A Study in Constitutional History.* 1922. New York: Da Capo Press, 1969.

Thomas, Norman C. "Voting Machines and Voter Participation in Four Michigan Constitutional Revision Referenda." *Western Political Quarterly* 21, no. 3 (1968):409–19.

Tomz, Michael, and Robert Van Houweling. "How Does Voting Equipment Affect the Racial Gap in Voided Ballots?" *American Journal of Political Science* 47, no. 1 (2003): 46–60.

Uhlmann, Michael. "Creating Constitutional Majorities: The Electoral College after 2000." In *Securing Democracy: Why We Have an Electoral College*, edited by Gary L. Gregg II. Wilmington, Del.: ISI, 2001, 150–65.

U.S. Census Bureau. *Voting and Registration in the Election of November 1996.* Washington, D.C.: U.S. Census Bureau, 1998.

U.S. Commission on Civil Rights. "Voting Irregularities in Florida During the 2000 General Election." 2001 (www.usccr.gov).

U.S. General Accounting Office. "Elections: Statistical Analysis of Factors That Affected Uncounted Votes in the 2000 Presidential Election." Report GAO-02-122. 2001 (www.gao.gov).

Vanderleeuw, James M., and Glenn H. Utter. "Voter Roll-off and the Electoral Context: A Test of Two Theses." *Social Science Quarterly* 74, no. 3 (1993):664–73.

Walker, Jack L. "Ballot Forms and Voter Fatigue: An Analysis of the Office Block and Party Column Ballots." *Midwest Journal of Political Science* 10, no. 4 (1966):448–63.

Wand, Jonathan N., Kenneth W. Shotts, Jasjeet S. Sekhon, Walter R. Mebane Jr., Michael C. Herron, and Henry E. Brady. "The Butterfly Did It: The Aberrant Vote for Buchanan in Palm Beach County, Florida." *American Political Science Review* 95 (2001):793–810.

Wattenberg, Martin P., Ian McAllister, and Anthony Salvanto. "How Voting Is Like Taking an SAT Test: An Analysis of American Voter Roll-Off." *American Politics Quarterly* 28, no. 2 (2000):234–50.

Weatherford, M. Stephen. "Measuring Political Legitimacy." *American Political Science Review* 86 (1992):149–66.

Weaver, Vesla. "Racial Profiling at the Polling Place: The Impact of Felony Disenfranchisement on Black Participation." Senior thesis, University of Virginia, 2001.

"What We'll Remember in 2050." *Chronicle of Higher Education,* January 5, 2001, B15–16.

Wilmerding, Lucius. *The Electoral College.* New Brunswick, N.J.: Rutgers University Press, 1958.

Winger, Richard. "Nader Wins Illinois, But Loses North Carolina." *Ballot Access News,* September 1, 2000, 1, 7.

Wolfinger, Raymond E., and Steven J. Rosenstone. *Who Votes?* New Haven: Yale University Press, 1980.

Wolfley, Jeannette. "Jim Crow, Indian Style: The Disenfranchisement of Native Americans." *American Indian Law Review* 16 (1991):167–202.

Yunker, John H., and Lawrence D. Longley. *The Electoral College: Its Biases Newly Measured for the 1960s and 1970s.* Beverly Hills, Cal.: Sage, 1976.

List of Contributors

Blair Bobier, a founder of the Pacific Green Party of Oregon, was the party's gubernatorial candidate in 1998 and initiated the national Green Party's effort to establish a Green "shadow cabinet." He has worked as a consultant for nonprofit organizations such as the Center for Voting and Democracy and the Northwest Democracy Institute. His law practice is in Corvallis, Oregon.

Mitchell Ceasar is the chair of the Democratic Party of Broward County, Florida. He has served as chairman of the Florida Democratic Party, a member of the Democratic National Committee, and vice chairman for the Democratic National Convention in 2000. He practices law in Plantation, Florida.

James Corey is assistant professor of history and political science at High Point University in North Carolina.

Cathy Dubin is former executive director of the Democratic Party of Palm Beach County, Florida. She was also a longtime aide to U.S. senator and 2000 Democratic vice presidential nominee Joseph Lieberman.

Victoria A. Farrar-Myers is associate professor of political science at the University of Texas–Arlington. She is coauthor of *Legislative Labyrinth: Congress and Campaign Reform* and author of numerous journal articles on campaign finance reform. As an APSA Congressional Fellow, she served as a legislative assistant to Representative Christopher Shays of Connecticut.

Michael A. Genovese holds the Loyola Chair of Leadership and is director of the Institute for Leadership Studies at Loyola Marymount University in Los Angeles. Genovese is the author of thirteen books on the presidency, a frequent media commentator, and is president of the Presidency Research Group.

Jess Gittelson serves as supervisor of the Voting Equipment Center for the Broward County Elections Office.

TeResa C. Green is assistant professor of political science and African American studies at Eastern Michigan University. She is editor of the book *African American Churches and Political Mobilization* and chairs the Political Science Panel for the Michigan Academy of Science, Arts, and Letters.

Mark Hoch is political director of the Republican Party of Palm Beach County and has taught at Palm Beach Community College.

Carolyn Jefferson-Jenkins is past president of the League of Women Voters of the United States, the first woman of color to head the nonpartisan political organization. She has been a member of the league since 1982 and part of its national leadership since 1994. She is the author of *The Road to Black Suffrage* and *One Man, One Vote: The History of the African-American Vote in the United States*.

Joan Karp is past president of the League of Women Voters of South Palm Beach County and has been a member of the league since 1965, first in Massachusetts and since 1994 in Florida. She testified before the Florida State Legislature regarding the 2000 election and electoral reforms. She has spent more than twenty years in the computer industry as a programmer, technical writer, and manager.

David C. Kimball is assistant professor of political science at the University of Missouri–St. Louis. He is coauthor of *Why Americans Split Their Tickets*.

Rhonda S. Kinney is chair of the Department of Political Science and former director of the Women's Studies Program at Eastern Michigan University. She has published widely and serves on the editorial boards of the *Academy of Educational Leadership Journal* and the *Academy of Strategic Management Journal*. She is coeditor of *Innovation and Entrepreneurship in State and Local Governments*.

Stephen Knack is senior research economist at the World Bank, where he specializes in governance and public sector reform. He has written several studies on American voting participation and is editor of *Democracy, Governance, and Growth.*

Martha E. Kropf is assistant professor of political science at the University of Missouri–Kansas City. She has written numerous journal articles on political behavior and social capital.

David Leahy was supervisor of elections for Miami-Dade County, Florida, from 1980 to 2002, and previously was assistant supervisor of elections and Miami-Dade County's ombudsman. Leahy served on the canvassing board that monitored Miami-Dade's recount in 2000.

Katherine McAndrew Keeney is a graduate student in political science at Southern Illinois University–Carbondale.

Jason E. Mitchell, after graduation from the University of Michigan in 1996, interned at the office of Michigan state senator Alma Wheeler Smith. Under the Jesse M. Unruh Assembly Fellowship Program, he works with the California Legislative Black Caucus and is an aide to California state assemblyman Jerome E. Horton.

Bruce I. Oppenheimer is professor of political science at Vanderbilt University. He is coauthor of *Sizing Up the State: The Unequal Effects of Equal Representation* and coeditor of *Congress Reconsidered.*

Chris Owens is a graduate student in political science at Texas A&M University.

Glenn W. Rainey Jr. is professor of political science and public administration and director of the Institute for Government at Eastern Kentucky University. He has published more than thirty essays and articles.

Jane G. Rainey is professor of political science at Eastern Kentucky University, where she teaches American and Russian politics. Her major research interests are politics and religion in the United States, politics of transition in the former Soviet Union, and civic education.

Gisela Salas was the assistant supervisor of elections and public information officer for Miami-Dade County from 1988 to 2003. A native Miamian and Cuban-American, Salas has worked in a number of departments with Miami-Dade County since 1977, including the County Manager's Office, Police Department, Personnel Department, and the Elections Department.

Paul D. Schumaker is professor of political science and chair of the Department of Political Science at the University of Kansas. He wrote *Critical Pluralism, Democratic Performance, and Community Power,* coauthored *Great Ideas/Grand Schemes,* and is also coeditor of *Choosing a President: The Electoral College and Beyond.*

Thomas R. Spencer is chairman of the Political Education Committee and member of the Executive Committee of the Republican Party of Miami-Dade County. He is also a member of the Presidents' Club of the Republican National Committee. He practices law in Miami and served as cocounsel for the 2000 Bush-Cheney campaign in the Florida recount.

Robert P. Watson is associate professor of political science at Florida Atlantic University and editor of the journal *White House Studies.* He has published 20 books and more than a hundred articles. He was project director and editor of *Report to the First Lady 2001,* which was presented to the White House. A frequent political commentator for such media outlets as CNN, MSNBC, and *USA Today,* Watson was a guest for CNN.com's coverage of the 2001 presidential inauguration and has served as a visiting scholar with numerous presidential foundations and universities.

Index